Lecture Notes in Computer Science 1199

Springer
*Berlin
Heidelberg
New York
Barcelona
Budapest
Hong Kong
London
Milan
Paris
Santa Clara
Singapore
Tokyo*

Dhabaleswar K. Panda   Craig B. Stunkel (Eds.)

Communication and Architectural Support for Network-Based Parallel Computing

First International Workshop, CANPC'97
San Antonio, Texas, USA, February 1-2, 1997
Proceedings

 Springer

Series Editors

Gerhard Goos, Karlsruhe University, Germany

Juris Hartmanis, Cornell University, NY, USA

Jan van Leeuwen, Utrecht University, The Netherlands

Volume Editors

Dhabaleswar K. Panda
The Ohio State University
Department of Computer and Information Science
Columbus, OH 43210-1277, USA
E-mail: panda@cis.ohio-state.edu

Craig B. Stunkel
IBM T.J. Watson Research Center
P.O. Box 218, Yorktown Heights, NY 10598, USA
E-mail: stunkel@watson.ibm.com

Cataloging-in-Publication data applied for

Die Deutsche Bibliothek - CIP-Einheitsaufnahme

Communication and architectural support for network based parallel computing :
first international workshop ; proceedings / CANPC '97, San Antonio, Texas,
USA, February 1997. Dhabaleswar K. Panda ; Craig B. Stunkel (ed.). - Berlin ;
Heidelberg ; New York ; Barcelona ; Budapest ; Hong Kong ; London ; Milan ;
Paris ; Santa Clara ; Singapore ; Tokyo : Springer, 1997
  (Lecture notes in computer science ; Vol. 1199)
  ISBN 3-540-62573-9

NE: Panda, Dhabaleswar K. [Hrsg.]; CANPD <1, 1997, San Antonio, Tex.>; GT

CR Subject Classification (1991): C.2, D.1.3,F.1.2, D.4.4

ISSN 0302-9743
ISBN 3-540-62573-9 Springer-Verlag Berlin Heidelberg New York

Typesetting: Camera-ready by author
SPIN 10548953   06/3142 – 5 4 3 2 1 0   Printed on acid-free paper

Preface

As the performance gap between commodity microprocessors and exotic high-end processors continues to close, microprocessor-based massively parallel processors (MPPs) are becoming commonplace for achieving supercomputer performance levels. Similarly, clusters of workstations connected by local area networks (LANs) are increasingly being employed as cost-effective parallel processing systems. Such configurations are often termed Networks of Workstations (NOWs) [1], Clusters of Workstations (COWs), or simply clusters [2].

Efficient and scalable parallel processing implies efficient communication and synchronization. Although the use of workstation technology can be relatively inexpensive, commodity workstation hardware and software components have not typically provided low latency, high bandwidth inter-node communication. Strategies for improving communication and synchronization fall into several categories, some of which are:

- Better interfaces between the processor and the network
- More efficient implementations of existing end-to-end protocols (e.g., TCP/IP)
- Light-weight end-to-end communication protocols
- High-performance interconnect technology and protocols
- Operating system and architectural support for communication and synchronization
- Architectural support for distributed shared memory
- Load balancing techniques
- Collective communication support

Unlike most MPP systems, NOW systems may operate in a "shared" environment and might consist of heterogeneous workstations and networks. Such systems may be also integrated with an existing computing environment like a department or a lab, all of which makes it more difficult to achieve optimal performance.

CANPC '97—the Workshop on Communication and Architectural Support for Network-based Parallel Computing—addresses these and other issues which have an impact on the effectiveness of clusters used as parallel systems. Potential authors submitted 10-page extended abstracts which were typically reviewed by 4 referees, including at least two program committee members. We were able to accept 19 papers out of a total of 36 submissions. We believe that the resulting selections comprise an important compilation of state-of-the-art solutions for network-based parallel computing systems. This CANPC workshop was sponsored by the IEEE Computer Society, and was held in conjunction with HPCA-3, the 3rd International Symposium on High-Performance Computer Architecture, held in San Antonio on Feb. 1-5, 1997. The workshop itself took place on Feb. 1-2.

We would like to thank all of the authors who submitted papers to this workshop. Special thanks go to the program committee and the other referees for providing us with high-quality reviews under tight deadlines. We thank Lionel Ni for his support of this workshop, including the use of his web-based review software which made our jobs considerably easier. Thanks to Rajeev Sivaram for porting and installing this software to our web server at Ohio State and maintaining it. Lastly, we thank Springer-Verlag for agreeing to an extremely tight publication schedule in order to provide the workshop attendees with these proceedings as they registered.

February 1997   Dhabaleswar K. Panda and Craig B. Stunkel

References

1. T. Anderson, D. Culler, and Dave Patterson. A Case for Networks of Workstations (NOW). *IEEE Micro*, pages 54–64, Feb 1995.
2. G. F. Pfister. *In Search of Clusters*. Prentice Hall, 1995.

CANPC'97 Program Committee

Dhabaleswar K. Panda, *Ohio State University* (co-chair)
Craig B. Stunkel, *IBM T.J. Watson Research Center* (co-chair)

Tilak Agerwala, *IBM, USA*
Henri Bal, *Vrije University, The Netherlands*
Adam Beguelin, *Carnegie Mellon University, USA*
Jehoshua Bruck, *Caltech, USA*
Al Davis, *University of Utah, USA*
David Du, *University of Minnesota, USA*
Jose Duato, *University of Politécnica de Valencia, Spain*
Sandhya Dwarkadas, *University of Rochester, USA*
Ian Foster, *Argonne National Lab, USA*
Michael Foster, *National Science Foundation, USA*
Ching-Tien Ho, *IBM Almaden Research Center, USA*
Lionel Ni, *Michigan State University, USA*
Steve Scott, *Cray Research, USA*
Marc Snir, *IBM T.J. Watson Research Center, USA*
Per Stenstrom, *Chalmers University, Sweden*
Vaidy Sunderam, *Emory University, USA*
Anand Tripathi, *NSF/Univ. of Minnesota, USA*
Thorsten von Eicken, *Cornell University, USA*
David Wood, *University of Wisconsin, USA*
Sudhakar Yalamanchili, *Georgia Tech, USA*

Referees

B. Abali
T. Agerwala
H. Bal
A. Beguelin
J. Bonney
J. Bruck
X. Chen
A. Davis
B. Dimitrov
D. C. DiNucci
J. M. Draper
D. Du
J. Duato
S. Dwarkadas
I. Foster
M. Foster
J. C. Gomez
W. J. Hahn
P. J. Hatcher
C.-T. Ho
M. A. Iverson
J. Kim
C.-T. King
M. Kaddoura
I. Kodukula
P. Leung

P. Marenzoni
E. Markatos
W. Meira Jr.
N. Mekhiel
R. G. Minnich
L. Ni
N. Nupairoj
K. Omang
K. Pingali
K. A. Robbins
S. Scott
R. Sivaram
H. Sivaraman
M. Snir
P. Stenstrom
X.-H. Sun
V. Sunderam
P. Sundstrom
A. Tripathi
J. S. Turner
T. von Eicken
D. Wood
S. Yalamanchili
H. Yamashita
X. Zhang

Table of Contents

Efficient Communication Mechanisms for Cluster Based Parallel Computing*

Al Davis, Mark Swanson, Mike Parker

Department of Computer Science
University of Utah
Salt Lake City, UT 84112, USA
ald@cs.utah.edu, swanson@cs.utah.edu, map@cs.utah.edu

Abstract. The key to crafting an effective scalable parallel computing system lies in minimizing the delays imposed by the system. Of particular importance are communications delays, since parallel algorithms must communicate frequently. The communication delay is a system-imposed *latency*. The existence of relatively inexpensive high performance workstations and emerging high performance interconnect options provide compelling economic motivation to investigate NOW/COW (network/cluster of workstation) architectures. However, these commercial components have been designed for generality. Cluster nodes are connected by longer physical wire paths than found in special-purpose supercomputer systems. Both effects tend to impose intractable latencies on communication. Even larger system-imposed delays result from the overhead of sending and receiving messages. This overhead can come in several forms, including CPU occupancy by protocol and device code as well as interference with CPU access to various levels of the memory hierarchy. Access contention becomes even more onerous when the nodes in the system are themselves symmetric multiprocessors. Additional delays are incurred if the communication mechanism requires processes to run concurrently in order to communicate with acceptable efficiency. This paper presents the approach taken by the Utah Avalanche project which spans user level code, operating system support, and network interface hardware. The result minimizes the constraining effects of latency, overhead, and loosely coupled scheduling that are common characteristics in NOW-based architectures.

1 Introduction

Minimizing communication latency is a critical design component of parallel processing systems since parallel programs communicate frequently. Reductions in communications latency permit increased levels of parallelism between finer grained components. The result is that communication latency is the key to achieving high levels of aggregate system performance and reasonable scalability. MPP (massively parallel processor) supercomputers achieve low communication latencies and are capable of high sustained bandwidths. MPP systems

---

* This work was supported by SPAWAR contract #N00039-94-C-0018 and ARPA order #B990.

achieve enhanced performance by providing support for synchronization between communicating programs. Even though today's MPP systems are all based on commodity microprocessors, the logic and packaging to support the communication and synchronization mechanisms are specialized for the low-volume supercomputer market. The result is that MPP systems achieve very high levels of performance but are too expensive.

The existence of relatively inexpensive high performance workstations and the emerging availability of high performance interconnect options provide compelling economic motivation to investigate cluster based multiprocessor architectures. If performance scalability can be achieved, then a wide range of performance options can be selected to suit the customer's needs. Unfortunately, several aspects of commercial workstations and networks are significant handicaps from the standpoint of low-latency communication in a multiprocessor cluster configuration. Workstation I/O architectures and networks have been designed for generality rather than performance. These problems span the entire system framework from code path lengths in applications, libraries, operating systems, protocol stacks and device drivers to physical delays in the processor, memory system, I/O controllers, network interface, and within the interconnect fabric. It is clear that these latency problems must either be drastically reduced or effectively hidden if clusters are to achieve acceptable levels of performance. The approach described here is an interesting hybrid in that it provides both significant latency reduction as well as a mechanism for hiding some of the remaining delays.

In clusters of workstations (COWs), the largest latency component is the software code path between the application code and the physical interconnect fabric on both the send and receive sides. The biggest leverage can be therefore be obtained from improved software message passing protocols and by reduced operating system overhead. Further reduction can be achieved by improved network interfaces that accelerate these protocols and tightly integrate the interconnection fabric with the processor and its memory system. Additional improvement can be achieved by improving the *percolation effect* caused by the significant compulsory miss penalty that the CPU incurs as the receiving application starts to access the communication data.

This paper describes the communications latency reduction approach taken by the Utah Avalanche project. The Avalanche machine supports both distributed shared memory as well as message passing based programming models. However, the focus in this paper is restricted to the message passing aspects of the system. The approach concentrates on latency reduction across the whole system and provides improvement in each of the possible areas, namely:

- A new set of efficient message passing protocols and the associated applications programming interface.
- A streamlined lightweight system call interface which reduces operating system overhead while retaining traditional levels of security.
- An improved network interface which is tightly coupled with the memory system, provides hardware support for the new protocols, and acts as a communication data cache to reduce the percolation effect.

These features are performed in a system setting which maximizes the use of commercial off-the-shelf (COTS) technology. The new network interface couples Hewlett-Packard's multiprocessor workstation technology to Myricom's interconnect fabric to achieve user to user message latencies that are less than 4 microseconds. A standard Unix operating system is used with only minor modifications to maintain traditional levels of security and safety. An additional benefit is that the protocol permits asynchronous message passing applications to be self synchronizing to alleviate the need for overhead intensive gang scheduling operations.

2 Message Latency

Quantifying message latency has been a non-standard process which varies with the focus of the particular experiment. The concern here is with total system performance and with the latency seen by communicating application programs. Latency is defined here to be the time between a sending application process initiating a send to the time the receiving application process can actually issue instructions which use the information contained in the message. Message latency is therefore the combined influence of several system components:

- **Interconnect Performance:** This includes the fall-through delay, delays imposed by connection set-up and tear-down, propagation delay, and the transit delay imposed by components in the transmission path.
- **Interconnect Behavior:** This includes overheads associated with maintaining the quality of service for aspects such as reliability, flow control, access control, packet size, and contention delays.
- **Network Interface:** Delays are influenced by the amount of software aid required to transport data in and out of the interface.
- **Memory System Effects:** In NOW architectures, the message data on the send side tends to reside in the cache while on the receive side the data is only useful when it is either in the cache or the processor registers. There is often a considerable delay incurred in moving the data between the cache and the network fabric.
- **System Overhead:** Protocol generality translates proportionately into software overhead. This includes a number of potentially hidden delays such as context switching, memory bus contention, and cache miss penalties in addition to the protocol code path lengths.

Numerous design decisions exist for each of these five areas. For NOW/COW systems utilizing commodity fabrics and processors, many of the choices are beyond the control of the system architect. The restriction is a choice based on cost and integration capability. The challenge is to maximize performance while minimizing cost by using commodity components. The use of shared media networks results in intractable latencies under heavy loads. A high capacity point to point interconnect fabric is currently the best option.

The Avalanche approach is to use Hewlett-Packard's symmetric multiprocessor (SMP) workstations and Myricom's Myrinet-II interconnect fabric coupled by a custom network interface called the *Widget*. Hewlett-Packard provides one to four processor workstation platforms based on their HP-7200 or PA-8000 microprocessors [7, 15]. While these processors vary significantly in their internal architecture, they both use the Runway [5] main memory bus. The Runway bus is a 64-bit, split transaction bus which supports cache coherence for SMP configurations. For HP7200 based systems, the clock speed is 120 MHz with a maximum sustainable bandwidth of 768 megabytes/second in 4-way systems. The results presented in this paper are based on the HP7200.

The Myrinet-II [4] fabric runs at 160 MHz and uses bidirectional, byte-wide, data paths in each link to provide a source routed, wormhole, point to point interconnect fabric. While the Runway bandwidth is 4.8 times that of the Myrinet, the system is reasonably well balanced since the Runway must support cache to cache, and cache to memory transactions as well as I/O. Myrinet switching is done using 8 or 16 link crossbar switches with a fall-through time of 110 ns. The source routing choice provides topology independence although the particular topology will affect latency. Cascaded switches have negligible impact on bandwidth but do increase fall-through delays. Finally, cost effective cascaded switch topologies for large systems will have blocking properties. The blocking probability and associated overhead will vary with aggregate load. The performance numbers reported in this paper are based on a single switch configuration and therefore model a non-blocking cluster of modest size.

The Myrinet provides reliable in-order message delivery, as well as internal error and flow control. The Avalanche protocols depend on this reliability and, to a lesser extent, on ordering guarantees. The tacit assumption is that the Myrinet is a totally reliable network. This assumption has proven reasonable in practice for clusters that are not geographically widely distributed. Increased inter-node distances will degrade performance, and a higher level error protocol is probably necessary. A version of TCP/IP for more distributed clusters is under development. The main defect of the Myrinet technology for NOW/COW systems is the network interface card, LaNai, which incurs several microseconds of latency on each side. Additional overheads are caused by the LaNai connecting an I/O controller rather than directly to the memory bus. The LaNai choice is reasonable for LAN applications but not for tightly coupled cluster organizations such as Avalanche. The LaNai interface also precludes coherent fabric transactions and does not efficiently support the improved protocols described in this paper.

The design of the fabric interface can have a dramatic effect on both latency and overhead[20]. The overhead incurred by the CPU interactions to send or receive a message are usually difficult or impossible to eliminate from the basic latency. The Avalanche choice has been to create a custom network interface capable of directly coupling the Myrinet to the Runway bus. The important difference between the Widget functionality and that of other memory to memory interconnect capabilities is that the Widget permits improved memory locality by providing cache coherent message handling, direct hardware support for the Avalanche protocols, and acts as a communication cache that is integrated into the receiver's memory hierarchy. From the perspective of the other processors and the memory controller in the SMP node, the Widget looks just like a processor. The downside of this approach is that the node loses a processor slot in order to achieve efficient communications. This does not need to be the case in general, but the current decision is imposed by the existing packaging options.

3 Communications and Scheduling Overhead

Overhead also results from many factors, including protocol complexity, fabric interface design and capabilities, and protocol implementation. For parallel applications, the largest overhead contributions come from data movement and from polling. Protocol design and implementation dictate the number of copy operations, with a practical minimum of two copies to move the data into and out of the communications fabric. Interface design also impacts the copy overhead. For example, DMA-capable interfaces eliminate the instruction execution overhead of these copies. Further integration of the interface into the memory system can reduce the cache, bus, and main memory overheads. Additionally, an interface which requires polling of device registers in order to check for message arrival is more latency intensive than an interface which permits arrival notifications to be posted as a cacheable memory object.

Operating system overhead is often a significant fraction of the communications overhead. System calls, context switch times, interrupt and polling overheads are all culprits. The Avalanche approach has been to provide minor modifications to a standard UNIX operating system kernel (BSD and HP-UX in this case). This provides lightweight system call and interrupt capabilities in order to retain TCP/IP levels of security without incurring the intractable latencies of traditional implementations. The result is increased efficiency without a corresponding reduction in safety.

Scheduling can impact parallel application performance in a number of ways. Delays in scheduling tasks can delay all tasks as they wait for synchronization. In a communications model where receiving tasks are required to extract messages from the fabric, delay in scheduling a receiving task can delay the sender of an otherwise non-synchronized communication. These effects have naturally led to concern that clusters of workstations running independent operating systems will exhibit poor parallel performance. Results from our own simulations [2] and from work done by Paikin, et. al. at the University of Illinois at Urbana show that it may be unnecessary to modify the kernel to perform coordinated scheduling.

Under high loads and with appropriate communication mechanisms, distributed parallel applications show a tendency to *self-schedule*. This improves performance significantly in terms of time-to-completion for single parallel ap-

---

[2] Space limitations prohibit presenting these measurements in this paper.

plications and in terms of throughput for multiple competing applications. An appropriate communication mechanism should provide a blocking message reception primitive for cases when the message is not yet available. It should also provide an inexpensive primitive for the case where the message is available. This form of co-scheduling is imprecise since send and receive processes may not be running concurrently. The communication mechanism must efficiently address the case where the receive process is not running. This will remove the synchronization requirement for the receiving process, and support asynchronous communications. Finally, this capability must be provided in a fashion that does not incur additional scheduling overhead elsewhere in the system.

4 Message Passing in Avalanche

Message passing in Avalanche takes a complete system approach to minimizing latency and overhead, and reduces the importance of coordinated scheduling. Lightweight, sender-based protocols[22] are used to reduce the software components of latency and overhead, and to allow simple hardware acceleration of common operations. Operating system involvement is retained in connection establishment and in message transmission. This kernel mediation on the send side permits protected use of the fabric by multiple processes. Operating system involvement in message reception is optional, at the discretion of the application. A custom network interface is used to lower overhead and to reduce processor involvement in data transfer between the fabric and the memory for both transmission and reception. Additional latency and overhead improvement is achieved by connecting the network interface directly to the memory bus rather than via an I/O adapter.

4.1 Sender-Based Protocols

The key concept of sender-based protocols[19] (SBPs) is a connection based mechanism that enables the sender to manage a reserved receive buffer within the receiving process' address space that is obtained when the connection is established. The sender directs placement of messages within that buffer via an offset within each packet header. The sender has no knowledge of the actual physical or virtual location of the buffer at the receiving end. A pointer to the base of the buffer is contained in the receive endpoint data structure established as part of the connection. This endpoint is identified by a field within each packet header. The sender can rely on an arriving message being placed within the buffer at the offset the sender has specified, as long as the offset lies within the buffer and the message would not extend past the end of the buffer. Given a reliable network, a message that is successfully sent will be received, since neither the network or the receiving processor/interface will drop the message. The protocol API provides a mechanism to permit the sender to know when the message has been sent on the send side. Sender and receiver cooperate to manage the buffer space. The receiver must inform the sender when receive buffer space can be reused, but this responsibility is left to a higher level protocol. For some communication patterns, standard techniques such as piggy-backed ACKs might be used. For others, buffer state is implicit in synchronization. For example, an RPC ACK implies that the request has been consumed.

The Avalanche implementation of SBPs is called *Direct Deposit*[18] (DD); it provides system call-based connection establishment and message transmission. Much of the security and safety overhead is isolated to connection setup time and is provided by going through the kernel. The use of a system call allows implementation of safe and atomic shared access to the communication interface for message transmission. It also complements the security of OS-mediated connections by allowing the kernel to limit a process' access to its own connections. While mechanisms to allow secure user-level transmission via a shared interface have been implemented, they often rely on some combination of added interface complexity, limited sharing of the interface, OS scheduling support and virtual memory mapping. Retaining the system call interface for sends provides safety and flexibility at overhead and latency costs that are modest (see Section 5.2).

DD does support user mode message reception. On message arrival, the Widget writes a *notification object*, or note, into a circular queue specified by the connection. This queue can be in kernel or user memory. Each note contains a valid flag, which the Widget sets when a message arrives. A user level receive consists simply of checking the valid flag of the next note. When it is set, the user extracts the message address, size, and connection identifier from the note. Several connections within a single process can share a single notification queue, at the discretion of the user. Message buffers can likewise be in kernel or user memory, to yield a completely user-mode receive capability. A system call is provided to allow a process to sleep and wait for the arrival of a message notification on a specified queue. When the Widget posts a note to a queue, for which a waiting process is sleeping, it generates an interrupt to cause the kernel to alert the sleeping process.

A key to the performance of DD and the Widget is that receive buffers and notification queues must reside in *wired* memory. Thus, the Widget can write to them when a message arrives. They need not be mapped by the TLB, as the Widget performs memory operations using physical addresses. The use of wired memory may be viewed as non-scalable. However, the cost of the extra DRAM required by this approach is a minor fraction of the system cost. It is a small price to pay for a significant increase in performance.

4.2   The Network Interface

As seen by the CPU, the Widget provides a simple interface supporting both DIO (processor mediated) and DMA transmissions. The CPU builds a transmission request block (TRB) in a memory queue and then issues a single write to a device register to initiate transmission by incrementing the count of outstanding TRBs. The TRB contains destination information (node, endpoint identifier, offset) and source information (message address and length). A TRB contains both physical and virtual source address information for a single page of a message. A long message utilizes a sequence of TRBs. Formation of the subsequent TRBs is overlapped with transmission of data described by earlier ones. DIO differs from DMA in that the source address specified is within a region of the Widget's on-board SRAM, to which the CPU would have copied the message data. Each DIO TRB is limited to describing only 128 bytes of data (this is the allocation unit within the Widget's on-board memory). CPU operations to initialize a TRB should hit in the cache after an initial miss. The Widget then reads the entire TRB in one bus transaction.

Completion of transmission of each TRB is signaled via a status bit in the TRB. Given a reasonable number of TRBs, the Widget will be finished with a TRB before the software needs to reuse the TRB. The software only incurs a single cache miss to determine that the TRB has been processed. A lightweight system call is provided to the user to query the status of transmission on a given connection.

The Widget and CPU generally do not interact at all on message reception. As described earlier, the Widget writes a note into memory when a message arrives. In some cases the receiver will block, waiting for message arrival notification. A status bit in the note indicates that the Widget should interrupt the CPU in this case. This is the only time in normal reception that the Widget interacts directly with the CPU.

4.3 Integrating the Network Interface into the Memory Hierarchy

The Avalanche Widget is a system memory bus resident interface. It operates as a peer with the CPU(s) in maintaining memory coherence. Both incoming and outgoing message data are moved into and out of the memory system using coherent bus transactions. The software need not flush or purge cache lines to ensure data consistency. This reduces both overhead and latency in the CPU, cache, bus, and memory system.

Incorporated into the Widget is a 256K SRAM buffer called the Shared Buffer (SB). The SB is used to stage outgoing messages and acts as a second level (1024 line, direct-mapped, physically indexed, 128 byte line) data cache for incoming message data. Outgoing messages are pipelined through the SB in units of 32 bytes (1 cache line) at a time. For long messages, the transmission of data can be overlapped while subsequent data is being fetched from the memory system. Variations in the time to acquire data are smoothed by this mechanism, providing a steady stream of data to the Myrinet.

For incoming messages, data is stored in the SB, and the Widget asserts ownership of the affected cache lines. If the message occupies a portion of a given cache line, the Widget merges the new data into the old value after gaining ownership of the line. The Widget then serves as a fast source for subsequent CPU accesses to these lines. Another benefit of buffering in the SB is that it allows data to be moved out of the Myrinet without waiting for the main memory to absorb the data. Once again, bus and memory bandwidth consumption are reduced, as is cache miss latency as seen by the CPU to access the data. Some messages are too long to be stored in the SB and must be placed in main memory. In this case, the SB allows the transaction to be pipelined.

5 Performance Results

The fundamental performance of communication primitives of an Avalanche system based on 120 MHz HP 7200 processors and a 160 MHz Myrinet are examined here. The results were obtained from execution-driven simulations using the Paint simulator[17]. Paint simulates the HP PA RISC 1.1[14] architecture and includes an instruction set interpreter and detailed cycle-level models of a first level cache, system bus, and memory system similar to those found in HP J-class systems. In addition, it contains a detailed cycle-level model of the Widget and a simple Myrinet simulator that models contention only at node inputs. For these particular experiments, a simple processor is modeled at 120 MHz, with non-blocking loads and stores. Most instructions (except floating point) take one cycle. The cache is direct mapped, virtually indexed, 128 KB with 32 byte lines. It provides single-cycle loads and stores, a one-cycle load-use penalty, and data streaming. The Runway bus is also modeled at 120 MHz. The memory system contains 4 banks and a 17 entry write buffer. The Myrinet is modeled at 160 MHz, giving nearly 160 MB/second bandwidth; fall through time for the single switch is 14 processor cycles (approximately 116 ns.), propagation delays are 1 cycle on each side of the switch. In the experiments, cache misses to main memory had an average latency of 30 cycles, while those serviced by the Widget's cache capability had an average latency of 16 cycles. The simulation environment includes a small BSD-based kernel, used to provide device driver and system calls which initialize the Widget, set up connections, and perform message send operations.

5.1 Latency

Latency is measured by starting programs on two nodes. A receiver program establishes a communication endpoint and enters a loop polling for incoming messages. The sender program connects to that endpoint, waits to ensure that the receiver will be polling, and then sends a number of messages. Figure 1 presents the latency in 120 MHz cycles for message sizes from 4 to 2K bytes in length. Time is measured from before the send system call to when the receiver has discovered the message's arrival and touched a word from each cache line comprising the message, causing those cache lines to be brought into first level cache. The latency columns are labeled either DIO or DMA and *cache* (meaning the Widget's caching capability is used), *nocache* (meaning that arriving data is moved to main memory), or *notouch* (where the receiver does not perform the touch of the incoming data to bring it into the first level cache).

Several interesting trends should be noted in these numbers:

– DIO is competitive with DMA for messages up to 256 bytes in length.

Fig. 1. Latency vs. Message Size

Message Size	DIO cache	DIO no cache	DMA cache	DMA no touch
4	382	390	400	401
16	399	403	411	412
32	413	422	422	423
64	466	501	508	484
128	574	663	587	524
256	786	923	777	635
512	1210	1443	1156	855
1024	2064	2496	1915	1291
2048	3796	4568	3446	2181

Fig. 2. Overhead vs. Message Size

Message Size	Receive			DMA Send			DIO Send		
	low	high	avg	low	high	avg	low	high	avg
4	65	129	71	146	148	146	117	147	141
16	65	129	71	146	148	146	119	151	143
32	65	65	65	146	148	146	124	156	148
64	65	129	84	146	148	147	134	166	158
128	65	152	78	146	152	147	154	186	178
256	65	150	82	146	168	153	250	350	311
512	65	150	82	145	154	147	503	573	566
1024	65	89	69	145	148	146	1089	1089	1089
4096	65	89	71	145	148	147	4278	4278	4278
8192	65	65	65	243	252	248	8436	8508	8453

- The efficacy of the Widget's cache capability becomes evident for medium sized (4 cache lines) and larger messages, resulting in latency reductions of 13% to 17%.
- Getting data into the first level cache is a significant portion of the actual latency. Comparing the DMA/cache latency with DMA notouch, the latter understates real latency by as much as 37%.

5.2 Overhead

Overhead results are reported in Figure 2. The receiver delays long enough for all messages to arrive, eliminating wait time within the library call. Timing starts before the receive library call and ends when it returns and the first cache line of message data has been referenced. This is an exact measurement of first-order message reception overhead. Second order effects such as bus/cache contention incurred as the messages arrive at the node are not measured by this experiment. Receive overhead is independent of message size and has a small range, averaging 65 to 84 cycles. This cost is very nearly optimal, and is dominated by fundamental references to three cache lines: the notification queue descriptor, the note at the head of the queue, and the first cache line of message data.

Sender overhead is the time spent in the send system call. Timing commences before each send call and ends when it returns. Send overhead for DMA mode is nearly constant up to 4K bytes. Then it increases by approximately 100 cycles. As explained in Section 4.2, each TRB can specify the transmission of up to 4K bytes of data. DMA sender overhead increases linearly at a rate of 100 cycles per 4K increment in message size. This is the time required to allocate and initialize a TRB and increment the Widget's count of outstanding TRBs. It is independent of whether the send interface is implemented within a system call or not. Subtracting this 100 cycles from the base time of 150 cycles gives an upper bound of 50 cycles on the cost imposed by using a system call. The 50 cycles includes the library call sequence and some bookkeeping which would exist even in a user-level IO approach.

In contrast, DIO sender overhead increases linearly at about 1 cycle, 8.33 nanoseconds, per byte increment in message size. As the 160 MHz Myrinet can optimally absorb one byte every 6.25 nanoseconds, one concludes that DIO cannot saturate the fabric. Data movement from the CPU over the system bus is the limiting factor for DIO transfers.

Another performance-critical operation is polling time. It is independent of message size and send mode. A non-blocking receive serves as the message arrival polling primitive on a specified notification queue. It simply returns a status value indicating there are no messages. A simple poll on a queue with no unconsumed messages takes 53 cycles if it causes a cache miss on the note structure, which is likely on the first poll. 19 cycles are required for subsequent polls as long the note remains in cache. The posting of a notification by the Widget will purge the stale note from the cache, resulting in the previously reported time for a receive. This poll is not minimal, since it uses the receive library call. More aggressive approaches, such as compiler-generated code, could reduce this to a couple of memory references and a conditional. Polling to determine if a send has completed is done via a system call and takes 49 cycles.

5.3 An Example Program

This section reports performance data for an example program, illustrating the effectiveness of the Widget's cache and the high volume of communication sustainable while still achieving speedup. The program used is an asynchronous version of a successive over-relaxation problem. It is *asynchronous* in that each node broadcasts its portion of the current solution vector as soon as it completes a sweep. The nodes only synchronize at time steps (each comprised of 5 sweeps). The solution converges more quickly, in terms of time steps, than with a more conventional approach where nodes exchange partial solutions only at the synchronization points. This comes at the cost of significant increases in the

Fig. 3. Asynchronous Update SOR Performance

# of Procs	Message Count	Message Data	Bus Utilization		Run Time		Runtime ratio
			cache	no cache	cache	no cache	
4	446	1.476	1.97	2.16	40.92	41.61	98.3
8	500	1.72	1.13	1.34	19.38	20.14	96.2
16	1225	1.85	1.157	1.388	10.61	11.44	92.7
32	2500	1.92	1.255	1.494	6.53	7.4	88.2

frequency and volume of communication. This is impractical for systems with high relative communication overheads (see the study by Chandra, et al.[8] for a detailed description of the program and evaluation on another architecture).

Figure 3 reports a number of metrics obtained from running the program on 4 different sized systems, with and without Widget cacheing enabled. The average count of messages per node is given, as well as the volume of data (in millions of bytes) sent by each node. This is followed by the bus utilization, in millions of cycles, for the cache/nocache cases, and the run time (minus program initialization time) for the cache/nocache cases, also in millions of cycles. The Widget cache decreases bus utilization by 8.8% to 16.7%. The improvement increases with processor count. When the Widget caches the data, it provides it directly to the CPU on a miss in the first level cache. This eliminates the extra trip from the Widget to memory. The lower latency of misses to the Widget cache compared to that of main memory is evidenced by the ratio of cache/nocache runtimes in the column labeled *Runtime ratio*. There is a clear trend towards lower run times as the number of processors is increased, which in turn drives up the communication to computation ratio. The lower latency afforded by the Widget cache clearly enhances the scalability range of the program.

6 Related Work

Many groups are currently researching efficient messaging for workstations. The Hamlyn[6] effort at Hewlett-Packard Labs is similar in many respects to the Avalanche approach. It utilizes a sender-based protocol, HP Runway-based workstations, and the Myrinet interconnect. Their interface uses an I/O controller LaNai rather than the system bus. They report a one-way message latency of 12.7 microseconds with a large portion of the time spent in the interface processor and in high-latency bus translation hardware. Illinois Fast Messages[16] is another I/O-bus resident system, in this case using SPARCstations and Myrinet. Their protocol uses a more traditional buffering approach. Their use of the I/O bus LaNai interface results in a 32 microsecond latency for small messages. U-Net[2] attempts to achieve many of the same goals as Avalanche, but using completely off-the-shelf hardware. They arrive at many of the same conclusions, such as the retention of system call interface for message transmission. Positioning the network interface on an I/O bus and the use of a processor in the fabric interface limits their latency to approximately 32 microseconds for a one cell ATM message.

Hewlett Packard's Afterburner[10] efforts have shown that the bottleneck for communication between machines is due to copy overhead. Sender Based protocols used in the Avalanche work are designed to eliminate any unnecessary copies of message data. Both the Princeton SHRIMP[11, 3] group and Digital Equipment Corporation with its Memory Channel[12] provide user-level messaging by mapping local memory pages to receiver memory pages. Message transmission becomes a series of simple stores to mapped pages, relying either on non-cacheable pages or the availability of a write-through mode in the cache to ensure that stores become visible to the network interface. This approach can deliver excellent latency for small messages (4.5 and 5.4 microseconds respectively). Neither provides the DMA capability to avoid CPU cycle stealing to support bulk transfers. Neither has the capability of serving incoming data to cache, or achieves the latency and bus utilization benefits exhibited by the Avalanche Widget.

Stanford's FLASH[13] architecture places the network interface on the memory bus by replacing the standard memory controller with the MAGIC (Memory And General Interconnect Controller) chip. The MIT Alewife[1] also places the network interface on the memory bus but connects to a custom memory controller. Both preclude the use of commercial workstation boards.

The two distinguishing features of Avalanche are its whole system approach, which attacks costs from the communication protocols all the way to the physical interconnect, and its treatment of interface card memory (the SB) as a second level communications cache to minimize the latency effects of memory percolation.

7 Conclusions

This paper has specifically described a set of design choices that have been made by the Utah Avalanche project which result in very low-latency message passing that is appropriate for NOW and COW style multiprocessing architectures. The approach, while specific to a particular commercial processor and fabric choice in the Avalanche implementation, is not vendor specific. It takes advantage of the fact that modern microprocessors are being designed to be used in both uniprocessor and small-way SMP product platforms. The primary feature that supports this capability is the provision of a system or memory bus that supports cache coherent transactions between the processors and the memory system. By providing an interconnect network interface that attaches directly to the coherent system bus, it is possible to significantly reduce the software overhead associated with message communication.

The paper has also described a new efficient communication protocol (DD) which further reduces message overheads and which provides the additional benefit of permitting the system to be insensitive to task synchronization delays.

These delays are imposed by systems which only support synchronous message transactions. The extremely efficient polling mechanism and low-latency for small messages make DD an excellent target for languages such as Split-C[9], and for message passing libraries such as Active Messages[21] and Thinking Machine Corporation's CMMD, that depend on such efficiency. The Avalanche network interface has also been designed to provide direct hardware support for these new protocols which significantly reduces software overheads on both the send and receive side while maintaining the level of security that is expected from existing TCP/IP based systems. The result is that message latency is reduced to approximately 3.5 microseconds and the need for overhead intensive gang scheduling mechanisms is unnecessary.

The results presented here are based on architectural simulations, but the chip design is underway as a .6 micron CMOS ASIC. The simulation timing models are based on currently available implementation data. A 32 node prototype system is expected to be operational in early 1998.

References

1. AGARWAL, A., BIANCHINI, R., CHAIKEN, D., AND JOHNSON, K. The MIT Alewife Machine: Architecture and Performance. In *Proceedings of the 22nd Annual International Symposium on Computer Architecture* (June 1995), pp. 2–13.
2. BASU, A., BUCH, V., VOGELS, W., AND VON EICKEN, T. U-Net: A User-Level Network Interface for Parallel and Distributed Computing. In *Proceedings of the 15th ACM Symposium on Operating Systems Principles* (December 1995).
3. BLUMRICH, M., ET AL. Virtual Memory Mapped Network Interface for the SHRIMP Multicomputer. In *Proceedings of the 21st Annual International Symposium on Computer Architecture* (April 1994), pp. 142–153.
4. BODEN, N., ET AL. Myrinet – A Gigabit-per-second Local-Area Network. *IEEE MICRO 15*, 1 (February 1995), 29–36.
5. BRYG, W., CHAN, K., AND FIDUCCIA, N. A High-Performance, Low-Cost Multiprocessor Bus for Workstations and Midrange Servers. *Hewlett-Packard Journal 47*, 1 (February 1996), 18–24.
6. BUZZARD, G., ET AL. An implementation of the Hamlyn sender-managed interface architecture. In *Proceedings of the Second Symposium on Operating System Design and Implementation* (October 1996).
7. CHAN, K., ET AL. Design of the HP PA 7200 CPU. *Hewlett-Packard Journal 47*, 1 (February 1996), 25–33.
8. CHANDRA, S., LARUS, J., AND ROGERS, A. Where is Time Spent in Message-Passing and Shared-Memory Programs? In *Proceedings of the 6th Symposium on Architectural Support for Programming Languages and Operating Systems* (Oct. 1994), pp. 61–73.
9. CULLER, D. E., ET AL. Parallel Programming in Split-C. In *Proceedings of Supercomputing '93* (Nov. 1993), pp. 262–273.
10. DALTON, C., ET AL. Afterburner: A Network-Independent Card Provides Architectural Support for High-Performance Protocols. *IEEE Network* (July 1993), 36–43.

11. DUBNICKI, C., IFTODE, L., FELTEN, E., AND LI, K. Software Support of Virtual Memory Mapped Communication. In *10th International Parallel Processing Symposium* (Apr. 1996).

12. GILLETT, R., AND KAUFMANN, R. Experience Using the First-Generation Memory Channel for PCI Network. In *HOT Interconnects Symposium IV* (Aug. 1996).

13. HEINRICH, M., ET AL. The Performance Impact of Flexibility in the Stanford FLASH Multiprocessor. In *Proceedings of the 6th Symposium on Architectural Support for Programming Languages and Operating Systems* (Oct. 1994), pp. 274–285.

14. HEWLETT-PACKARD CO. *PA-RISC 1.1 Architecture and Instruction Set Reference Manual*, February 1994.

15. HUNT, D. Advanced Performance Features of the 64-bit PA-8000. In *COMPCON '95* (1995), pp. 123–128.

16. PAIKIN, S., LAURIA, AND CHIEN, A. High Performance Messaging on Workstations: Illinois Fast Messages (FM) for Myrinet. In *Proceedings of Supercomputing '88* (1995).

17. STOLLER, L., KURAMKOTE, R., AND SWANSON, M. PAINT- PA Instruction Set Interpreter. Tech. Rep. UUCS-96-009, University of Utah - Computer Science Department, September 1996.

18. STOLLER, L., AND SWANSON, M. Direct Deposit: A Basic User-Level Protocol for Carpet Clusters. Tech. Rep. UUCS-95-003, University of Utah - Computer Science Department, March 1995.

19. SWANSON, M., AND STOLLER, L. Low Latency Workstation Cluster Communications Using Sender-Based Protocols - Computer Science Department. Tech. Rep. UUCS-96-001, University of Utah, March 1996.

20. THEKKATH, A., AND LEVY, H. Limits to Low-Latency Communications on High-Speed Networks. *acm Transactions on Computer Systems 11*, 2 (May 1993), 179–203.

21. VON EICKEN, T., CULLER, D. E., GOLDSTEIN, S. C., AND SCHAUSER, K. E. Active Messages: a Mechanism for Integrated Communication and Computation,. In *Proceedings of the 19th Annual International Symposium on Computer Architecture* (May 1992), pp. 256–266.

22. WILKES, J. Hamlyn - an interface for sender-based communication. Tech. Rep. HPL-OSR-92-13, Hewlett-Packard Research Laboratory, Nov. 1992.

Stream Sockets on *SHRIMP*

Stefanos N. Damianakis, Cezary Dubnicki, Edward W. Felten

Department of Computer Science, Princeton University, Princeton NJ 08544, USA
{snd,dubnicki,felten}@cs.princeton.edu

Abstract. This paper describes an implementation of stream sockets for the *SHRIMP* multicomputer. *SHRIMP* supports protected, user-level data transfer, allows user-level code to perform its own buffer management, and separates data transfers from control transfers so that data transfers can be done without the interrupting the receiving node's CPU. Our sockets implementation exploits all of these features to provide high performance. End-to-end latency for 8 byte transfers is 11 microseconds, which is considerably lower than all previous implementations of the sockets interface. For large transfers, we obtain a bandwidth of 13.5 MBytes/sec, which is close to the hardware limit when the receiver must perform a copy. Further experiments with the public-domain benchmarks ttcp and netperf confirm the performance of our implementation.

1 Introduction

A wide variety of distributed applications rely on the Berkeley stream sockets model for interprocess communication. The stream socket interface provides a connection-oriented, bidirectional byte-stream abstraction, with well-defined mechanisms for creating and destroying connections and for detecting errors.

In this paper, we describe an implementation of the sockets interface on the *SHRIMP* multicomputer. Our implementation is compatible with the stream sockets interface; it properly detects broken connections and correctly implements the **select** call.

Our sockets library performs much better than all previous sockets implementations for small transfers, with an end-to-end latency of 11 microseconds for an 8-byte transfer. Small transfers are important because they are very common in many applications [15]. For large transfers our implementation obtains a bandwidth of 13.5 MBytes/sec, which is close to the hardware limit when the receiver must perform a copy.

We achieve high performance by taking advantage of the features of the underlying *SHRIMP* architecture. *SHRIMP* provides low-latency protected user-level communication, without imposing any buffer management semantics, and without requiring an interrupt for each message. These properties allow packages like our sockets library to customize their buffer management and control transfer strategies to optimize performance.

We measured the performance of our implementation on a prototype *SHRIMP* machine, using custom micro-benchmarks in addition to two well-known benchmarks: ttcp and netperf.

2 *SHRIMP* Hardware

The *SHRIMP* multicomputer is a network of commodity systems. Each node is a Pentium PC running the Linux operating system. The network is a multicomputer routing network [22] connected to the PC nodes via custom-designed network interfaces. The *SHRIMP* network interface closely cooperates with a thin layer of software to form a communication mechanism called virtual memory-mapped communication (VMMC) [10]. This mechanism delivers excellent performance and supports various message-passing packages and applications effectively [11].

The prototype system consists of four interconnected nodes. Each node is a DEC 560ST PC containing an 60 MHz Intel Pentium processor with an external 256 Kbyte second-level cache, and 40 MBytes of main DRAM memory. Peripherals are connected to the system through the EISA expansion bus, which has main memory mastering capability and a maximum burst bandwidth of 33 MBytes/sec.

Main memory data can be cached by the CPU as write-through or write-back on a per-virtual-page basis, as specified in process page tables. The caches snoop DMA transactions and automatically invalidate corresponding cache lines, thereby keeping consistent with *all* main memory updates, including those from EISA bus masters.

The network connecting the nodes is an Intel routing backplane consisting of a two-dimensional mesh of Intel Mesh Routing Chips (iMRCs) [22], and is the same network used in the Paragon multicomputer. The backplane supports deadlock-free, oblivious wormhole routing, and preserves the order of messages from each sender to each receiver.

In addition to the fast backplane interconnect, the PC nodes are connected by a commodity Ethernet, which is used for diagnostics, booting, and exchange of low-priority messages.

The custom network interface [3, 4] is the system's key component. It connects each PC node to the routing backplane and implements the hardware support for VMMC.

3 Virtual Memory Mapped Communication

Virtual memory-mapped communication (VMMC) addresses the need for a basic multicomputer communication mechanism with extremely low latency and high bandwidth. VMMC achieves this by allowing applications to transfer data directly between two virtual memory address spaces over the network. This mechanism efficiently supports applications and common communication models such as message passing, shared memory, RPC, and client-server communication.

The VMMC mechanism consists of several calls to support user-level buffer management, various data transfer strategies, and transfer of control.

3.1 Import-Export Mappings

In the VMMC model, an *import-export mapping* must be established before communication begins. A receiving process can *export* a region of its address space as a receive buffer together with a set of permissions to define access rights for the buffer. In order to send data to an exported receive buffer, a user process must *import* the buffer with the appropriate permissions. After a successful import, a sender can transfer data from its virtual memory into an imported receive buffer at user-level without further protection checking and without entering the kernel. The *SHRIMP* implementation forces page granularity for all import-export mappings.

The *unexport* and *unimport* primitives can be used to destroy existing import-export mappings. Before completing, these calls wait for all currently pending messages using the mapping to be delivered.

3.2 Protection

Communication in VMMC is protected in two ways. First, communication may take place only after the receiver gives the sender permission (by calling *export*) to transfer data to a given area of the receiver's address space. Import and export requests are matched by a trusted daemon process.

Second, at send initiation, the *SHRIMP* implementation uses the hardware virtual memory management unit (MMU) to verify permission to send data to a receive buffer. For more details please see [5].

3.3 Transfer Strategies

The VMMC model defines two user-level transfer strategies: *deliberate update* and *automatic update*. Deliberate update is an explicit transfer of data from a sender's memory to a receiver's memory. In automatic upate there is no explicit send operation; all writes performed to the local memory are automatically propagated to the remote memory (by the *SHRIMP* hardware). In order to use automatic update, a sender *binds* a portion of its address space to an imported receive buffer, creating an *automatic update binding* between the local and remote memory.

An important distinction between these two transfer strategies is that under automatic update, local memory is "bound" to a receive buffer at the time a mapping is created, while under deliberate update the binding does not occur until an explicit send command is issued. Automatic update is optimized for low latency, and deliberate update is designed for flexible import-export mappings and for reducing network traffic.

Automatic update is implemented by having the *SHRIMP* network interface hardware snoop all writes on the memory bus. If a write is to an address that has an automatic update binding, the hardware builds a packet containing the destination address and the written value, and sends it to the destination node. The hardware can combine writes to consecutive locations into a single packet.

Deliberate update is implemented by having a user-level program execute a sequence of two accesses to addresses which are decoded by the *SHRIMP* network interface board on the node's expansion bus (the EISA bus). These accesses specify the source address, destination address, and size of a transfer. The ordinary virtual memory protection mechanisms (MMU and page tables) are used to maintain protection [5]. The hardware requires that both source and destination addresses are word aligned.

VMMC guarantees the in-order, reliable delivery of all data transfers. but does not include any buffer management since data is transferred directly between user-level address spaces. This gives libraries and applications the freedom to use as little buffering and copying as needed.

The VMMC model assumes that receive buffer addresses are specified by the sender, and received data is transferred directly to memory. Hence, there is no explicit receive operation. CPU involvement in receiving data can be as little as checking a flag, although the hardware also supports a notification mechanism.

3.4 Notifications

The *notification* mechanism is used to transfer control to a receiving process, or to notify a receiving process about external events. It consists of a message transfer followed by an invocation of a user-specified, user-level handler function. The receiving process can associate a separate handler function with each exported buffer, and notifications only take effect when a handler has been specified.

Notifications are similar to UNIX signals in that they can be blocked and unblocked, they can be accepted or discarded (on a per-buffer basis), and a process can be suspended until a particular notification arrives. Unlike signals, however, notifications are queued when blocked.

4 Shrimp Sockets

The *SHRIMP* socket API is implemented as a user-level library, using the VMMC interface. It is compatible, and seamlessly integrated with the Unix stream sockets facility [16]. We introduce a new address family, **AF_SHRIMP**, to support the new type of stream socket.

We implement three variations of the socket library, two using deliberate update and one using automatic update. The first protocol performs two copies, one on the sender to eliminate the need to deal with data alignment, and the other on the receiver to move the data into the user memory. We can improve the performance by eliminating the send-side copy, leading to a one-copy protocol. Our current protocol uses two-copies for unaligned transfers in order to minimize small message latency. The automatic-update protocol always does two copies, since the sender-side copy acts as the send operation.

On *SHRIMP*, it is not possible to eliminate the receive side copy without violating the protection requirements of the sockets model. Such a protocol would require a page of the receiver's user memory to be exported; the sender could

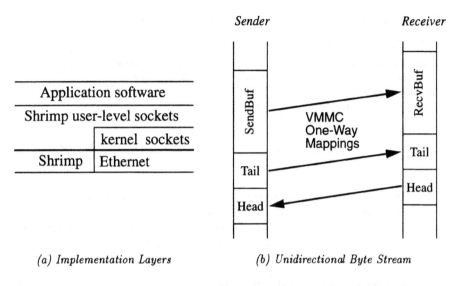

(a) Implementation Layers   (b) Unidirectional Byte Stream

Fig. 1. Socket Diagrams

then clobber this page at will. This is not acceptable in the sockets model, since the receiver does not necessarily trust the sender.

4.1 Implementation

The user-level library's socket descriptor table contains one entry for each open socket, regardless of the socket type. When non-*SHRIMP* sockets are used, our library passes calls through to the regular `libc` socket calls, while still maintaining a descriptor table entry. Also, our library uses calls to the regular `libc` socket functions in order to bootstrap the *SHRIMP* connection. Figure 1a illustrates the software layers in our implementation.

We use a straightforward implementation of circular buffers in order to manage each socket's incoming and outgoing data. First, we describe how to implement a simple unidirectional byte stream on *SHRIMP*. Then we show how we use this simple structure as the building block for our library.

The byte stream is managed by a circular buffer that consists of a data buffer and the head and tail indices. In order to implement a simple unidirectional byte stream the sender and receiver each allocate a copy of the circular queue and cross map the three components. The tail index and buffer are mapped from the sender to the receiver and the head index is mapped from the receiver to the sender (see Figure 1b).

Figure 2 illustrates how this simple queue structure can be used to transfer bytes. The sender writes the buffer and the tail index and only reads the head index, while the receiver only reads the buffer and tail index and writes the head index. Since writes to the index variables are always exclusive, race conditions are eliminated.

```
simple_send(msg)                        simple_recv(buf)
{                                       {
  wait until buffer space is available    wait until data is available
  copy msg into sendbuf                   copy data from recvbuf to buf
  transfer sendbuf data to receiver       update head pointer
  update tail pointer                     transfer head pointer to sender
  transfer tail pointer to receiver     }
}
```

Fig. 2. *Pseudo code for simple send and recv*

In order to construct a bidirectional byte stream we use two unidirectional byte streams described above: one for sending bytes and one for receiving bytes. This basic underlying implementation is simple, straightforward, and works very well with *SHRIMP*'s VMMC communication mechanism.

4.2 Connection Setup and Shutdown

During connection establishment, the implementation uses a regular TCP socket connection to exchange the data required to establish two VMMC mappings (one in each direction). The TCP socket remains open, and is used to detect certain errors, such as node failure. To import a buffer a process must obtain the following information about the remote process and node:

- **IPaddr**: the node's IP address
- **squID**: similar to a process ID, obtained by a call to the *SHRIMP* library
- **bufferID**: identifies which exported buffer to import

The two VMMC mappings are established when the server process is in **accept** and the client process is in **connect**. Our implementations of these functions call an internal routine **Shrimp_Setup** that does the following:

- **pack** local data describing process and node
- **allocate buffers** for incoming and outgoing data
- **export** the receive buffer
- **client** process
    1. *TCP-send* the node's local id structure
    2. *TCP-receive* the remote node's id structure
    3. *import* the receive buffer (from the server)
- **server** process
    1. *TCP-receive* the remote node's id structure
    2. *TCP-send* the node's local id structure
    3. *import* the receive buffer (from the client)

The transfer strategy, deliberate or automatic update, is determined (using compile time defines) in **Shrimp_Setup**. When this function completes on both nodes, the two processes are ready to communicate using the *SHRIMP* hardware.

When a connection is terminated (using **close**) the specified socket's descriptor table entry is freed and the associated VMMC mapping is removed.

4.3 send

send must copy the user data into the local circular buffer and initiate the transfer to the remote node. For deliberate update this requires an explicit *SHRIMP* call to initiate data transfer. Two calls are required if the data wraps around the circular buffer. When automatic update is used, copying the data into the circular buffer automatically triggers the send. Once the data is sent, the sender sends a one-word message to update the receiver's tail pointer. The pseudo-code for **send** is as follows:

- **check** that socket is valid and alive
- **verify** that space is available for the remote node to receive data; if not, spin until space becomes available
- **send** data to remote node with automatic or deliberate update
- **update** remote node's circular buffer tail pointer

4.4 recv

recv must copy data that is in the incoming buffer to the user-specified buffer. Once it consumes the data, it updates the **head** pointer on the remote node. Each call costs one copy (or two, depending on the state of the circular buffer) and a one-word message to update the pointer. The pseudo code for **recv** is as follows:

- **check** that socket is valid and alive
- **verify** that data is available to receive; if not, wait for data to arrive
- **copy** data from socket library's circular buffer into user buffer
- **update** remote node's circular buffer start pointer

4.5 select

select is the most complex function in the library because it deals with both TCP and *SHRIMP* sockets. It uses notifications in order to detect the arrival of new *SHRIMP* data. **select** uses a null user-level notification handler.

When a buffer is exported, notifications are optionally activated, and a user-level handler is specified. Each exported buffer's notifications can be in one of three states:

- *ignore*: notifications are dropped
- *accumulate*: notifications are queued for later delivery

– *deliver:* accumulated and incoming notifications are delivered

Since notifications are implemented using interrupts we do not want the common case to pay the notification processing cost. To achieve this initially all of the socket library's buffers *ignore* notifications. `select` must first *queue* notifications for the sockets in question.

The algorithm for our user-level `select` uses the kernel version of select, which we denote `SELECT`. `SELECT` returns when I/O occurs or any signal is trapped. Since signals are used to implement notifications, `SELECT` also traps them. But, when `SELECT` completes it returns no indication of which, if any, signals have occurred. This leads to the following implementation of our user-level `select`:

– *deliver notifications*: turn on notifications for Shrimp socket data
– *check for new data*: check the Shrimp socket data structures to see if any data has arrived
– *loop* until data has arrived:
  • call `SELECT`, i.e. block in the kernel for a notification or other I/O, with a timeout. The timeout is required because a notification can arrive after checking for data but before calling `SELECT`; therefore we use a timeout in tandem with the loop.
  • *check for new data*: check the Shrimp socket data structures and exit loop if any new data has arrived
– *ignore notifications*: return notifications to the fast common case

4.6 Integration with `libc`

We integrated our library with `libc` by renaming the corresponding functions in `libc` to all uppercase. In order to keep things simple, we did this directly in the binary object modules of `libc`. Where necessary, our library is able to call the original socket functions.

5 Performance Issues

5.1 Sending and Aligning Bytes

Socket communications operate at the byte level: all sends and receives specify byte counts, and there is no guaranteed relationship between the alignment of the send and receive buffers. The *SHRIMP* hardware is most efficient when transferring words, so byte transfers are best done by transferring a little extra data.

In addition, *SHRIMP* requires that all deliberate update transfers be word aligned. This requirement complicates the implementation. On the sending side, if the data is copied from the user buffer to the socket library's circular buffer, then the alignment problem goes away, since the extra copy into the library's buffer forces proper byte alignment. We can eliminate this extra copy by encoding byte alignment and send it along with the data; the receiver must decode this information when removing data from its buffer.

5.2 Deliberate vs. Automatic Update

We must choose when to use the deliberate update strategy and when to use automatic update. Automatic update is clearly faster for small transfers so we use automatic update to transfer control information (i.e. the circular buffers' index values).

For transferring message data, the choice is less clear-cut. Deliberate update has slightly higher asymptotic bandwidth, but automatic update is convenient to use and does not restrict buffer alignment.

When we use automatic update, the sender transmits the message data to the receiver by simply copying the data from the user memory to the send-side communication buffer. We do not count this as a data copy since this acts as the data transfer. The benefit of this transfer mechanism is that no explicit send operation is required. Thus, every automatic update protocol does only one copy, on the receive side.

5.3 Caching Effects

Our experience with *SHRIMP* shows that communication performance can be affected by the caching strategy used for send-buffer and receive-buffer memory; communication performance is better with write-through caching [2]. We do not want to change the caching strategy for the application's data, since that would probably degrade the application's performance. However, we can safely change the caching mode for pages that consist entirely of our internal data buffers.

6 Measurements

This section describes the performance measurements we obtain using our implementation of sockets. All tests are performed on a prototype four-node *SHRIMP* system. Each node is a 60 MHz Pentium PC running Linux 1.2.8. We use gcc 2.6.3 with all optimizations enabled (-O3).

We report the performance for three different implementations of the socket library. The three implementations differ only in the data transfer mechanism:

- **DU+1copy**: deliberate update with only one copy. The receiver moves the incoming data from the library's internal buffer to the user's buffer. For the current implementation, this places alignment restrictions on the sender.
- **DU+2copy**: deliberate update with two copies. The sender copies the data from the source to the library's internal buffer and the receiver moves the incoming data from the library's internal buffer to the user's buffer.
- **AU+1copy**: automatic update with one copy. The receiver moves the incoming data from the library's internal buffer to the user's buffer. Note that the sender also does a copy from the source to the library's internal buffer but this copy is not counted because it acts as the actual data transfer.

Finally, we use the following three metrics from [19] to characterize performance:

r_∞ = peak bandwidth for infinitely large packets
$n_{\frac{1}{2}}$ = packet size to achieve $\frac{r_\infty}{2}$ bandwidth
l = one way packet latency

6.1 Micro-Benchmarks

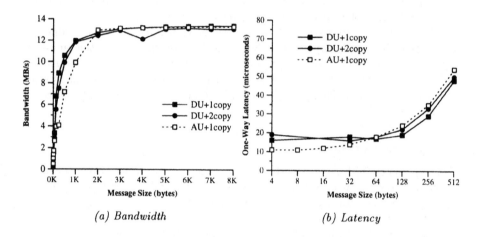

(a) Bandwidth   (b) Latency

Fig. 3. *Socket Micro-benchmarks*

To determine the bandwidth performance of our sockets library, we measure the time required for a large number of consecutive transfers in the same direction. Figure 3a shows the results. All three implementations have similar performance. For large messages, performance is very close to the raw hardware one-copy limit of about r_∞=13.5 MBytes/sec. Further, all three of the performance curves have a steep rise indicating that peak performance is obtained quickly: $n_{\frac{1}{2}}$=256 bytes.

Figure 3b shows the latency for small transfers, measured using a ping-pong test. For small messages, we incur a one-way latency of $l = 11$ μsec, or about 7 μsec above the hardware limit. This extra time is spent equally between the sender and receiver performing procedure calls, checking for errors, and accessing the socket data structure.

6.2 Ttcp

Ttcp is a public-domain benchmark originally written at the Army Ballistics Research Lab. Ttcp measures network performance using a one-way communication test in which the sender continuously pumps data to the receiver. The performance of our library as reported by ttcp appears in Figure 4a. Ttcp obtained a peak bandwidth of r_∞=12.4 MBytes/sec using 7 KByte messages. Once again, the bandwidth rises quickly as the message size increases: $n_{\frac{1}{2}}$=512 bytes.

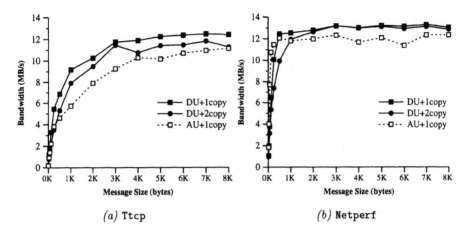

(a) Ttcp   *(b)* Netperf

Fig. 4. *Socket Bandwidth*

6.3 Netperf

Netperf (Revision 1.7) is a public domain benchmark from Hewlett-Packard. Figure 4b shows the performance of our library as reported by the TCP stream test. The peak bandwidth is about r_∞=13 MBytes/sec and $n_{\frac{1}{2}}$=256 bytes.

6.4 Discussion of Results

Our sockets implementation achieves low latency because of customized buffer management and the low software overhead of VMMC on *SHRIMP*. The available user-to-user bandwidth grows fast with the message size; $n_{\frac{1}{2}}$ is between 256 and 512 for all experiments. The bandwidth curves in Figures 3 and 4 show that automatic update closely tracks deliberate update, to within 7% - 17%. Yet for small messages (Figure 3b), automatic update's latency is 30% - 40% less than deliberate update's. Furthermore, all the bandwidth curves continue level beyond the 8K limit of the graphs; we have tested messages up to 64K. However, the maximum bandwidth is limited because we must use a memory copy.

The results for all of the experiments are consistent: the **AU+1copy** implementation performs best for small transfers, and the **DU+1copy** implementation is better for large transfers. The crossover point is at a message size of 256 bytes. This indicates that a hybrid implementation, which switches between transfer modes, based on the transfer size, would provide the best performance. We expect to implement this approach in the near future.

However, we have implemented a second hybrid approach: using deliberate update to transfer the buffer data and automatic update to transfer the index values. This results in practically no change in the latency and only a small improvement (less than 6%) in bandwidth.

7 Future Work

The implementation we described does not allow open sockets to be preserved across **fork** and **exec** calls. With **fork**, the problem is arbitrating socket access between the two resulting processes. **exec** is difficult because *SHRIMP* communicates through memory and **exec** allocates a new memory space for the process. Maeda and Bershad discuss how to implement **fork** and **exec** correctly in the presence of user-level networking software [18]. We intend to follow their solution.

Our current implementation ignores all **fcntl** calls, passing them through to the underlying kernel socket. While this behavior is correct is some cases, in others it is not. We intend to implement a better **fcntl** that handles all of the **fcntl** directives correctly.

Finally, our current implementation does not support asynchronous I/O to sockets. Doing so would require a straightforward use of *SHRIMP* notifications, but we have not implemented it yet.

8 Related Work

We have previously presented this work in [9] and its results were summarized in [11]. Several groups have studied how to support the socket interface on experimental high-performance network interfaces.

The most closely related work is by Rodrigues et al. [21] who have a user-level implementation of sockets using *active messages* [24]. Their sockets can take advantage of receives that are posted before sends, which allows them a zero-copy implementation. They obtain similar bandwidth numbers, despite using different operating system, CPU, and networking hardware. Because of different network interface we obtain a significantly lower small message latency.

U-Net [23] describes an architecture for user-level communications which is independent of the network interface hardware. Using Sun SparcStations and Fore Systems ATM interfaces, they measured a TCP one-way latency of 78 μsec and a bandwidth of 14.4 MBytes/sec for 4 KByte packets.

Boden et al. [6] describe an implementation of TCP/IP using the Myrinet API. This implementation had a minimum user-to-user latency of over 40 μsec, which is considerably larger than ours. Two factors contribute to this: first, they implement full TCP/IP while we support the stream socket interface directly; second, their underlying hardware has a higher communication latency than ours.

Even with the "restriction" of building a compatible message passing library we obtain performance comparable to "unrestricted" APIs. To illustrate this, consider the following measurements of two APIs that are not compatible with sockets. Myricom's custom API using their interconnect results in a latency of 40 μsec and a peak bandwidth of 27 MBytes/sec. Illinois Fast Messages (FM) [19] also implement a custom API using the Myrinet hardware. FM sacrifices some features available in the Myricom API and some peak bandwidth in order to reduce the small-message latency by a factor of almost two. Their one-way latency is 24 μsec while they obtain a peak bandwidth of 19.6 MBytes/sec.

Wilkes's "sender-based" communication in the Hamlyn system [25] supports user-level message passing, but requires application programs to build packet headers. They have not tried to implement message-passing libraries using the underlying communication mechanism.

Several projects have tried to lower overhead by bringing the network all the way into the processor and mapping the network interface FIFOs to special processor registers [7, 13, 8]. While this is efficient for fine-grain, low-latency communication, it requires the use of a non-standard CPU, and it does not support the protection of multiple contexts in a multiprogramming environment. The Connection Machine CM-5 implements user-level communication through memory-mapped network interface FIFOs [17, 12]. Protection is provided through the virtual memory system, which controls access to these FIFOs. However, there are a limited number of FIFOs, so they must be shared within a partition (subset of nodes), restricting the degree of multiprogramming. Protection is provided between separate partitions, but not between processes within a partition. Since the application must build packet headers, message passing overhead is still hundreds of CPU instructions.

Other high-performance networking libraries have been implemented on *SHRIMP*. Bilas [2] describes two implementations of remote procedure call, one that is compatible with SunRPC [14] and one that is not. The SunRPC-compatible library achieves latency and bandwidth comparable to our sockets implementation. One layer of this RPC implementation implements a bidirectional stream which can be viewed as a specialized implementation of our sockets library. Alpert [1] describes an implementation of the NX/2 [20] message-passing library for SHRIMP; it also achieves latency similar to ours.

9 Conclusion

Our sockets implementation was able to achieve very low latency by exploiting the features of *SHRIMP*. The freedom to use customized buffer management strategies allows us to design a very efficient implementation of bidirectional streams. The separation of control transfer from data transfer allows us to avoid receive-side interrupts.

These results correspond to the strengths of each transfer strategy. Larger messages benefit from deliberate update's DMA transfers, while automatic update snoops the writes on the memory bus and thus is better at handling smaller transfers.

The impact of a memory copy on bandwidth must not be overlooked. As I/O buses and networks get faster, the effect of a memory copy will become more pronounced. We believe the next important step in improving sockets performance is to develop a general zero-copy implementation.

Our sockets implementation, and implementations of other message-passing facilities on *SHRIMP* [1, 2] demonstrate that *SHRIMP* has met its goal of providing flexible, very high performance communication.

Acknowledgments

We would like to thank Kai Li, Matt Blumrich, Liviu Iftode, Rob Shillner, and the rest of the *SHRIMP* Group at Princeton for their many useful suggestions that contributed to this work.

This project is sponsored in part by ARPA under contract N00014-95-1-1144, by NSF under grant MIP-9420653, by Digital Equipment Corporation and by Intel Corporation. Felten is supported by an NSF National Young Investigator Award.

References

1. Richard Alpert and Edward W. Felten. Design and Implementation of NX Message Passing Using SHRIMP Virtual Memory Mapped Communication. Technical Report TR-507-96, Dept. of Computer Science, Princeton University, January 1996.
2. Angelos Bilas and Edward W. Felten. Fast RPC on the SHRIMP Virtual Memory Mapped Network Interface. Technical Report TR-512-96, Dept. of Computer Science, Princeton University, February 1996.
3. M. Blumrich, K. Li, R. Alpert, C. Dubnicki, E. Felten, and J. Sandberg. A Virtual Memory Mapped Network Interface for the Shrimp Multicomputer. In *Proceedings of 21th International Symposium on Computer Architecture*, pages 142–153, April 1994.
4. Matthias A. Blumrich. *Network Interface for Protected, User-Level Communication*. PhD thesis, Dept. of Computer Science, Princeton University, June 1996. Available as technical report TR-522-96.
5. Matthias A. Blumrich, Cezary Dubnicki, Edward W. Felten, and Kai Li. Protected, User-Level DMA for the SHRIMP Network Interface. In *Proc. 2nd Intl. Symposium on High-Performance Computer Architecture*, pages 154–165, February 1996.
6. Nanette J. Boden, Danny Cohen, Robert E. Felderman, Alan E. Kulawik, Charles L. Seitz, Jakov N. Seizovic, and Wen-King Su. Myrinet: A Gigabit-per-Second Local Area Network. *IEEE Micro*, 15(1):29–36, February 1995.
7. S. Borkar, R. Cohn, G. Cox, T. Gross, H.T. Kung, M. Lam, M. Levine, B. Moore, W. Moore, C. Peterson, J. Susman, J. Sutton, J. Urbanski, and J. Webb. Supporting Systolic and Memory Communication in iWarp. In *Proceedings of 17th International Symposium on Computer Architecture*, June 1990.
8. William J. Dally. The J-Machine System. In P.H. Winston and S.A. Shellard, editors, *Artificial Intelligence at MIT: Expanding Frontiers*, pages 550–580. MIT Press, 1990.
9. Stefanos Damianakis, Cezary Dubnicki, and Edward W. Felten. Stream Sockets on SHRIMP. Technical Report TR-513-96, Dept. of Computer Science, Princeton University, February 1996.

10. Cezary Dubnicki, Liviu Iftode, Edward W. Felten, and Kai Li. Software Support for Virtual Memory-Mapped Communication. In *Proceedings of the IEEE 8th International Parallel Processing Symposium*, April 1996.

11. Edward W. Felten, Richard Alpert, Angelos Bilas, Matthias A. Blumrich, Douglas W. Clark, Stefanos Damianakis, Cezary Dubnicki, Liviu Iftode, and Kai Li. Early Experience with Message-Passing on the Shrimp Multicomputer. In *Proceedings of 23th International Symposium on Computer Architecture*, May 1996.

12. FORE Systems. *TCA-100 TURBOchannel ATM Computer Interface, User's Manual*, 1992.

13. Dana S. Henry and Christopher F. Joerg. A Tightly-Coupled Processor-Network Interface. In *Proceedings of 5th International Conference on Architectur al Support for Programming Languages and Operating Systems*, pages 111–122, October 1992.

14. Internet Request for Comments RFC 1057, Internet Network Working Group. *RPC: Remote Procedure Call Protocol Specification, Version 2*, June 1988.

15. Kimberly K. Keeton, Thomas E. Anderson, and David A. Patterson. LogP: The Case for Low-Overhead Local Area Networks. In *Hot Interconnects III*, August 1995.

16. Samuel J. Leffler, Marshall Kirk McKusick, Michael J. Karels, and John S. Quarterman. *The Design and Implementation of the 4.3BSD Unix Operating System*. Addison Wesley, 1989.

17. C.E. Leiserson, Z.S. Abuhamdeh, D.C. Douglas, C.R. Feynman, M.N. Ganmukhi, J.V. Hill, D. Hillis, B.C. Kuszmaul, M.A. St. Pierre, D.S. Wells, M.C. Wong, S. Yang, and R. Zak. The Network Architecture of the Connection Machine CM-5. In *Proceedings of 4th ACM Symposium on Parallel Algorithms and Architectures*, pages 272–285, June 1992.

18. Chris Maeda and Brian N. Bershad. Protocol Service Decomposition for High-Performance Networking. In *Proceedings of 14th ACM Symposium on Operating Systems Principles*, pages 244–255, December 1993.

19. Scott Pakin, Mario Lauria, and Andrew Chien. High Performance Messaging on Workstations: Illinois Fast Message (FM) for Myrinet. In *Supercomputing '95*, November 1995.

20. Paul Pierce. The NX/2 Operating System. In *Proceedings of Third Conference on Hypercube Concurrent Computers and Applications*, pages 384–390, January 1988.

21. Steven H. Rodrigues, Thomas E. Anderson, and David E. Culler. High-Performance Local-Area Communication With Fast Sockets. In *Proc. of Winter 1997 USENIX Symposium*, January 1997.

22. Roger Traylor and Dave Dunning. Routing Chip Set for Intel Paragon Parallel Supercomputer. In *Proceedings of Hot Chips '92 Symposium*, August 1992.

23. Thorsten von Eicken, Anindya Basu, Vineet Buch, and Werner Vogels. U-Net: A User-Level Network Interface for Parallel and Distributed Computing. In *Proceedings of 15th ACM Symposium on Operating Systems Principles*, pages 40–53, December 1995.

24. Thorsten von Eicken, David E. Culler, Seth Copen Goldstein, and Klaus Erik Schauser. Active Messages: A Mechanism for Integrated Communication and Computation. In *Proceedings of 19th International Symposium on Computer Architecture*, pages 256–266, May 1992.

25. John Wilkes. Hamlyn – An Interface for Sender-Based Communications. Technical Report HPL-OSR-92-13, Hewlett-Packard Laboratories, November 1993.

A Simple and Efficient Process and Communication Abstraction for Network Operating Systems

David C. DiNucci

MRJ, Inc., NAS Systems Division
NASA Ames Research Center, M/S T27A-2
Moffett Field, CA 94035-1000

Abstract. Process and communication abstractions in current uniprocessor or SMP OSs are poorly suited for processors which may be connected by relatively high-latency, low-bandwidth interconnects. Cooperative Data Sharing (CDS) is a subroutine-level interface designed to target both shared-memory and distributed-memory multiprocessors. CDS1 supports a single simple communication abstraction in which data is not copied unless required by the user program or the target architecture, yet it still supports the use of data forwarding to compensate for high-latency interconnects (when the consuming process is known in advance) and/or remote retrieval of data for demand-driven applications. The ability to write portable heterogeneous programs is also supported, as is communication-initiated subroutine execution. Its utility and small size makes it well suited to partial kernel-level implementation.

1 Introduction

An operating system must present a consistent virtual machine to the user. That virtual machine should hide as many unimportant features of the physical machine as possible. However, features of the physical machine only become unimportant if a satisfactory virtual machine can be developed which can be efficiently implemented on any realistically-probable physical machine.

Tying individual computers together into a network does not in itself create a new virtual machine. Although significant success has been achieved in providing virtual global file systems over networks, creating processes on different processors and communicating between them is a different story. Currently, the programmer is (and must be) cognizant of the individual machines and the individual copies of the operating system. Some higher-level tools, such as PVM [10] and P4, have been created atop traditional operating systems to help deal with the complexities of creating, managing, and communicating between processes on distributed processors, but they have succeeded in spite of their host operating systems rather than because of them, and their advantages are realized only during the time that a program is executing under the control of that tool.

The goal, then, is to extend the virtual machine abstraction supported by an operating system into one which can span several physical machines. Although tools like PVM and MPI [19] provide some experience on which to base some of the functionality required, these interfaces themselves are not suitable. First, the message-passing paradigm on which they are based relies on copying, as is illustrated by the fact that modification of the communicated data, by either the sender or receiver, after communication is complete is guaranteed to leave the data in the other process unaffected. Second, the interfaces provided by these tools are are too large, and (especially with MPI) were not built with the goal of a minimal subset upon which other functionality could be constructed, as a kernel must be. Third, these tools do not fully take advantage of the fact that all or many of the processes which are communicating may be part of the same user program, and therefore, just as separate threads in a single process, do not necessarily require kernel-level protection from each other.

This paper will describe an interface called CDS1, the kernel layer of a package called Cooperative Data Sharing, or CDS [6] [7], as a virtual machine which will allow the construction of multi-process programs which can portably and efficiently execute on one or more processors which may be very close (e.g. sharing memory) or very distant (e.g. over a wide-area network). This interface has been prototyped as a user layer on top of Unix, and it is expected that such a layer will be useful for portability even if some systems are able to migrate some of this functionality into the OS kernel for efficiency, as this paper will recommend.

The remainder of this paper will be written from the viewpoint of Unix, but it is expected that much of the content will also apply to other OS environments. Section 2 will outline current practice and the problems that must be surmounted, section 3 describes design choices made in this work to address these problems, and section 4 contains a brief description of the entire CDS1 interface. Section 5 then gives some brief performance figures from a prototype, section 6 compares CDS with some other systems with similar goals, and section 7 offers some conclusions.

2 Current Practice and Problems

This section describes some of the problems with the virtual machine abstraction offered by operating systems like Unix when extended to multiple physical machines with high-latency interconnects over a wide area. Two types of abstraction will be addressed here; processes and inter-process communication.

2.1 Process model

Unix creates new processes through the use of the **fork** operation, which creates a new process by effectively making a copy of an existing process, complete with state such as open files, stack, heap, and program counter. The process ID of the child and a status code for the creation is delivered to the parent as part of the creation process, thereby requiring that the parent block during creation. It is common practice for a child process to execute very little code before calling **exec**, which then re-starts the process from some other executable file, re-initializing almost all of the program state. The user must use an entirely different and more heavyweight approach (e.g. 'execute remote shell' command) when starting a process across a network or in an unshared process space. Each process within a Unix virtual machine is given a unique integer process ID which is visible to all users and processes through the use of OS calls.

Although clever, **fork** works well only in the sort of environment for which it was designed—i.e. a uniprocessor or coherent local shared-memory system, with MMU hardware to accomodate copy-on-write. The state dependences present in the semantics and common usage make it unrealistic to extend the environment to include a high-latency interconnect. In a process space which could reside on hundreds of widely distributed machines, the requirement to ensure that each process is uniquely and globally identified is extremely cumbersome and unnecessary. In an environment where user programs are often composed of multiple processes, the effects of global process IDs and synchronous process creation become even more problematic.

2.2 Inter-Process Communication

Unix offers two primary kinds of inter-process communication: files, primarily used for persistent communication, and pipes, used for more direct, non-persistent communication between processes started in a parent/child or sibling relationship. Sockets, a more general version of pipes, provide for communication with remote processes and processes initiated from different parents. Shared-memory segments (shm) and message queues (msg) were later added to allow an efficient and portable method for communicating between processes with access to common shared memory.

Sockets provide the most consistent method of communicating between processes in a workstation network environment, in a way that is relatively independent of their relative locations, but sockets are definitely not the most efficient method for that communication in some cases. In addition, the portable protocols currently available for sockets have contrary goals. UDP/IP allows connectionless communication with datagram boundaries, but does not ensure reliable transfer. TCP/IP requires connections before communication, but does not include datagram boundaries, and does guarantee reliable transfer. Neither interface supports asynchronous message transmission. Also, sockets do not lend themselves to demand-driven or load-balancing applications, where a message may be consumed by any one of several processes, depending upon which is prepared to consume it first.

Both shared-memory segment IDs and message queue IDs currently utilize a global name space across the system with no practical means of management. Also, in spite of their title, message queues, like shared-memory segments, only aid in communicating between processes with access to common shared memory.

Ideally, the user should not need to be cognizant of the relative locations of processes in order to know which form of communication to use. He/she should be able to specify to the OS the requirements of the communication, and any information which might allow the OS to optimize that communication on the available hardware. Such specifications could include: (1) the process which is expected to consume the communication (by the producer), (2) the process which is expected to produce the communication (by the consumer), (3) the address in local memory where the data should reside upon receipt (or the lack of any positional requirement), (4) the declaration that there will be no further local access to the communicated data, (5) the desire to queue data in the source or destination process, and (6) the expectation that the communicated data will be locally modified.

3 CDS1 Design Philosophy/Foundation

The top-level goal of CDS1 is to implement a simple, small user interface which addresses the problems mentioned in the previous section in a portable and efficient manner. Since "ease of use" is a very subjective metric, its maximization is not a primary goal of CDS1, but it is expected to be the goal of interfaces built upon CDS1 (e.g. CDS2, MPI, Linda, or HPF), so CDS1 must be powerful enough to implement such interfaces. This section describes and explains some design choices that were made during the development of CDS1 in light of these goals. The CDS1 interface itself is described in a later section.

Communication was designed to obey five primary constraints: (1) a single set of interfaces with consistent semantics should support communication regardless of whether it is facilitated by the use of data copying or data sharing, so that the user can program to the virtual, rather than the physical, machine; (2) the user should have good visibility and control of the operations which may result in remote actions; (3) operations which may result in the execution of remote actions should be available in an asynchronous form; (4) some form of "demand-driven" communication should be available which allows several processes to compete for access to data; and (5) protection between the kernel and the user program, and between separate user programs, must be enforced.

3.1 Data Sharing

Any interface which allows communication without copying must necessarily allow multiple processes to access the same data *in situ*. This is accomplished by communicating pointers to data rather than the data itself. If a pointer is passed to a process which does not have direct access to the data, the data could either be moved to the receiving process piecemeal as the pointer is dereferenced, or as a unit with the pointer. In this work, the latter approach has been used as a result of constraint 2 above, and to allow compensation for latency by allowing the user to explicitly forward data in this way to the process which will be using it next even before it is actually referenced. It also reduces the reliance on specialized hardware to implement the former semantics.

To maximize the chances that the process receiving the pointer will have shared access to the data item to which it is pointing, the sender must acquire the pointer from a special CDS1 malloc-like call. This also allows CDS1 to know the length of the region when communication is necessary and to keep a reference count with the region so that (for example) a **free** will not actually free the memory if there are other current pointers to the region (in other processes).

This form of communication would ordinarily have a loosely defined semantics, since modification of the communicated data by one process might or might not be detectable by the other process, depending upon whether the processes are actually pointing to the same data or to copies. In some other systems, like Mach [3] and Treadmarks [15], an MMU detects when one of the processes attempts to modify physically shared data, and a copy could be made at that time if necessary. CDS1 instead simply requires the user to call a special function before modifying communicated data, after which any number of modifications can be made. If this function finds a reference count of zero, it does nothing, otherwise it can make a copy or even block temporarily. This serves the same purpose as MMU detection except that it does not exact the overhead involved with setting up an MMU and does not restrict the granularity of data transfer or modification detection to page-sized regions. It also helps further to enforce constraint 2, since possibly-expensive copying will not take place without the user's explicit invitation. Failure by the user to inform CDS1 before modifying communicated data is considered a program error.

Identifying regions only by raw pointers can cause problems. For example, if CDS1 is required to make a copy before a modification, as described above, a pointer to the new item will need to be returned to the user code, and any temporary variables there which hold the old pointer will need to be updated. A logical solution is to provide the user a handle to an object containing the pointer, and to have CDS1 update the latter when a copy is made. But unless the user is to be restricted from all access to the data except through CDS1 calls (which would yield unacceptable overhead), the user would eventually need access to the pointer anyway, leading to the same problem. The use of an object handle would have other advantages, however, such as allowing CDS1 to keep extra information in the object which could help in remapping the pointer as it moves from one process to another. In the end, the decision was made to give the user a pointer to an object, where the first element in the object is a pointer to the region, which is visible to the user. The object may contain other members which are not visible. The user is explicitly allowed (in C) to cast the object pointer to be a pointer to a pointer to the region, with the assumption that a pointer to a structure can be cast to a pointer to its first element.

3.2 Demand-Driven Communication and Message-Handlers

The "demand-driven" property mentioned in constraint 4 requires that processes be able to compete for access to data, which in this case means access to region pointers. In other words, there must be some repositories for pointers which can be accessed by several processes. Such repositories are called communication cells, or just cells, and are used to facilitate all pointer passing between processes. At its simplest, a cell can be considered as a global (i.e. accessible from any process) variable of type "region pointer" with an associated empty-full bit.

Whenever a pointer is deposited into the cell by a process, the bit is set "full". When data is removed from a "full" cell, the bit is optionally set "empty" or is unchanged. When the user attempts to remove data from an "empty" cell, the attempt blocks until the cell becomes full. Such a cell can also be considered as a single-element queue. By extending this data structure to a multi-element queue, more standard forms of queued communication can also be performed.

The cell construct also provides an anchor point for "message handlers"—i.e. user routines that are automatically invoked as the result of communication— by allowing the user to associate with the cell both a function and a high or low threshold at which the function should be called. However, allowing these functions to be invoked asynchronously, to preempt threads, and/or to execute in separate threads can lead to severe portability problems, especially among systems without efficient thread mechanisms. It was therefore decided to separate the concept of the thread and the handler. That is, a handler in CDS1 is always made to execute in the thread in which it is declared to CDS1. This may be the same thread running the user program (e.g. in a single-threaded system), so a priority system is provided to help the user to allocate the thread between handlers and the mainline. CDS1 will precisely preempt threads (i.e. during calls to CDS1) to allow other handlers or mainline to run, based on these priorities. If the user has a mechanism for initiating other threads, he/she is free to bind CDS1 handlers to those threads instead.

3.3 Data Communication

Passing pointers facilitates asynchronous communication protocols, as required in constraint 3. The user process can continue to have local access to the region while the kernel uses a communication link to copy the region to another processor. As long as the user process follows the protocol of informing CDS1 before modifying the region, the kernel can move the region data directly from the communication heap to the interconnect while the user process continues execution. In effect, the user and the kernel are sharing access to data in the communication buffers of a message-passing system.

This asynchrony is confounded by any problems which may arise in transferring the data across the interconnect, since the user program will have already continued on before an error code is returned. CDS1 provides two avenues to help the user deal with this. First, CDS1 will place a special region containing information about the erroneous transfer, called an error region, into a cell of the user's choice when an error is detected. Second, CDS1 allows the user to explicitly manage the amount of space allocated to the communication heap and communication cells in each process to minimize the likelyhood that communication will fail due to lack of space on the receiver. Because the user is responsible for managing this buffer space, CDS1 implementations can be made even more efficient by allowing a "sending" processor to always assume that a distant "receiving" processor has sufficient buffer space, thereby obviating the need for extra housekeeping messages to check or reserve space on the receiver. If such housekeeping is desired, it can be built on top of CDS1.

Although the CDS1 pointer-based approach to communication can be much more efficient that traditional message-passing in some cases, it can also be less efficient. Theoretically, message passing only needs to perform a single copy to move data from any location (heap, stack, or static) in one process to any location in another, even though it is rarely implemented so efficiently. CDS1 pointer-based communication must perform two copies for such a transfer: one to the communication heap, and one from that heap. Therefore, standard send and receive style primitives still serve an important purpose, and are included in CDS1 in a consistent style primarily for those cases where the process must communicate data to or from its private stack, heap, or static storage. These are still defined in terms of a copy to or from a region and then a transfer of a region pointer, but the region is never made visible to the user, so standard message-passing optimizations are possible.

3.4 Data Conversion

Heterogeneous systems, in which different processes use different data formats, require the user to specify the data type of the communicated data so that it can be translated properly. Some systems (like MPI) require users to construct these data types as opaque objects, adding complexity, and require their use during every communication just in case data must be converted, adding overhead. CDS1 provides tools to allow the user program to recognize when conversion is necessary, and to perform that conversion explicitly with the use of user-constructed type descriptors. In this way, higher-level interfaces can perform automatic conversion if desired, and can perform that conversion before, after, or before and after the communication, but programs which are not meant to ever execute in a heterogeneous environment do not need to pay overhead for this capability. Although the conversion could be performed outside of the CDS1 kernel, the necessary routines are included in the kernel anyway for use with send/receive, where the conversion must be performed internally.

3.5 Inter-Process Protection and Addressing

Existing threads packages gain efficiency by minimizing protection between different parts of the same program—i.e. between a user and him/herself. CDS1 attempts to benefit from the same approach—e.g. by not protecting against corruption of the comm heap by other parts of the same program. However, protection between processes, and/or protection between user processes and the kernel, can be imposed where required or requested without altering the communication semantics by using possibly-less efficient implementation approaches. For example, all communication between protected processes can be implemented by copying, or an MMU can be employed in a manner similar to Treadmarks to detect illegal update attempts to common regions.

Many of the drawbacks of process creation on Unix-like systems can be overcome by abandoning the copy semantics of **fork** and exercising more strict control over a process's identity. In CDS1, the kernel provides a process's ID only to that process and its children. Since communication requires the initiating process to have the other process's ID, and because the process ID of a child is not automatically provided to the parent process, such programs have three important properties. First, process initiation does not require that any information be passed from the child to the parent, so it can be implemented as a non-blocking operation. Second, a child process is essentially invisible until it voluntarily communicates its process ID to another process (usually its parent) using standard communication mechanisms, so until it does so, it is guaranteed a communication-free window of opportunity to perform any required initialization. Finally, a process can have some control over its visibility by restricting the distribution of its process ID. In a sense, a process ID acts as a capability, allowing access to the communication cells in the process.

4 CDS1 Description

This section describes the CDS1 abstract virtual machine which embodies the decisions outline above, and to which the user is expected to program. The machine models described are process, communication, translation, and error.

4.1 Process Model

A CDS1 program consists of a set of CDS1 processes. The root process is created directly by the user. Any CDS1 process can create others by calling **enlist** and specifying a file containing the executable and the processor or processors on which to execute the new process. Each new process must call **init** to inform CDS1 of the services (e.g. comm heap garbage collection, in-order communication) which it expects to be available, and **init** returns the process ID of the process, the process ID of the parent process, and a list of the requested services which are not implemented. Another function, **myinfo**, returns the same values as **init** but doesn't initialize.

A process is free to explicitly transfer process IDs that it knows to other processes, using the normal communication mechanism to be described shortly. The user can address the program as a whole (i.e. the root process and all processes initiated by it) through the OS for management and control functions.

Process IDs are treated as integers. Because of their limited scope, different process IDs may be used by different processes to denote the same process, and the same process ID may be used by different processes to denote different processes. To facilitate this flexibility, process IDs must be translated into and back out of an internal form when they are communicated between processes. This translation is performed just as foreign data formats are translated by the copy and send routines described later.

4.2 Communication Model

Communication is facilitated by adding two constructs to the usual code and data for each process: a set of logically-public **comm cells** and a logically-private

comm heap. Each process explicitly manages the number of its comm cells and the size of its comm heap using the **cagrow** and **cafree** functions.

The function of the comm cells is to provide a global name space and some minimal storage through which communication can take place. Each comm cell in a process has an integer name, which is unique to the cells within that process. (Cells allocated at one time have sequential integer names to make management simple.) A cell in any process can be addressed by any (other) process by combining the integer cell name with the process ID, though restrictions on the operations which can be performed on a cell by outside processes may be specified to **cagrow** when the cell is created.

The comm heap is a memory area which is designed to contain dynamically-allocated sequences of bytes called regions. Each region is identified by a region ID, which is a structure pointer which may be cast to a pointer to a pointer to the first byte within the region.

Each cell can hold zero or more regions, organized as a queue. All communication within CDS is performed by (virtually) copying regions to and from cells, using the following eight primitives (see Figure 1):

rgalloc	Creates a region on the comm heap
rgfree	Destroys a region on the comm heap
deq	Copies first region from cell into comm heap, then removes that region from cell
enq	Adds copy of a region from comm heap to the end of a cell, and optionally destroys that region in the comm heap
read	Copies first region from cell into comm heap
write	Removes all regions from a cell, then performs **enq**
zap	Removes all regions from a cell
rgmod	Performs no externally-visible action, but this must be called before a region is modified the first time after the region has been processed with a **read**, **write**, **enq**, or **deq**

When a process is first created, it is provided with one comm cell (named 0) and a small comm heap. The parent process can optionally provide an initial region to **enlist** which is implicitly **enq**d into cell 0 of the child at initiation. It is the user process's responsibility to resize the comm heap as necessary to ensure that future incoming regions can be properly accommodated. Failure to do so may cause some communications to result in error conditions.

The **read** and **deq** primitives each have a time-out argument to regulate the time spent waiting for a region. If a special time-out value of **cds1_PENDING** is supplied, these primitives always return immediately, but the **read** or **deq** request remains in force. The region ID returned in this case cannot be used for anything other than **rgfree** until validated with a call to the **rgwait** or **rgwaitany** routine. These two routines also take a time-out argument, after which time they return a "no success" error code and can optionally perform an automatic **rgfree**. This **cds1_PENDING** facility allows the calling program to perform computation while incurring the latency for the request to be sent to a possibly-remote processor and for the data to be returned. In this case, the

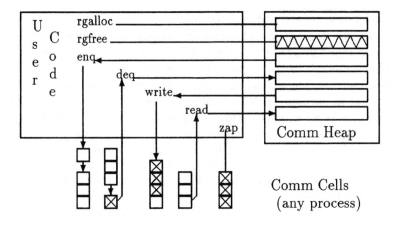

Fig. 1. The seven CDS1 communication primitives

initial **deq** or **read** plays the role of a prefetch operation.

To facilitate the communication of data which resides in a process's address space (i.e. not on the comm heap), CDS1 provides two composite functions, **send** and **recv**. **send** has the exact semantics of creating a region in the comm heap, copying data from the process's address space to the region, **enq**ing the region, and **free**ing the region. **recv** has the exact semantics of **deq**ing a region, copying the data from the region to the process's address space, and **free**ing the region. As their names imply, these functions provide message-passing-like semantics on top of the lower-level CDS1 primitives, and the cell name plays a role similar to the tag in other message-passing systems.

The presence or absence of a region within a cell can be used to model the availability or unavailability of a lock in a traditional shared-memory system. To initialize this model, a region is first **malloc**'d and **written** into a cell. A process which needs to modify the region **deq**s it from the cell (effectively acquiring the lock), performs **rgmod** (to inform the system that modification will take place), modifies the data within the region, then **write**s the region back into the cell (effectively relinquishing the lock). A process which only needs to read the contents of a region just **read**s the region from the cell. Both the **deq** and the **read** will block if another process has the region for modification.

Communication in CDS1 is perhaps most naturally considered as the migration of regions from one process to another, with each region's readiness or current state being represented by its presence in a particular cell or set of cells. If there is just one "version" of the region, which must go through a set of sequential queries and updates, then only one region should exist in that set of cells at any one time, using the shared-memory techniques described in the previous paragraph. The message-passing paradigm described above models a situation where a region can have multiple versions, with newer versions being created before older ones are accessed and destroyed.

For very simple programs, a fixed set of cells may be used for communication. For more complex programs, it is the responsibility of a process to allocate and communicate its cell names to other processes which will need to access them.

Three multicast routines are also provided: enqm, writem, and sendm. These are identical in function to their counterparts (enq, write, and send) except that they may be given a list of (*pid,cell*) pairs in a single invocation.

enq and write are actually macros, which call a more general routine called put. put is like enq and write, but has an additional argument called *qlike* which is a flag telling whether the cell should act like a queue (for enq) or not (for write). Similarly, enqm and writem are macros which call a putm routine, deq and read are macros which call a get routine, and send and recv are macros which call the cput (i.e. "copy and put") and getc (i.e. "get and copy") routines.

4.3   Data Copying and Translation Model

CDS1 provides three copy routines—copytorg, copytofromrg, copyrgtorg— that optionally translate and repack data while copying it between a region and user space or another region. In some rare implementations of CDS1, these functions may be the only method of accessing the data within regions, because the comm heap may not be directly accessible from the user program (e.g. to allow more efficient interface with the parallel interconnect and/or minimize the number of locked user pages in virtual memory). The copy functions take a region ID and offset, a pointer to a buffer, a copy descriptor, and a translation table as arguments.

A copy descriptor is an integer array which describes the types and lengths of the fields to be copied and/or skipped when executing the copy function. CDS1 does not supply functions for the creation of copy descriptors—they are constructed by the user outside of CDS1. Specifically, a copy descriptor is a sequence of triples of the form (*adjust, type, repl*) where *adjust* is an integer displacement in bytes, *type* is one of the CDS1 atomic type descriptors (or, if negative, a negated offset as described below), and it repl is a non-negative integer, optionally ORed with cds1T_EOT. The triples are processed sequentially (i.e. *adjust* is added to the buffer pointer and *repl* elements of type *type* are copied) until a *repl* with the cds1T_EOT flag set is encountered. If a negative *type* is encountered, processing of the current copy descriptor is temporarily suspended while the copy descriptor -*type* triples away is processed *repl* times.

A translation table is an integer which dictates how the data of each type should be modified as it is copied. A separate function, transtab, which takes two process IDs as arguments, is used to determine the table to use to translate between the internal data formats used by those processes. A table of zero always performs no translation, except for process IDs (i.e. type cds1T_PID) which are always translated between their integer form and an expanded processor-independent form within the region.

4.4 Handler Model

A process may make one or more cells active by specifying a handler and an integer high- or low-water mark for those cells, using the **handler** function. A handler is a user-supplied routine (i.e. function or subroutine), which is requested whenever a condition (dependent on the water mark) occurs. Specifically, if a high-water mark is specified, the handler will be requested whenever the number of regions in the cell is greater than the water mark after a region has been added to the cell (with **enq** or **write**). If a low-water mark is specified, the handler will be requested whenever the number of regions in the cell is less than or equal to the water mark at the time that a process attempts to remove a region from the cell. Note that a high-water mark of 1 will request the handler whenever a region is enqueued to the cell, and a low-water mark of 0 will request a handler before a region is removed from an empty cell. The handler associated with a high-water mark will generally begin by **deq**ing a region from the corresponding cell, and a handler associated with a low-water mark will generally end by **enq**ing a new region to the corresponding cell.

Although each handler request should eventually result in that handler being invoked (i.e. called), the handler is not necessarily invoked at the time of the request. Handlers run in the same thread as their owner, so invocations are delayed until the currently-executing routine (i.e. process mainline or handler) performs a CDS1 function, and until the priority of the requested handler is greater than or equal to the priority of the current routine. The active and blocked priority of a routine is specified with the **handler** or **priority** function. When a handler routine is invoked, no currently-executing routine will be serviced further until the new routine concludes (i.e. returns), regardless of priority—i.e. handler routines are stack based. CDS1 also provides a function, **allow**, to temporarily lower the priority of the current routine until all waiting handler requests are serviced. If a user wants handlers to run in a separate thread, they can initiate a separate thread (using mechanisms unknown to CDS1) and provide it with a low CDS1 priority to allow handlers to run there.

4.5 Error Model

Some errors can be detected by CDS1 locally and immediately upon a caller's request for a CDS1 service, and these are reported to the caller immediately as error return codes. Errors which may occur at some later time, or which may originate from a distant process, are reported in the form of error regions which are **enq**d into a cell of the user's choosing, called the error cell. A handler can be installed on the error cell as with any other, so errors can be handled by the user program when they are reported.

4.6 Summary of CDS1 Operations

CDS1 consists of 28 functions. The above text has described 24 of them: **enlist**, **init**, **cagrow**, **cafree**, and **myinfo** for process initiation and startup; **put**, **get**, zap, and putm for communication; rgalloc, rgfree, rgwait, rgwaitany, and rgmod for manipulating regions; transtab, copyfrom, copyto, and copytofrom for performing copying and translation; handler, priority, and allow for specifying and manipulating handlers; and cput, cputm, and getc operations composed from the above. In addition, 8 macros are provided, as described: enq, deq, read, write, enqm, writem, send, and recv.

The four remaining functions are rgrealloc, rglen, sizeof, and block. rgrealloc attempts to change the size of a region without copying it. rglen returns the length of a region. sizeof returns the number of bytes which would be copied by a copy descriptor. Finally, block never returns, but allows handlers to execute, playing a role similar to XtAppMainLoop in X.

5 Performance

The CDS1 interface has been prototyped on a network of Suns and on a network of multiprocessor SGI Challenge (90MHz R8000) workstations. The implementation is built on top of the native OS, and uses shared memory segments for internode communication and UDP/IP over FDDI, HiPPI, and/or Ethernet for intranode communication. No OS-specific code is used, other than vendor-offered low-latency locking mechanisms. A simple program which passes regions (i.e. pointers) in a circle among three processes on the SGI was used for these timings.

Passing a single region (i.e. enq+deq) between processes on different processors of the same node averages $23.4\mu sec$ (i.e. about 43,000 passes/sec) regardless of region size. This could conceivably be sped up by using even faster locks, or some of the "lock-free queue" technology currently used for SGI's native MPI implementation. At last measure, CDS1 outperforms SGI's native MPI for passing any region longer than about 25 bytes in this "no copy required" scenario.

Putting the three processes on different nodes yields about a 1msec latency over HiPPI or FDDI. Figure 2 shows bandwidths. The performance appears to be restricted by (1) the relatively complex memory allocation scheme currently used to manage the communication heap, (2) the overhead of IP (which is avoided in SGI native MPI over HiPPI), and (3) the queuing overhead discussed above.

6 Comparison with Other Work

The communication model within CDS is probably best described as software-implemented distributed-shared messages with copy-on-write. It is related to distributed shared-memory [16] with release consistency [15]. A similar approach was taken in the C Region Library (CRL) [13], but queues and region premigration (i.e. where the data producer moves the data to the processor of the next consumer) are not available there and only SPMD applications are supported. Some similarities also exist to Cooperative Shared Memory [11]. Treadmarks also has many similar goals to CDS1. Research on zero-copy communica-

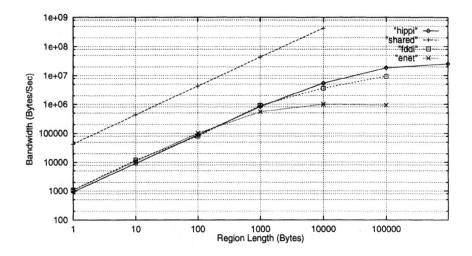

Fig. 2. Bandwidths for various region sizes

tion has also been performed by the traditional OS community in the context of TCP/IP [5].

The handler model is similar to the **hrecv** function in the Intel NX library [12], and the notion of using high-priority messages as a replacement for interrupts was used in the Occam language [14]. The concurrently-developed "Remote Queues" (RQ) system [4] similarly provides global access to queues.

The communication model is also similar to that used in the Reactive Kernel (RK) [2] and Zipcode [18], with the addition of shared region access and remote region retrieval. Comparisons can also be made with the "Generative Communication" of Linda [9], replacing associative matching with explicit association through cell names, though Linda does not facilitate the sharing of messages, the elimination of copying in shared memory, or the ability to explicitly forward messages to their destination.

Generic Active Messages (GAM) [17] and Nexus [8] have traditional message-passing semantics, but are also designed as a substrate to higher-level interfaces.

7 Conclusions

CDS1 demonstrates a single communication mechanism which possesses many of the advantages of both message-passing (e.g. compensation for latency by allowing producers to forward data to consumers, queuing of communication, and automatic handler invocation) and of shared-memory (e.g. globally-retrievable data, non-copy communication, and allowance for simultaneous readers). Although it is difficult to address factors such as optimal communications granularity for different architectures with this level of interface, CDS1 provides the basic functionality required to program efficiently in an architecture-independent manner. A prototype of CDS1 has been implemented on a hybrid architecture (networked SMPs) with promising results.

References

1. C. Amza, A.L. Cox, S. Dwarkadas, P. Keleher, H. Lu, R. Rajamony, W. Yu, W. Zwaenepoel, "TreadMarks: Shared Memory Computing on Networks of Workstations", IEEE Computer, Vol. 29,No. 2, pp. 18-28, February 1996.
2. W. C. Athas, C. Seitz, "Multicomputers: Message-Passing Concurrent Computers," Computer 21(8), pp 9-24 (August 1988)
3. B. N. Bershad, M. J. Zekauskas, "Shared Memory Parallel Programming with Entry Consistency for Distributed Memory Multiprocessors", CMU-CS-91-170, Carnegie Mellon University, September 1991.
4. E. Brewer, F. Chong, L. Liu, S. Sharma, J. Kubiatowicz, "Remote Queues: Exposing Message Queues for Optimization and Atomicity", SPAA '95, Santa Barbara CA, ACM, pp.42-53
5. H. K. J. Chu, "Zero-Copy TCP in Solaris", Proc. USENIX 1996 Annual Technical Conf., San Diego, January 1996, USENIX
6. D. DiNucci, "CDS", http://www.nas.nasa.gov/NAS/Tools/Projects/CDS/
7. D. DiNucci, "Cooperative Data Sharing: A Layered Approach to an Architecture-Independent Message-Passing Interface", 2nd MPI Developer's Conf., Notre Dame, July 1996, IEEE, pp. 58-65
8. I. Foster, C. Kesselman, R. Olson, and S. Tuecke, "Nexus: An interoperability toolkit for parallel and distributed computer systems", ANL/MCS-TM-189, Argonne National Laboratory, 1994.
9. D. Gelernter, "Generative Communication in Linda", ACM ToPLaS, 1 (1985), pp 80-112
10. A. Geist et. al, "PVM: Parallel Virtual Machine", MIT Press, 1994, ISBN 0-262-57108-0
11. M. Hill, J. Larus, S. Reinhardt and D. Wood, "Cooperative Shared Memory: Software and Hardware for Scalable Multiprocessors", ACM TOCS, 11(4):300-318, Nov. 1993
12. Paragon User's Guide, Intel Corporation.
13. K. Johnson, M. F. Kaashoek, and D. Wallach, "CRL: High-Performance All-Software Distributed Shared Memory", TR LCS-TM-517, MIT Laboratory for Computer Science, March 1995.
14. G. Jones, M. Goldsmith, "Programming in occam 2", Prentice-Hall (1988)
15. P. Keleher, A. Cox, S. Dwarkadas, W. Zwaenepoel, "An Evaluation of Software-Based Release Consistent Protocols", to appear JPDC.
16. K. Li, P. Hudak, "Memory Coherence in Shared Virtual Memory Systems", ACM Transactions on Computer Systems, 7(4), pp 341-359, November 1989.
17. L. Liu, D. Culler, "Evaluation of the Intel Paragon on Active Message Communication", Proc. Intel Supercomputer Users Group (ISUG) Conf., June 1995.
18. A. Skjellum, A., and C. H. Still, "Zipcode and the Reactive Kernel for the Caltech Intel Delta prototype and nCUBE/2," in Proc. Sixth Dist. Memory Computing Conf. (DMCC6), pages 26-33. IEEE Comp. Society, Los Alamitos, CA, April 1991.
19. M. Snir, S. Otto, S. Huss-Lederman, D. Walker, J. Dongarra, "MPI: The Complete Reference", MIT Press, 1994, ISBN 0-262-57104-8.

Efficient Adaptive Routing in Networks of Workstations with Irregular Topology *

F. Silla, M. P. Malumbres, A. Robles, P. López and J. Duato

Facultad de Informática
Universidad Politécnica de Valencia
P.O.B. 22012. 46071 - Valencia, SPAIN
E-mail: {fsilla,mperez,arobles,plopez,jduato}@gap.upv.es

Abstract. Networks of workstations are rapidly emerging as a cost-effective alternative to parallel computers. Switch-based interconnects with irregular topologies allow the wiring flexibility, scalability and incremental expansion capability required in this environment. The irregularity also makes routing and deadlock avoidance on such systems quite complicated. Current proposals avoid deadlock by removing cyclic dependencies between channels. As a consequence, many messages are routed following non-minimal paths, increasing latency and wasting resources. In this paper, we propose a general methodology for the design of adaptive routing algorithms for networks with irregular topology. These routing algorithms allow messages to follow minimal paths in most cases, reducing message latency and increasing network throughput. The methodology is based on the application of the theory of deadlock avoidance proposed in [14], which increases routing flexibility by allowing cyclic dependencies between channels. As an example of application, we propose an adaptive routing algorithm for Autonet. It can be implemented either by duplicating physical channels or by splitting each physical channel into two virtual channels. In the former case, the implementation does not require a new switch design. It only requires changing the routing tables and adding links in parallel with existing ones, taking advantage of spare switch ports. In the latter case, a new switch design is required but the network topology is not changed. Preliminary evaluation results show that the new routing algorithm is able to increase throughput for random traffic by a factor of up to 2.8 with respect to the original algorithm, also reducing latency.

1 Introduction

Wormhole switching [7] has become the most widely used switching technique for multicomputers. Wormhole switching only requires small buffers in the nodes through which messages are routed. Also, it makes the message latency largely insensitive to the distance in the network. See [26] for a detailed analysis of wormhole.

* This work was supported by the Spanish CICYT under Grant TIC94–0510–C02–01

The main drawback of wormhole switching is that blocked messages remain in the network, therefore wasting channel bandwidth. In order to reduce the impact of message blocking, physical channels may be split into virtual channels by providing a separate buffer for each virtual channel and by multiplexing physical channel bandwidth. The use of virtual channels can increase throughput considerably by dynamically sharing the physical bandwidth among several messages [8]. However, it has been shown that virtual channels are expensive, increasing node delay [6].

An alternative approach consists of using adaptive routing [18]. However, deadlocks may appear if the routing algorithms are not carefully designed. A deadlock occurs in an interconnection network when no message is able to advance toward its destination because the network buffers are full. As routing decisions must be taken in a few nanoseconds in wormhole networks, a practical way to avoid deadlock is to design deadlock-free routing algorithms. A simple and effective approach to avoid deadlocks consists of restricting routing so that there are no cyclic dependencies between channels [7]. A more efficient approach consists of allowing the existence of cyclic dependencies between channels while providing some escape paths to avoid deadlock [13, 14]. The resulting routing algorithms are more flexible, usually increasing performance. As a consequence, some recent router implementations like the MIT Reliable Router [10, 11] and the Cray T3E router [30] are based on these techniques, implementing escape paths as dedicated virtual channels. Additionally, there has been a considerable interest on these issues. Several researchers developed alternative theories of deadlock avoidance, proposing sufficient conditions [1, 23, 31, 19] and necessary and sufficient conditions [15, 16, 29, 24] for deadlock-free adaptive routing.

Recently, several switch-based interconnects like Autonet [28], Myrinet [3] and ServerNet [20] have been proposed to build networks of workstations for cost-effective parallel computing. Typically, these switches support networks with irregular topologies. Such irregularity provides the wiring flexibility required in local area networks, also allowing the design of scalable systems with incremental expansion capability. The irregularity also makes routing and deadlock avoidance on such systems quite complicated. Current proposals avoid deadlock by removing cyclic dependencies between channels. As a consequence, many messages are routed following non-minimal paths, therefore increasing latency and wasting resources.

In this paper, we propose a general methodology for the design of adaptive routing algorithms for networks with irregular topology. As an application of this methodology, we propose an adaptive routing algorithm for Autonet networks. This algorithm allows messages to follow minimal paths in most cases, reducing message latency and increasing network throughput. The proposed routing algorithm does not require a new switch design. It can be implemented simply by changing the routing tables and adding links in parallel with existing ones, taking advantage of spare switch ports. The proposed routing algorithm can also be implemented by splitting physical channels into virtual ones. However, this approach would require a new switch design supporting virtual channels.

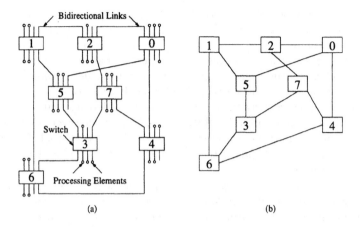

Fig. 1. (a) A network with switch-based interconnect and irregular topology; (b) the corresponding graph G.

The paper is organized as follows. Section 2 introduces switch-based networks with irregular topologies. Section 3 describes a general methodology for the design of adaptive routing algorithms for networks with irregular topology. As an example, this methodology is applied to the Autonet routing algorithm. Section 4 describes the routing algorithm proposed in Autonet, showing how adaptivity can be increased in Section 5. The performance of the new routing algorithm is evaluated in Section 6. Finally, some conclusions are drawn.

2 Switch-Based Networks with Irregular Topologies

Switch-based networks consist of a set of switches where each switch can have a set of ports. Each port consists of one input and one output link. A set of ports in each switch are either connected to processors or left open, whereas the remaining ports are connected to ports of other switches to provide connectivity between the processors. Such connectivity is typically irregular and the only thing that is guaranteed is that the network is connected. Typically, all links are bidirectional full-duplex and multiple links between two switches are allowed. Such a configuration allows a system with a given number of processors to be built using less number of switches than a direct network while allowing a reasonable number of external communication ports per processor. Figure 1(a) shows a typical network of workstations using switch-based interconnect with irregular topology. In this figure, it is assumed that switches have eight ports and each processor has a single port.

The switch may implement different switching techniques: wormhole, virtual cut-through, or ATM. However, wormhole switching is used in recently proposed networks like Myrinet and ServerNet. So, we will restrict ourselves to wormhole switching in this paper. Several deadlock-free routing schemes have been proposed in the literature for irregular networks [28, 3, 20, 27]. Routing in irregular topologies can be performed by using source routing or distributed routing. In the former case, each processor has a routing table that indicates the sequence of ports to be used at intermediate switches to reach the destination node. That information is stored in the message header [3]. In the latter case, processors and switches require routing tables. The use of table lookup routing allows the use of the same switch fabric for different topologies. However, some network mapping algorithm must be executed in order to fill those tables before routing can be performed. The details of the mapping algorithm greatly depend on the underlying hardware support.

Once a message reaches a switch directly connected to its destination processor, it can be delivered as soon as the corresponding link becomes free. So, we are going to focus on routing messages between switches. The interconnection network I between switches can be modeled by a multigraph $I = G(N, C)$, where N is the set of switches, and C is the set of bidirectional links between the switches. Figure 1(b) shows the graph for the irregular network in Figure 1(a).

3 A Design Methodology for Adaptive Routing Algorithms

In this section, we propose a general methodology for the design of adaptive routing algorithms for networks with irregular topology. This methodology is very simple. Given an interconnection network and a deadlock-free routing function defined on it, it is possible to add physical channels in parallel with the existing ones. Alternatively, it is possible to split physical channels into two virtual channels. In both cases, the graph representation of the network contains the original and the new channels. Then, the routing function is extended in such a way that newly injected messages can use the new channels without any restriction as long as the original channels are used exactly in the same way as in the original routing function. However, once a message reserves one of the original channels, it can no longer reserve any of the new channels.

Deadlock-freedom can be informally proved by contradiction as follows. Suppose that there is a deadlocked configuration. In this configuration, messages cannot occupy the original channels because the original routing function is deadlock-free and once a message has entered the original set of channels, it cannot return to new channels. So, all the blocked messages must occupy new channels. However, those messages can escape from deadlock by using the original channels because the original routing function is able to deliver messages from any source to any destination. Deadlock freedom can be formally proved by using the theory proposed in [14]. This result is valid for any topology. It is also valid regardless of whether the additional channels are physical or virtual ones. This routing strategy is similar to the one proposed in [9] except that it is valid for any topology and it does not require keeping track of the number of dimension reversals.

4   The Autonet Routing Algorithm

In this section, we briefly describe the deadlock-free routing scheme used in Autonet networks [28]. In addition to providing deadlock-freedom, it provides adaptive communication between nodes in an irregular network. The Autonet routing algorithm is distributed, and implemented using table-lookup. When a message reaches a switch, the destination address stored in the message header is concatenated with the incoming port number and the result is used to index the routing table at that switch. The table lookup returns the outgoing port number that the message should be routed through. When multiple routes exist from the source to the destination, the routing table entries return alternative outgoing ports. In case multiple outgoing ports are free, the routing scheme selects one port randomly.

In order to fill the routing tables, a breadth-first spanning tree (BFS) on the graph G is computed first using a distributed algorithm. This algorithm has the property that all nodes will eventually agree on a unique spanning tree. Routing is based on an assignment of direction to the operational links. In particular, the "up" end of each link is defined as: 1) the end whose switch is closer to the root in the spanning tree; 2) the end whose switch has the lower ID, if both ends are at switches at the same tree level (see Figure 2). Links looped back to the same switch are omitted from the configuration. The result of this assignment is that each cycle in the network has at least one link in the "up" direction and one link in the "down" direction.

To eliminate deadlocks while still allowing all links to be used, this routing uses the following up/down rule: a legal route must traverse zero or more links in the "up" direction followed by zero or more links in the "down" direction. Thus, cyclic dependencies between channels are avoided because a message cannot traverse a link along the "up" direction after having traversed one in the "down" direction. Such routing not only allows deadlock-freedom but also adaptivity. The lookup tables can be constructed to support both minimal and non-minimal adaptive routing. However, in some cases, up/down routing is not able to supply any minimal path between some pairs of nodes, as shown in the following example.

Figure 2 shows the example irregular network shown in Figure 1(a). Switches are arranged in such a way that all the switches at the same tree level are at the same vertical position in the figure. The root switch for the corresponding BFS spanning tree is switch 0. The assignment of "up" direction to the links on this network is illustrated. The "down" direction is along the reverse direction of the link. Note that every cycle has at least one link in the "up" direction and one link in the "down" direction. It can be observed that all the alternative minimal paths are allowed in some cases. For example, a message transmitted from switch 7 to switch 0 can be either routed through switch 4 or switch 2. In some other cases, however, only some minimal paths are allowed. For example, a message transmitted from switch 2 to switch 5 can be routed through switch 0 but it cannot be routed through switch 1. It should be noted that any transmission between adjacent switches is always allowed to use the link(s) connecting them,

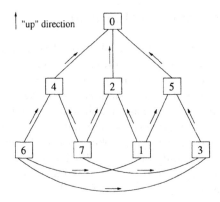

Fig. 2. Link direction assignment.

regardless of the direction assigned to that link. However, when two switches are located two or more links away, it may happen that all the minimal paths are forbidden. This is the case for messages transmitted from switch 4 to switch 1. The shortest path (through switch 6) is not allowed. All the allowed paths (through switches 0, 2, and through switches 0, 5) are non-minimal.

5 Increasing Adaptivity

The routing scheme used in Autonet networks allows partially adaptive communication between switches. However, it does not always provide minimal paths. Some minimal paths are not allowed because messages traveling along them should go through a link in the "up" direction after having traversed a link in the "down" direction, contrary to the basic routing rule. This "down" to "up" conflict may occur more than once in these minimal paths.

In this section we present a routing strategy that allows messages to use these forbidden routes. This mechanism also increases adaptivity and throughput. It is based on the methodology proposed in Section 3. We can follow two different approaches. In the first approach, physical channels are not split into virtual channels. Instead, the channels in the network are duplicated, taking advantage of spare switch ports. This approach requires adding more wires but it does not require a new switch design. In the second approach, physical channels are split into virtual channels. This approach does not require more wires but current switches do not support virtual channels. In both cases, the additional channels will be used to circumvent the "down" to "up" conflicts that prevent routing using minimal paths. Thus, the routing algorithm must be extended in order to use the new channels.

In figure 2 we can see that the legal path from switch 4 to switch 1 is non-minimal, since messages must travel through switch 0, thus requiring three hops.

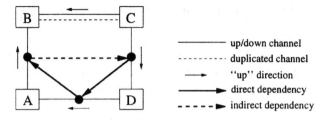

Fig. 3. Extended channel dependency graph.

As indicated in the previous section, there exists an illegal path through switch 6 that is minimal, requiring only two hops. This route is illegal because it requires one transition from "down" to "up" direction. Once channels have been either duplicated or split into virtual channels, messages can arrive at switch 1 with only two hops by using the new channels. These channels must be direction-less.

Since new channels are direction-less, they can be used in both directions, as a shortcut. However, if direction-less channels are used without restrictions, the new routing algorithm may not be deadlock-free, as it can be seen in Figure 3. This figure shows part of the extended channel dependency graph [14] for a fragment of an irregular network consisting of four switches. The "up" direction of the channels is also displayed. A new direction-less channel connecting switches B and C has been added (shown with a dashed line). If a message is routed through the "up" channel from A to B, the direction-less channel from B to C, and the "up" channel from C to D, it produces the indirect dependency shown in the figure. Thus, there is a cycle in the graph. Hence, a routing algorithm that imposes no restriction on the use of new channels may not be deadlock-free.

Using the methodology proposed in Section 3, the new routing algorithm can be stated as follows: Original (up/down) channels can be used according to the up/down rule. New channels can only be used if the message arrives at the switch through a new channel or if the message is injected into the network at the current switch. However, once a message has reserved an "up" or "down" channel, it cannot use any of the new channels again. When the routing table provides both, up/down and new channels, a higher priority has been assigned to the new ones, since they allow messages to be routed with higher flexibility.

Once channels have been duplicated or split into virtual channels, new channels can be used by messages traveling to any destination. For example, in Figure 2, messages traveling from switch 5 to switch 6 can be transmitted through new channels until they reach their destination. They can also change to the up/down channel in the hop from switch 1 to switch 6, or they can even reach their destination through up/down channels from their source. The same occurs for messages from switch 6 to switch 5. Routing messages in this way increases adaptivity considerably, since the number of possible paths between two switches increases.

As indicated in Section 3, the proposed routing scheme is deadlock-free. It is also livelock-free. Effectively, we know that the up/down routing scheme revisited in Section 2 is livelock-free. The new channels can only be used if a message has arrived at a switch through one of the new channels. Additionally, new channels can be used to forward messages along paths that are equal in length or shorter than the basic up/down paths. Thus, the new routing scheme is livelock-free.

6 Performance Evaluation

In this section, we evaluate the performance of the routing strategy proposed in Section 5. We will refer to this routing scheme as minimal adaptive (MA) when implemented by duplicating physical links. We have also evaluated the up/down scheme for the same network for comparison purposes. We will refer to this routing scheme as UD.

As the MA routing scheme requires the duplication of all the physical channels in the network, cost increases accordingly. Thus, in order to perform a fair comparison, a third routing scheme was evaluated. This scheme also duplicates all the channels but labels them in the same direction as the original up/down routing. The additional channels are used exactly in the same way as the original ones. We will refer to this routing scheme as UD-2.

As mentioned in Section 3, an alternative approach consists of splitting physical channels into two virtual channels. We have also studied this option. We will refer to as UD-2cv the routing scheme in which physical channels are split into two virtual channels, and both of them use up/down routing. Note that we do not divide the irregular network into two different virtual networks, since messages at a switch can use any of the two outgoing virtual channels independently of the incoming virtual channel they arrived through. Similarly, we have labeled as MA-2cv the routing scheme that uses the two virtual channels exactly in the same way as the physical channels are used in MA. In this case, both virtual channels do not have the same functionality, as the two physical channels in MA cannot be used in the same way.

It is important to note that we assume that virtual channel multiplexing can be efficiently implemented. In practice, implementing virtual channels is not trivial because link wires can be long, increasing signal propagation delay and making flow control more complex. This issue would require further research, analyzing techniques like channel pipelining and/or block acknowledgment.

Instead of analytic modeling, simulation was used to evaluate the routing algorithms. Our simulator models the network at the flit level. The evaluation methodology used is based on the one proposed in [14]. The most important performance measures are latency and throughput. The message latency lasts since the message is introduced in the network until the last flit is received at the destination node. Latency is measured in clock cycles. Traffic is the flit reception rate, measured in flits per node per cycle. Throughput is the maximum amount of information delivered per time unit (maximum traffic accepted by the network).

Message latency should also include software overhead at source and destination processors (system call, buffer allocation, buffer-to-buffer copies, etc.). This overhead traditionally accounted for a high percentage of message latency [25, 21]. However, we did not considered such an overhead because some recent proposals reduce and/or hide that overhead, thus exposing hardware latency [17, 2, 22, 12]. So, we only considered network hardware latency in this study.

6.1 Network Model

The network is composed of a set of switches. Network topology is completely irregular and has been generated randomly. However, for the sake of simplicity, we imposed three restrictions to the topologies that can be generated. First, we assumed that there are exactly 4 nodes (processors) connected to each switch. Also, two neighboring switches are initially connected by a single link. That link is duplicated later in order to implement the MA and the UD-2 routing algorithms. Finally, all the switches in the network have the same size. We assumed 12-port switches, thus leaving 8 ports available to connect to other switches. Among them, only 4 ports are used when the topology is randomly generated. The remaining ports are left open and may be used for link duplication. We have evaluated networks with a size ranging from 16 switches (64 nodes) to 64 switches (256 nodes). For each network size, several distinct irregular topologies have been analyzed.

In order to apply the UD scheme, the spanning tree for the network must be computed. The root switch is chosen as the switch whose average distance to the rest of the switches is the smallest one. After rooting the network, links are labeled with their corresponding direction, according to the rules described in Section 2. Then, the routing table for the up/down scheme is computed. In order to apply the MA scheme, the path lengths obtained by using the up/down routing algorithm (routing distances) are compared with the real distances between switches. First, all the channels in the network are duplicated. Then, routing tables are computed in this way: a message generated at a switch can leave the switch through a new channel if the routing distance from the next switch up to the destination switch is less than the routing distance from the source to the destination. This rule prevents messages from being routed through paths that are longer than the basic up/down paths. Finally, the routing table for the UD-2 scheme is also computed. The routing tables for the UD-2cv and MA-2cv routing schemes are the same tables used in the case of UD-2 and MA, respectively, but considering virtual channels instead of physical links.

Each switch has a routing control unit that selects the output channel for a message as a function of its destination node, the input channel and the output channel status. Table look-up routing is used. UD, UD-2, MA, UD-2cv or MA-2cv routing strategy can be chosen. The routing control unit can only process one message header at a time. It is assigned to waiting messages in a demand-slotted round-robin fashion. When a message gets the routing control unit but it cannot be routed because all the alternative output channels are busy, it must wait in the input buffer until its next turn. A crossbar inside the switch allows multiple messages traversing it simultaneously without interference. It is configured by the routing control unit each time a successful routing is made. We assumed that it takes one clock cycle to compute the routing algorithm, or to transmit one flit across a crossbar or a physical channel.

6.2 Message Generation

Message traffic and message length depend on the applications. For each simulation run, we considered that message generation rate is constant and the same for all the nodes. Once the network has reached a steady state, the flit generation rate is equal to the flit reception rate (traffic). We have evaluated the full range of traffic, from low load to saturation. On the other hand, we have considered that message destination is randomly chosen among all the nodes. This pattern has been widely used in other performance evaluation studies [8, 5, 4]. For message length, 16-flit, 32-flit, 64-flit and 128-flit messages were considered.

6.3 Simulation Results

For each network size, we have analyzed several distinct randomly generated irregular topologies. However, the average latency values achieved by each topology for each traffic rate are almost the same. The only differences arise when the networks are heavily loaded, close to saturation. Additionally, the throughput achieved by all the topologies is almost the same. Hence, we will show the results obtained by one of those topologies, chosen randomly.

Figure 4 shows the average message latency versus traffic for each routing scheme on a randomly generated irregular network with 16-switches. Message size is 16 flits. As can be seen, when duplicating the available bandwidth, the MA routing scheme triples throughput when compared with the UD strategy. The UD-2 routing scheme only doubles throughput. Moreover, the latency achieved by MA is lower than the one for UD and UD-2 for the whole range of traffic. Thus, most of the improvement achieved by MA is due to the additional routing flexibility provided by this scheme and the use of shorter paths. This behavior of the MA scheme reduces contention and balances channel utilization.

When virtual channels are used instead of duplicating the available bandwidth, both UD-2cv and MA-2cv perform better than the UD strategy. MA-2cv almost doubles the throughput of the UD scheme, reaching a value close to that of the UD-2 scheme.

The MA routing scheme scales very well with network size. Figures 5 and 6 show the results obtained for networks with 32 and 64 switches, respectively. For 64 switches, throughput increases by factors of 3.7 and 1.8 with respect to the UD and UD-2 schemes, respectively, when the MA scheme is used. Latency is also reduced for the whole range of traffic. With respect to the use of virtual channels, it can be seen that the UD-2cv routing scheme doubles throughput and reduces latency with respect to the UD scheme. However, when the MA-2cv routing scheme is used, throughput is tripled and latency is also reduced with respect to the UD scheme. When network size increases, the performance

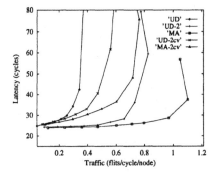

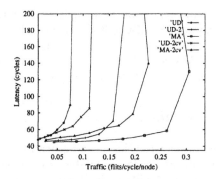

Fig. 4. Average message latency versus traffic for an irregular network with 16 switches. Message length is 16 flits.

Fig. 5. Average message latency versus traffic for an irregular network with 32 switches. Message length is 16 flits.

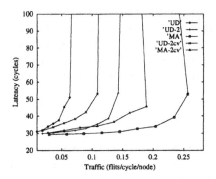

Fig. 6. Average message latency versus traffic for an irregular network with 64 switches. Message length is 16 flits.

Fig. 7. Average message latency versus traffic for an irregular network with 64 switches. Message length is 32 flits.

improvement achieved by the MA and MA-2cv schemes also increases, because there are larger differences among the real distance between any two switches and the routing distance imposed by the up/down mechanism. The MA and MA-2cv routing schemes allow messages to traverse minimal paths in most cases. It is worth to note that for large networks, the MA-2cv scheme achieves a higher throughput than the UD-2 scheme, despite the fact that network bandwidth is half the value available for the latter scheme.

Finally, Figures 7, 8 and 9 show the influence of message size on the behavior of the routing schemes. These results show the robustness of the MA and MA-2cv routing schemes against message size variation. As can be seen, the UD and UD-2 routing schemes achieve a slightly better throughput when message size is larger. In these routing schemes, link contention is significant. The MA routing

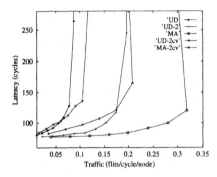

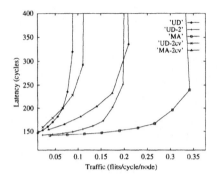

Fig. 8. Average message latency versus traffic for an irregular network with 64 switches. Message length is 64 flits.

Fig. 9. Average message latency versus traffic for an irregular network with 64 switches. Message length is 128 flits.

scheme also achieves a slightly better throughput when message size is larger. Anyway, the MA routing scheme achieves the maximum throughput and lowest latency for all message sizes. With respect to the use of virtual channels, UD-2cv and MA-2cv schemes achieve a throughput value that is almost independent of message size. However, they exhibit a higher latency than UD-2 or MA.

7 Conclusions

In this paper, a simple and general methodology for the design of adaptive routing algorithms for switch-based interconnects with irregular topologies has been proposed. Additionally, it has been shown that the resulting routing algorithms are deadlock and livelock-free. As an example, this methodology has been used to improve the performance of Autonet networks. Two alternative implementations have been analyzed. The first one does not require changing the switch design. It takes advantage of spare switch ports, duplicating the links of the network. Also, routing tables should be updated according to the new algorithm. The second implementation approach consists of splitting physical channels into two virtual channels. In this case, the topology remains unchanged, but the switch design must be revised.

The new routing algorithm allows the use of the new channels to newly injected messages. When a message arrives at a switch on a link connected to a processor or on a new channel, it is allowed to use new channels at the current switch as well as the original ones. However, once a message uses one of the original channels, it cannot use again any of the new channels. This simple strategy allows most messages to follow minimal paths, reducing message latency and increasing throughput.

The performance of the new routing algorithm has been evaluated, comparing it with the original Autonet algorithm as well as an extension of Autonet that uses the new channels according to the same basic routing rules. The evaluation study was performed on networks with 16, 32 and 64 switches, using random traffic and different message lengths. Despite the simplicity of the proposed approach, the new routing algorithm increases throughput by a factor of 2 to 3.7 with respect to the original Autonet routing algorithm, depending on network size. Latency is also reduced in all the cases for the whole range of network load. Different message sizes have been evaluated, showing that the throughput achieved by the new algorithm is almost independent of message length. The original Autonet algorithm, however, is more sensitive to message length, decreasing throughput by a small amount when messages become shorter. Finally, for large networks, the new routing scheme with virtual channels achieves a higher throughput than the up/down scheme with duplicated channels, despite the fact that network bandwidth is half the value available for the latter scheme.

As for future work, we plan to apply the proposed design methodology to other basic routing algorithms. Also, we plan to investigate the implementation of virtual channels when wires are long.

References

1. P. E. Berman, L. Gravano, G. D. Pifarré and J. L. C. Sanz, "Adaptive deadlock- and livelock-free routing with all minimal paths in torus networks," in *Proceedings of the 4th ACM Symposium on Parallel Algorithms and Architectures*, June 1992.
2. M. A. Blumrich, K. Li, R. Alpert, C. Dubnicki, E. W. Felten and J. Sandberg, "Virtual memory mapped network interface for the SHRIMP multicomputer," *Proceedings of the 21st International Symposium on Computer Architecture*, pp. 142–153, April 1994.
3. N. J. Boden, D. Cohen, R. E. Felderman, A. E. Kulawik, C. L. Seitz, J. Seizovic and W. Su, "Myrinet - A gigabit per second local area network," *IEEE Micro*, pp. 29–36, February 1995.
4. R. V. Boppana and S. Chalasani, "A comparison of adaptive wormhole routing algorithms," in *Proceedings of the 20th International Symposium on Computer Architecture*, May 1993.
5. A. A. Chien and J. H. Kim, "Planar-adaptive routing: Low-cost adaptive networks for multiprocessors," in *Proceedings of the 19th International Symposium on Computer Architecture*, May 1992.
6. A. A. Chien, "A cost and speed model for k-ary n-cube wormhole routers," in *Proceedings of Hot Interconnects'93*, August 1993.
7. W. J. Dally and C. L. Seitz, "Deadlock-free message routing in multiprocessor interconnection networks," *IEEE Transactions on Computers*, vol. C–36, no. 5, pp. 547–553, May 1987.
8. W. J. Dally, "Virtual-channel flow control," *IEEE Transactions on Parallel and Distributed Systems*, vol. 3, no. 2, pp. 194–205, March 1992.
9. W. J. Dally and H. Aoki, "Deadlock-free adaptive routing in multicomputer networks using virtual channels," *IEEE Transactions on Parallel and Distributed Systems*, vol. 4, no. 4, pp. 466–475, April 1993.
10. W. J. Dally, L. R. Dennison, D. Harris, K. Kan and T. Xanthopoulus, "The Reliable Router: A reliable and high-performance communication substrate for parallel

computers," in *Proceedings of the Workshop on Parallel Computer Routing and Communication*, pp. 241–255, May 1994.

11. W. J. Dally, L. R. Dennison, D. Harris, K. Kan and T. Xanthopoulos, "Architecture and implementation of the Reliable Router," in *Proceedings of Hot Interconnects II*, August 1994.

12. B. V. Dao, S. Yalamanchili and J. Duato, "Architectural support for reducing communication overhead in pipelined networks," *Third International Symposium on High Performance Computer Architecture*, February 1997.

13. J. Duato, "On the design of deadlock-free adaptive routing algorithms for multicomputers: Design methodologies," in *Proceedings of Parallel Architectures and Languages Europe 91*, June 1991.

14. J. Duato, "A new theory of deadlock-free adaptive routing in wormhole networks," *IEEE Transactions on Parallel and Distributed Systems*, vol. 4, no. 12, pp. 1320–1331, December 1993.

15. J. Duato, "A necessary and sufficient condition for deadlock-free adaptive routing in wormhole networks," in *Proceedings of the 1994 International Conference on Parallel Processing*, August 1994.

16. J. Duato, "A necessary and sufficient condition for deadlock-free adaptive routing in wormhole networks," *IEEE Transactions on Parallel and Distributed Systems*, vol. 6, no. 10, pp. 1055–1067, October 1995.

17. T. von Eicken, D. E. Culler, S. C. Goldstein and K. E. Schauser, "Active messages: A mechanism for integrated communication and computation," in *Proceedings of the 19th International Symposium on Computer Architecture*, June 1992.

18. P. T. Gaughan and S. Yalamanchili, "Adaptive routing protocols for hypercube interconnection networks," *IEEE Computer*, vol. 26, no. 5, pp. 12–23, May 1993.

19. L. Gravano, G. D. Pifarré, P. E. Berman and J. L. C. Sanz, "Adaptive deadlock- and livelock-free routing with all minimal paths in torus networks," *IEEE Transactions on Parallel and Distributed Systems*, vol. 5, no. 12, pp. 1233–1251, December 1994.

20. R. Horst, "ServerNet deadlock avoidance and fractahedral topologies," in *Proceedings of the International Parallel Processing Symposium*, pp. 274–280, April 1996.

21. J.-M. Hsu and P. Banerjee, "Performance measurement and trace driven simulation of parallel CAD and numeric applications on a hypercube multicomputer," *IEEE Transactions on Parallel and Distributed Systems*, vol. 3, no. 4, pp. 451–464, July 1992.

22. V. Karamcheti and A. A. Chien, "Do faster routers imply faster communication?," in *Proceedings of the Workshop on Parallel Computer Routing and Communication*, May 1994.

23. X. Lin, P. K. McKinley and L. M. Ni, "The message flow model for routing in wormhole-routed networks," in *Proceedings of the 1993 International Conference on Parallel Processing*, August 1993.

24. X. Lin, P. K. McKinley and L. M. Ni, "The message flow model for routing in wormhole-routed networks," *IEEE Transactions on Parallel and Distributed Systems*, vol. 6, no. 7, pp. 755–760, July 1995.

25. R. J. Littlefield, "Characterizing and tuning communications performance for real applications," in *Proceedings of the First Intel DELTA Applications Workshop*, February 1992.

26. L. M. Ni and P. K. McKinley, "A survey of wormhole routing techniques in direct networks," *IEEE Computer*, vol. 26, no. 2, pp. 62–76, February 1993.

27. W. Qiao and L. M. Ni, "Adaptive routing in irregular networks using cut-through switches," in *Proceedings of the 1996 International Conference on Parallel Processing*, August 1996.

28. M. D. Schroeder et al., "Autonet: A high-speed, self-configuring local area network using point-to-point links," Technical Report SRC research report 59, DEC, April 1990.

29. L. Schwiebert and D. N. Jayasimha, "A universal proof technique for deadlock-free routing in interconnection networks," in *Proceedings of the Symposium on Parallel Algorithms and Architectures*, pp. 175–184, July 1995.

30. S. L. Scott and G. Thorson, "The Cray T3E networks: adaptive routing in a high performance 3D torus," in *Proceedings of Hot Interconnects IV*, August 1996.

31. C. Su and K. G. Shin, "Adaptive deadlock-free routing in multicomputers using only one extra channel," in *Proceedings of the 1993 International Conference on Parallel Processing*, August 1993.

A Deadlock Avoidance Method for Computer Networks

Bulent Abali

IBM Thomas J. Watson Research Center,
P.O.Box 218, Yorktown Heights, NY 10598
`abali@watson.ibm.com`

Abstract. A deadlock avoidance method that minimizes the number of turn restrictions in wormhole routed networks is described. Fewer restrictions generally result in lower message latency and higher network bandwidth. The method is based on recursive partitioning of a graph model of the network and then removing interpartition edges to eliminate cycles. The method is applicable to a variety of network topologies including bidirectional multistage networks (BMIN), hypercubes, meshes, and irregular networks. In comparison to other algorithms, the method produces fewer or same number of turn restrictions on a set of benchmark networks.

1   Introduction

The main contribution of this paper is a deadlock avoidance method that minimizes the number of turn restrictions in wormhole routed networks. Fewer restrictions result in lower message latency and higher network bandwidth in general. Wormhole routing [1], a form of cut-through switching, is increasingly being used for clustering of workstations and in local area networks. Examples of wormhole routed networks are Tandem ServerNet [2] for clustering PCs, IBM SP [3, 4] for clustering RISC workstations, Myricom Myrinet, Fiber Channel Standard (FCS) switches, FDDI switches, and switched Ethernet [5].

An important issue in wormhole routed networks is deadlock avoidance. Deadlocks may occur whenever there is a cyclical dependency between message packets on the network links interconnecting the switches. Multiple packets block each other's path in the network and wait indefinitely for paths to be cleared. There are two main techniques for avoiding deadlocks in wormhole routed networks: virtual channels [1] and turn restrictions. Virtual channels eliminate cyclical dependencies by implementing multiple "virtual" channels passing through the same physical link. Virtual channels require replication of buffers in the switches and therefore they may increase switch complexity and delay (see [6] for example). Turn restrictions prohibit message packets from using particular input-output port combinations in particular switches in order to eliminate cyclical dependencies. The Turn Model [7], ServerNet [2], SP networks [3, 4, 8], the *e–cube* algorithm, and many other routing algorithms implement turn restrictions in some form. Turn restrictions serve a similar purpose to the "No Left Turn" traffic signs posted at street intersections. The signs prohibit some of the alternative routes, but at least the traffic will flow freely.

In this paper, we describe a method for minimizing the number of turn restrictions in wormhole routed networks. The method is based on a well known graph partitioning

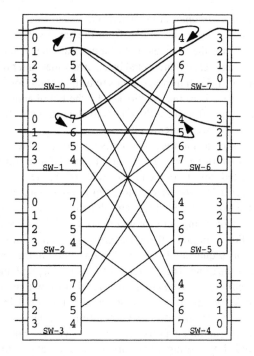

Fig. 1. A BMIN with 8 switches. An example cycle of four messages is also shown.

algorithm called Kernighan-Lin partition heuristic [9]. The method is applicable to many network topologies including bidirectional multistage networks (BMIN), hypercubes, meshes, and irregular networks. In comparison to other algorithms, the method produces fewer or same number of turn restrictions on a set of benchmarks, as summarized in Table 1. For example, it produces as few as 26 turn restrictions for the BMIN topology shown in Fig. 1, which compares well to the previously known 48 restrictions described in [8], and subsequently described 32 in [10].

2 Deadlocks

We will illustrate our method on a bidirectional multistage network (BMIN) shown in Fig. 1. We chose this BMIN, because it is one of the challenging topologies for which no fewer than 32 turn restrictions were published. However, the method does not depend on this particular topology and it can be used on other topologies as well. The BMIN topology shown in the figure is identical to the SP switch board [3, 4], which interconnects processors and/or other switch boards. The BMIN consists of eight 4 × 4 bidirectional cross–point switches. Each link interconnecting a pair switches is a full duplex bidirectional link, allowing simultaneous message transmission in both directions. All of the networks discussed in this paper have full duplex bidirectional links.

BMINs allow for *turn–around* routing where a message entering a switch from one side may turn around and leave the switch from the same side, as shown in Fig. 1. Deadlocks may occur since the head and tail of a message may span several switches. For example, four messages each represented by an arrow may enter the BMIN simultaneously as shown in Fig. 1. Each message wants to turn–around from particular switch, however finding its intended destination blocked by the tail of another message. Since no message can retreat, it will wait for the others to clear its path. Result is a deadlock in which the four messages wait indefinitely.

Typically, BMINs such as fat–trees avoid this deadlock problem by allowing turns in only one direction—turning only from "up" to the "down" direction [11], since processors are connected only to one end (i.e. side) of the tree. For example, Fig. 1 is a typical fat–tree for a 16 processor system with nodes connected along one side. However, it is possible to connect 32 processors along both sides of the BMIN to reduce the network cost, thus motivating our examination of the deadlock scenario of Fig. 1.

The deadlock in Fig. 1, in graph theoretic terms is a *cycle* of directed edges (arcs). A cycle is a contiguous sequence of input and output ports in the network, where the first and the last port is the same. The existence of a cycle in a graph may be determined by the well known *depth–first search* algorithm [12] that we will not describe here.

To avoid deadlocks we must ensure that set of routes used in the network are *acyclic*. One way to accomplish this is by prohibiting messages from turning around from a particular set of input/output ports in particular switches. For example, the cycle in Fig. 1 can be avoided by putting a "no turn" restriction at one of the four corners from which messages turn. Turn restrictions for the SP networks are first described in [8]. Horst describes turn restrictions for ServerNet in [2]. Glass and Ni describe turn restrictions for meshes in [7]. Qiao and Ni describe turn restrictions for irregular topologies in [5]. Note that Duato [13] describes sufficient conditions for deadlock-free routing that allows cyclic dependencies in adaptive networks, if there exists a connected acyclic channel subset in the network. However, Duato's proposal is not applicable to non-adaptive networks.

Note that there 12 different ways to make an internal turn in each switch, excluding entering and exiting from the same bidirectional port. Here, an internal turn refers to the ports 4–7 of the BMIN in Fig. 1. We make the assumption that every processor eventually receives its messages. Hence, final destinations –external ports 0, 1, 2, and 3– cannot participate in any cycles, and we will not consider them in further discussions. There are 8 switches in the BMIN, and therefore the total number of internal turns is 96.

Exhaustively searching for a minimal set of turn restrictions is a difficult task, since there are 2^{96} possible ways to restrict the turns. In the method of [8] one column of switches, either the left or the right column of switches allow for no turns at all (either the switches 0,1,2,3 or 4,5,6,7 in Fig. 1). This method restricts a total of 48 turns out of a possible 96 turns. The number of restrictions are subsequently reduced to 32 [10].

3 Deadlock Avoidance by Graph Partitioning

This paper's method of finding the turn restrictions is based on recursive partitioning of a graph model of the network and then removing inter-partition edges to eliminate cyclic

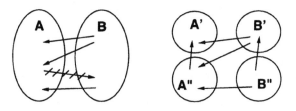

Fig. 2. Finding restrictions by graph partitioning and eliminating cycles.

FIND_RESTRICTIONS($G(V, E)$)
input: graph representation of the network
output: a set of turn restrictions
1   CYCLE_DETECT(G)
     if no cycles in G **then**
          return empty set.
     endif
2   Partition V in to set of vertices A and B such that
          A and B have nearly equal number of vertices
          AND the number of arcs from A to B is minimum
          AND partition constraints are satisfied.
3   Remove the set of arcs TR from A to B
4    $TR \leftarrow TR + \text{FIND\_RESTRICTIONS}(G_A)$
5    $TR \leftarrow TR + \text{FIND\_RESTRICTIONS}(G_B)$
6   return TR

Fig. 3. The pseudo-code for finding turn restrictions

dependencies, as illustrated in Fig. 2. We used the Kernighan-Lin heuristic procedure for graph partitioning [9], although other graph partitioning algorithms may be used as well. The objective of graph partitioning algorithms is to minimize the cut size, which is the number of edges between the partitions. This is the essence of our method. Smaller cut size leads to fewer turn restrictions.

A directed graph representation $G(V, E)$ of the network is used where graph vertices V represent the *network links*, and each directed edge (arc) in E represents an *input–output connection* in a switch. For example, 4 bidirectional internal ports of the BMIN is represented by 4 vertices representing switch input links, and 4 vertices representing switch output links, and a total of 12 arcs from 4 input vertices to 4 output vertices representing every possible connection. We assume that messages will not enter and exit from the same bidirectional port, since it serves no useful purpose.

The method is described by the pseudo–code in Fig. 3. In Step 2, vertices of the graph are partitioned in to 2 equal size vertex sets A and B (Fig. 2). Here, the most important issue is minimizing the cut size: We must split vertices V so that the number of arcs from set A to set B ($A \rightarrow B$) is as small as possible. The cut size of $B \rightarrow A$ is not important. We describe in Section 3.1 how cut size can be minimized.

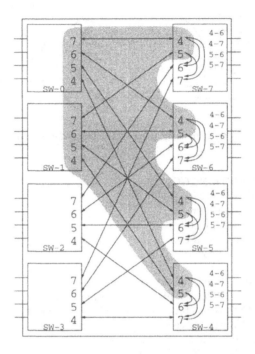

Fig. 4. Arcs removed between the two subgraphs to avoid cycles.

In Step 3, the arcs $A \rightarrow B$ are removed from the graph (indicated by dashed arrows Fig. 2). The removed arcs correspond to turn restrictions, since each arc represents an input–output connection in a switch. Since the remaining arcs between A and B are only in one direction ($B \rightarrow A$), no cycle spanning both A and B can exist. This observation is a key to our method. The two subgraphs A and B are then recursively partitioned (Steps 4,5) and more arcs are removed until no subsubgraph with a cycle (Step 1) remains in the network.

We now illustrate the method on the BMIN shown in Fig. 1. The BMIN is partitioned in to two set of vertices (e.g. links) shown in Fig. 4. Links in the shaded area represent one partition and links in the unshaded area represent the other partition. The arcs from one subgraph (shaded) to the other subgraph (unshaded) are removed. We represent the removed arcs with arrows in Fig. 4. This is the first partition, and it results in 16 turn restrictions: namely (input $\rightarrow$ output) $4 \rightarrow 6$, $4 \rightarrow 7$, $5 \rightarrow 6$, $5 \rightarrow 7$ in switches 4, 5, 6, and 7. Messages may not enter and exit from the restricted input–outputs. The first subgraph is further partitioned in to two subsubgraphs, and the arcs $4 \rightarrow 5$ in switches 4, 5, 6, and 7 are removed. Likewise, the second subgraph is partitioned and the arcs $6 \rightarrow 7$ are removed. The final result has a total of 24 turn restrictions $4 \rightarrow 5$, $4 \rightarrow 6$, $4 \rightarrow 7$, $5 \rightarrow 6$, $5 \rightarrow 7$, $6 \rightarrow 7$ in switches 4, 5, 6, 7 as shown in Fig. 5. This is a better result than the 48 restrictions described in [8] and 32 restrictions described in [10].

There are few noteworthy observations in Fig. 5, (1) although the turn restrictions on all 4 switches are identical in this particular example, this may not happen in general,

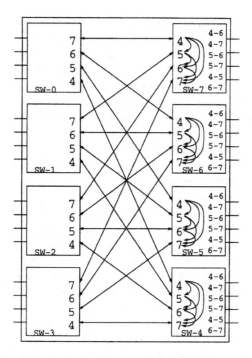

Fig. 5. The entire set of turn restrictions found by this paper's method. Restrictions are represented by arrows

(2) the 24 turn restrictions make some switches unreachable. For example, switch 3 is unreachable from switches 0, 1, 2. To deal with this problem we may use *partitioning constraints* which we will discuss later in Section 4.4.

3.1 Partitioning Step

The graph partitioning is an NP–complete problem. However, many good heuristics exist for graph partitioning. We used the well known Kernighan–Lin (KL) [9] heuristic in the partitioning step (Step 2). KL has been extensively used in many applications including VLSI circuit design, linear programming, and sparse matrix computations. We modified the KL algorithm to handle directed graphs and to reduce the cut size only in one direction. We will only present a sketch of the algorithm here. Details can be found in [9].

The modified KL algorithm starts with a randomly selected initial partition of two vertex sets A and B. The objective of the algorithm is to find two subsets A' and B' of same size (where $A' \subset A$, $B' \subset B$), such that exchanging the two subsets between A and B reduces the cut size. Here, cut size is defined as the number of arcs incident from set A to set B. After two subsets A', B' are exchanged between A and B, the procedure is repeated iteratively until no further reduction in cut size can be obtained. We assume that arcs do not have any associated weights. For characterizing heterogenous networks with differing switch and link capacities, one may use weighted arcs as well. Then, the cut size may be defined as the sum of the weights of arcs incident from set A to set B.

Given two randomly selected initial sets A, B, and $n = min(|A|, |B|)$, we determine the two vertices $a_1 \in A$ and $b_1 \in B$ such that exchanging them would correspond to the maximum possible reduction in cut size of $A \rightarrow B$. Call this reduction *the partial gain g_1*. In [9] it is described how maximum partial gain can be determined fast. We temporarily exchange vertices a_1 and b_1 between sets A and B, and "lock" them meaning that they will not be moved again in this iteration.

We now determine the two vertices $a_2 \in A - \{b_1\}$ and $b_2 \in B - \{a_1\}$ such that exchanging them would correspond to the maximum possible gain g_2 in cut size of $A \rightarrow B$. Continuing in this manner, we identify all the vertex pairs (a_3, b_3), (a_4, b_4), $\ldots (a_n, b_n)$ and their respective gains $g_3, g_4, \ldots, g_n$.

We now determine the k that maximizes the sum $G = \sum_{i=1}^{k} g_i$. If total gain $G > 0$, we then commit the vertex exchanges $(a_1, b_1), \ldots (a_k, b_k)$, and we undo the exchanges $(a_{k+1}, b_{k+1}), \ldots (a_n, b_n)$, i.e. we move back the vertex pairs for steps $k + 1$ through n to their original set. The procedure is then repeated with the newly formed sets A and B. However, if total gain $G \leq 0$ it means that we arrived at a local minimum in the previous iteration and we cannot further reduce the cut size. We undo all the exchanges for $i = 1, \ldots, n$, and terminate the procedure.

Few observations: (1) A partial gain g_i may be negative due to lack of a better choice. However, this may lead to positive gains g_j later $(j > i)$, resulting in a positive total gain G. Therefore, the algorithm can climb out of some local minimums. (2) Cut size decreases monotonically. (3) Due to the randomized initial selection of vertex sets, we must execute the algorithm several times, and use the best result.

Algorithm – Topology	BMIN	3-cube	Irregular	4x4 Mesh
This paper's method	26	12	14	
SP32 (Sethu et al [8])	32			
SP48 (Sethu [10])	48			
3-cube ex. (Horst [2])		12		
ET (Qiao and Ni [5])			37	
ET* (see text)	36		36	
Turn Model (Glass and Ni [7])				18
e-cube (dimension ordered)		24		36
Lower Bound (see text)	24	12	14	18

Table 1. Number of turn restrictions produced by several algorithms on benchmark networks.

4 Results

We compared our method to several algorithms on a set of network topologies. Table 1 compares the number of turn restrictions determined by various algorithms. All of the networks discussed here have full duplex bidirectional links interconnecting the switches and processors.

Switch	Turn Restrictions
0	7→4, 7→5
1	6→7
2	5→4, 6→4, 6→7, 7→4
3	5→4, 5→6, 5→7, 6→4, 6→5, 6→7
4	4→7, 5→4, 5→6, 5→7
5	5→4, 5→6, 6→4, 6→5
6	5→4, 6→4
7	4→7, 5→7, 6→7

Table 2. The 26 BMIN turn restrictions produced by this paper's method.

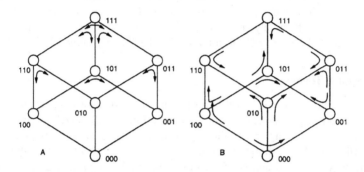

Fig. 6. Two different sets of turn restrictions for a 3-dim hypercube

4.1 BMIN

For the BMIN topology shown in Fig. 1 implementation of our method produced a minimum of 26 turn restrictions shown in Table 2. This is the best result obtained out of a few hundreds runs, each started with a different randomly selected initial partition. Note that this result has every switch reachable from every other switch unlike the 24 restriction example shown in Fig. 5. Note that we derived a lower bound of 24 turn restrictions for the BMIN in Fig. 1 using the method described in Section 4.2.

4.2 Hypercube

Horst [2] gives an example of a 3 dimensional hypercube with 12 turn restrictions when describing Tandem ServerNet, as shown in Fig. 6A. The number of restrictions are distributed as 0,0,0,2,0,2,2,6 in nodes 0–7, respectively. Turn restrictions are represented by arrows in the figure.

Application of our method also gives 12 restrictions, as shown in Fig. 6B. The number of restrictions are distributed as 1,1,2,2,2,2,1,1 in nodes 0–7, respectively. The distribution of turn restrictions is an issue of concern. With evenly distributed restrictions, one would expect the network to perform better in terms of latency and bandwidth. From that point of view, Fig. 6B is a better solution than Fig. 6A.

Note that for a 3–cube, 12 turn restrictions is the necessary minimum for a cycle free network. We can determine a lower bound for any network by counting *turn–disjoint* cycles. Turn–disjoint means that no pair of cycles in the counted set share any turns. For example, in a hypercube no two cycles of length 4 turn from the same corner, hence they are turn-disjoint: The 3–cube has 6 faces (each face is a 2–subcube). Each one has 2 cycles of length 4 along its perimeter. One cycle runs in the clockwise direction and the other runs in the counter–clockwise direction. Each cycle can be eliminated with one turn restriction. Therefore a total of 12 turn restrictions is necessary in a 3–cube. We can generalize this reasoning to n dimensional hypercubes. There are $2^{n-3}n(n-1)$ two subcubes in n-cube, with each 2-subcube having two cycles in opposite directions. Therefore, $2^{n-2}n(n-1)$ turn restrictions are the minimum necessary.

Note that the well known *e-cube* routing algorithm, which is also known as *dimension ordered routing* allows routing of messages from smaller dimension to larger dimension. Therefore, *e-cube* effectively implements $n(n-1)/2$ turn restrictions per node in n−cube. That is 24 turn restrictions total in a 3-cube. Table 1 summarizes the results.

4.3 Irregular Topology

Qiao and Ni [5] describe an algorithm for finding turn restrictions in irregular network topologies. Their algorithm is based on finding an Eulerian Trail (ET) in the network. If messages are sent along an ET, then no deadlocks can occur since the ET is cycle free by definition. Then "shortcuts" in the ET are found in order to reduce the number of turn restrictions. Qiao and Ni [5] demonstrate the ET algorithm on the topology shown in Fig. 7. The ET algorithm produces 37 turn restrictions for this topology. We describe here the algorithm ET* inspired by ET. ET* is easier to describe and implement. ET* produces 36 turn restrictions for this particular example. In comparison, our graph partitioning based approach produces 14 turn restrictions. (This is the best result obtained out of a few hundred runs.) Results are summarized in Table 1. The turn restrictions produced by our method are shown in Fig. 7 by arrows. Note that 14 turn restrictions are the minimum necessary for this topology. This lower bound is determined by counting turn–disjoint cycles in the network, as described in Section 4.2.

We now describe the ET* algorithm. A *trail* is a sequence of unidirectional links of the network in which all the links in the sequence are distinct. An *Eulerian trail* is a trail that contains all the links of the network. For example, Fig. 8 shows an Eulerian trail for the network in Fig. 7. The notation ij denotes the link from node i to node j. By definition an Eulerian trail has no cycles, hence messages sent along the trail cannot deadlock. For example, processor 0 can send a message to processor 1 along the trail $05 \rightarrow 54 \rightarrow 43 \rightarrow 38 \rightarrow 71$ (each processor i not shown in the figure is connected to switch i.)

Although the method routing messages along the trail is deadlock-free, it does not take advantage of the fact that switch 0 is directly connected to switch 1, hence there exists a *shortcut* to the intended destination. Shortcuts are created by adding arcs to the trail. A message may take a shortcut if does not cause any cycles. In the ET* algorithm, we allow a shortcut only if it is in the direction of the Eularian trail (forward shortcut). We do not allow backward shortcuts in order to avoid possible cycle(s). We define a shortcut from ij to jk as forward, if ij is before jk in the trail, otherwise it is a backward

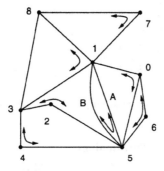

Fig. 7. Irregular topology of Qiao and Ni, and the turn restrictions determined by this paper's method

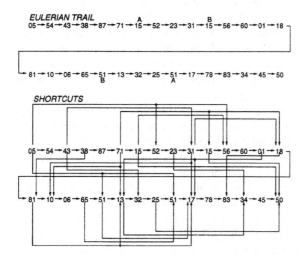

Fig. 8. A Eulerian trail and forward shortcuts added to the trail

shortcut. For example, the shortcut 05 → 52 is allowed. However, the shortcut 45 → 52 is not permitted since it is a backward shortcut that creates a cycle.

The arcs of the final graph represent the permitted turns. For example, 05 → 52 in Fig. 8 means that, switch 5 can forward messages incoming from switch 0 to switch 2. Arcs missing from the graph are the turn restrictions. For example, 45 → 52, missing from the figure, indicates that switch 5 can not forward messages from switch 4 to switch 2. By counting the missing arcs, we arrive at the figure of 36 turn restrictions. Note also that application of ET* algorithm to the BMIN in Fig. 1 produces 36 turns restrictions. Results are summarized in Table 1.

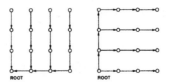

Fig. 9. Up and down trees for identifying turns that should not be removed

4.4 2-D Mesh (Constrained Partitioning)

We applied our graph partitioning based method to 2-D meshes as well, since meshes are one of the well known and studied network topologies. We first describe related work and then we describe the constrained partitioning procedure.

The *e-cube* routing algorithm prevents deadlocks by routing the messages along the x-axis first and then y-axis next. Thus, *e-cube* allows East to South turns (ES), and WS, EN, WN, EW, WE, NS, SN turns. The NE, NW, SE, and SW turns are not permitted. The *turn model* of Glass and Ni [7] implements fewer turn restrictions. In the "West First" turn model, the NW and SW turns are not permitted. In an $n \times m$ processor mesh the turn model requires $2(n-1)(m-1)$ turn restrictions. This is also the minimum number necessary for meshes which we can determine by counting the turn disjoint cycles, as described in Section 4.2

Our method, when applied without constraints, does not work at all for a mesh. The turn restrictions always make one or more nodes unreachable from another node, just as was the case for the BMIN in Fig. 5. In a 4 × 4 mesh, multiple runs with different initial partitions always resulted in 10–15% of the node pairs disconnected. The best way to avoid a cycle is to disconnect the network elements, which our method does very well in this case. Of course, this defeats the purpose of having a network. Due to its relatively long diameter, a mesh is disconnected easily when partitioned without constraints. We thus devised a constrained partitioning procedure to solve this problem.

Before partitioning we designate some turns as "cannot be restricted", so that there always exists a path between every node pair in the network, i.e. the graph stays connected. Then, during the partitioning step (Section 3.1) we ensure that those arcs (i.e. turns) do not appear in the cut from vertex set A to B.

The graph of constrained arcs (turns) should be acyclic, and the following strategy is devised to identify those arcs. A "down" spanning tree of the network and an "up" spanning tree of the network rooted at one node is created, such as shown in Fig. 9 for a 4 × 4 mesh. Every node is reachable from every other node by going up in the "up tree" towards the root, and then going down in the "down tree" towards the final destination. The turns used in the two trees are marked as "cannot be restricted", and then the partitioning step is applied. A tree is cycle free by definition, therefore constrained arcs cannot form a cycle.

5 Conclusions

In this paper we described a deadlock avoidance algorithm for minimizing turn restrictions in wormhole routed networks with arbitrary topology. The method is based on recursive partitioning of the channel dependence graph of the network and removing interpartition edges to make the graph acyclic. We used the KL graph partitioning algorithm to minimize the cut size between partitions, i.e. to minimize the number of turn restrictions.

We compared the method to existing algorithms on a small set of benchmark networks, and observed that fewer turn restrictions are usually obtained. We have preliminary (not presented here) results—simulated and measured on real systems—that show that fewer turn restrictions lead to lower latency and higher bandwidth. Further simulations of various networks are needed to validate this relationship and quantify performance improvement.

A strength of our method is that it does not require new hardware, switch design, or topology. The method can be easily applied to existing networks by changing the route tables.

Acknowledgements

We are grateful to anonymous reviewers for their valuable comments and criticism, Caroline Benveniste for preliminary results of simulation, and Mike Rosenfield for his support.

References

1. W. J. Dally and C. L. Seitz, "Deadlock-free message routing in multiprocessor interconnection networks," *IEEE Trans. on Computers*, vol. C-36, pp. 547–553, May 1987.
2. R. Horst, "ServerNet Deadlock Avoidance and Fractahedral Topologie0s," in *Proc. 10th Int. Parallel Processing Symp. (IPPS'96)*, pp. 274–280, April 1996.
3. C. B. Stunkel et al, "The SP2 High-Performance Switch," *IBM Systems Journal*, vol. 34, no. 2, pp. 185–204, 1995.
4. B. Abali and C. Aykanat, "Routing Algorithms for IBM SP1," *Lecture Notes in Computer Science, Springer–Verlag*, vol. 853, pp. 161–175, 1994.
5. W. Qiao and L. M. Ni, "Adaptive routing in irregular networks using cut–through switches," in *Proc. 25th Int. Conf. Parallel Processing (ICPP)*, August 1996.
6. A. A. Chien, "A cost and speed model for k-ary n-cube wormhole routers," in *Proc. Hot Interconnects'93*, August 1993.
7. C. Glass and L. M. Ni, "The turn model for adaptive routing," in *Proc. 19th Int. Ann. Symp. Computer Architecture*, pp. 278–287, 1992.
8. H. Sethu, R. F. Stucke, and C. B. Stunkel, "Technique for accomplishing deadlock free routing through a multi–stage cross–point packet switch." U.S. Patent 5,453,978, issued 9/26/1995.
9. B. W. Kernighan and S. Lin, "An efficient heuristic procedure for partitioning graphs," *Bell System Tech. J.*, vol. 49, pp. 291–307, 1970.
10. H. Sethu, "Routing Restrictions." unpublished.
11. I. D. Scherson and C.-H. Chien, "Least Common Ancestor Networks," in *Proc. 7th Int. Parallel Processing Symp.*, pp. 507–513, 1993.
12. T. H. Cormen, C. E. Leiserson, and R. L. Rivest, *Introduction to Algorithms*. NY: McGraw-Hill, 1990.
13. J. Duato, "A new theory of deadlock-free adaptive routing in wormhole networks," *IEEE Trans. Parallel and Distributed Systems*, vol. 4, no. 2, pp. 1320–1331, 1993.

Extending ATM Networks
for Efficient Reliable Multicast

Jonathan S. Turner, jst@cs.wustl.edu
Washington University, St. Louis

Abstract

One of the important features of ATM networks is their ability to support multicast communication. This facilitates the efficient distribution of multimedia information streams (such as audio and video) to large groups of receivers. Because ATM networks do not provide reliable delivery mechanisms, it is up to end systems to provide end-to-end reliability where it is needed. While this is straightforward for point-to-point virtual circuits, it is more difficult for multicast virtual circuits. This paper proposes extensions to the hardware of ATM switches that enables end systems to implement reliable multicast in a more efficient and scalable manner than is otherwise possible. We essentially provide a *network assist* to enable end systems to implement reliable multicast more effectively. With our approach, the amount of work that must be done by any receiver in a reliable multicast is independent of the number of participants in the multicast and the amount of work that must be done per packet transmission by any sender, is independent of the number of participants in the multicast. Of course, in large multicasts, a given packet may have to be transmitted multiple times and the number of such transmissions does depend on the number of participants. However, one can show that even under very conservative assumptions this effect does not limit scalability to any significant extent. The proposed reliable multicast mechanisms are being implemented in a scalable ATM switch support 2.4 Gb/s transmission links.

1 Introduction

Efficient multicast communication is a key feature of ATM network technology. Originally designed to support distribution of multimedia information streams (audio and video), it can also be useful for more general distributed computing applications. However, because such applications generally require reliable data delivery, end systems must provide mechanisms for ensuring reliable transport over the unreliable communication channels provided by ATM networks. While providing reliable transport is straightforward for point-to-point communication channels, it is more complex in the context of multicast channels which may have hundreds, thousands or even millions of participants.

This paper develops an approach to reliable multicast communication in ATM networks. Our objective is to provide *scalable* mechanisms by which we

---

[0] This work was supported by the Advanced Research Projects Agency.

mean mechanisms in which the amount of work done by senders and receivers in a multicast connection is independent of the total number of participants. Reliable multicast can be implemented entirely by mechanisms in end systems or by some combination of mechanisms in end systems and the network. Our approach is to provide a *network assist* to enable end systems to implement reliable multicast more effectively. There are actually four distinct aspects of the proposed reliable multicast support.

- *Redundant acknowledgement suppression* elimates redundant acknowledgements in a multicast connection, so that a sender receives just a single positive acknowledgement for each packet sent and at most one negative acknowledgement.
- *Targeted retransmission* ensures that packet retransmissions are forwarded only to the receivers that did not get a packet when it was first sent.
- *Dynamic channel sharing* allows multiple senders in a many-to-many multicast to dynamically share a single virtual circuit without the occurrence of packet loss due to cell interleaving of the different packets. This is accomplished using a dynamic virtual circuit subchannel assignment technique.
- *Path trace/retrace* is used in applications with multiple senders and allows control cells used in the reliable multicast protocol to accumulate path information that can be later used by cells going in the reverse direction to retrace the path back to the original sender.

These mechanisms can be used separately or in combination to provide reliable multicast for one-to-many and many-to-many applications. In addition, the dynamic channel sharing mechanism addresses a general issue for many-to-many virtual circuits and is of value even where fully reliable transmission is not required.

There is a substantial literature on providing reliable multicast mechanisms in networks. One of the earliest contributions was [3]. Some selected recent contributions include [1, 5, 7, 8, 9, 10, 11]. Much of the more recent work is directed toward multicast in the context of the internet protocol suite and shifts much of the responsibility for recovering lost data onto the receivers. The recent paper by Floyd, Jacobson, et. al. [6] is a good example of receiver-based recovery. They also advocates the use of application-specific reliable multicast mechanisms, rather than more general mechanisms supported at lower levels. While some of the prior work is applicable in the ATM context, there seems little prior work directly related to extending ATM switching mechanisms to assist in the implementation of reliable multicast.

In section 2, we describe the acknowledgement suppression mechanisms that enable scalable reliable one-to-many multicast. Section 3 describes the mechanisms used to support many-to-many multicast with consistent delivery order using one end system as a relay. Section 4 describes how the relay can be eliminated (at the cost of sacrificing consistent delivery order). Section 5 outlines how the mechanisms are being implemented in the Washington University Gigabit Switch. Section 6 gives a brief performance analysis.

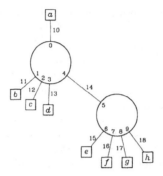

Fig. 1. Reliable Multicast Message Transmission

2 Reliable One-to-Many Multicast

Our basic approach to achieving reliable one-to-many multicast is illustrated in Figure 1. To send a packet to end systems b through h, end system a sends the packet on a reliable multicast virtual circuit, through the two ATM switching systems, shown in the figure. The packet is delineated by start and end of packet cells (these, and the other control cells required, can be implemented using a variant of the ATM Resource Management cell type). The ATM switches note the passage of the start and end cells, and when acknowledgement cells are received from the downstream neighbors, they propagate only the last acknowledgement cell expected. The acknowledgement cells are originated by the receiving end systems; the switches merely propagate them selectively, so that the sender receives only one acknowledgement indicating that all destinations have received the message. If the acknowledgement is not received until after a timeout has expired, source a can send the packet again, preceded by a new start cell. The switches propagate the retransmitted packet, only to those downstream neighbors that did not acknowledge the original transmission, so that destinations that received the first copy will not have to process a duplicate.

To allow end systems to pipeline multicast packet transmissions through the network, all control cells processed by the switches (start, end, ack) contain *transmission slot numbers* which are used to access stored state information relevant to a particular packet. Individual data cells do not contain slot numbers, but the data cells are assumed to be sent using AAL 5 (or something equivalent) and include the slot number or an equivalent transport protocol sequence number somewhere in the end-to-end protocol header. A receiver acknowledges a packet only if it is correctly received (as indicated by an end-to-end error check).

The switches maintain a state machine for each transmission slot, to keep track of which downstream neighbors have acknowledged a given packet and which have not. One version of this state machine is shown in Figure 2. In the state diagram, the state $ack(i)$ denotes all states in which i acknowledgements (out of a total expected number of d) have been received. Assuming the state machine starts in state $ack(d)$, the arrival of a start cell, places it in state $ack(0)$. In

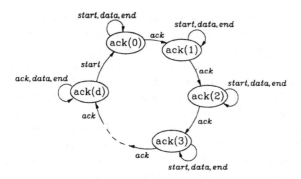

```
upstream_neighbor = input link and VCI on which packets arrive
downstream_neighbor = link and VCI on which a received ack arrived
output_set = set of output (link, VCI) pairs to which packets
              are to be forwarded
type = type of the cell being processed (data, start, end, ack)
i = slot number in the control cell being processed
    (i is undefined if processing data cell)
currslot = slot number in last start cell processed
status[j] = status of slot j (options are ack(0) ... ack(d))
ackset[j] = subset of downstream_neighbors that have ack'ed slot j

if type = start and status[i] = ack(d) then
    status[i] = ack(0)
    ackset[i] = {}
    currslot = i
    forward cell to output_set
if type = start and status[i] != ack(d) then
    currslot = i
    forward cell to (output_set - ackset[i])
if type = data then
    forward cell to (output_set - ackset[currslot])
if type = end then
    forward cell to (output_set - ackset[i])
if type = ack then
    ackset[i] = ackset[i] + {downstream_neighbor}
    update status[i]
    if status[i] = ack(d) then
        forward ack to upstream_neighbor
    else
        discard cell
```

Fig. 2. State Machine for Monochromatic Algorithm

this state it forwards data cells and the end cell. When the first acknowledgement is received, it notes which downstream neighbor acknowledged the cell and proceeds to state $ack(1)$. Additional acknowledgements trigger further transitions. The transition to state $ack(d)$ also triggers the forwarding of an acknowledgement to the upstream neighbor. When in state i for $i < d$, new start, data or end cells are simply forwarded to those downstream neighbors that have not yet acknowledged the packet. The program fragment in the figure shows the processing that would be done at a typical switch in a reliable multicast connection in response to the various types of cells. Note that `status[j]` need not really be a separate variable, since its value is implied by the value of `ackset[j]`. We've chosen to show it separately only for clarity of exposition.

Unfortunately, the state machine in Figure 2 is deficient in two respects. First, consider what happens if a given switch completes a packet and goes to state $ack(d)$, sends its acknowledgement to its upstream neighbor, and then the acknowledgement is lost before it reaches the upstream neighbor. Eventually, the sender will retransmit the packet beginning with a new start cell. The switch whose acknowledgement was lost should recognize this situation and simply convert the start cell to an acknowledgement cell and return it, discarding the subsequent data and end cells. However, the state machine as written, will treat this as a new transmission and forward it on to the downstream neighbors. Sequence numbers in the transport level packet can prevent the receiving end systems from being confused by this redundant transmission, but they will be forced to do some unnecessary work. The more important problem with this approach however, is that its correctness requires that the sender never initiate a retransmission if there is any possibility of the receiver still sending an acknowledgement. There are cases where the combination of a slow receiver, lost control cells and unlucky timing can result in the sender thinking a packet has been correctly received, when in fact, it has been lost.

To correct this problem, we add a *color bit* to the slot numbers carried in the various control cells. We require that senders alternate the color of consecutive packets sent with the same slot number. This leads to the state machine shown in Figures 3 and 4. Here, `cell_color` represents the color bit of the control cell being processed and `currcolor` represents the color bit of the most recent start cell. In this algorithm, the state machine is in either the leftmost or rightmost state when propagating a packet for the first time. As acknowledgements of the proper color are received, the state machine moves to the other end. Thus, when processing red packets, `ack(i)` designates states in which i acknowledgements have been received, while when processing black packets, it designates states in which i acknowledgements are still expected. To distinguish this algorithm from the original, we refer to it as the *bichromatic* algorithm and the original as the *monochromatic* algorithm. Note that the bichromatic algorithm correctly handles lost acknowledgements and its correctness is independent of timing considerations [1]

---

[1] The author thanks Andy Fingerhut for convincing him that the deficiencies of the monochromatic algorithm should be corrected and showing how they could be corrected withot adding any state.

78

```
if status[i] = ack(0) then
    if type = start and cell_color = red then
        ackset = {}
        currslot = i
        currcolor = red
        forward cell to output_set
    else if type = start and cell_color = black then
        convert cell to ack and return to upstream_neighbor
    else if type = data or type = end then
        forward cell to output_set
    else if type = ack and cell_color = red then
        ackset[i] = ackset[i] + {downstream_neighbor}
        discard cell
    else if type = ack and cell_color = black then
        discard cell
else if status[i] = ack(d) then
    if type = start and cell_color = black then
        ackset = output_set
        currslot = i
        currcolor = black
        forward cell to output_set
    else if type = start and cell_color = red then
        convert cell to ack and return to upstream_neighbor
    else if type = data or type = end then
        forward cell to output_set
    else if type = ack and cell_color = black then
        ackset[i] = ackset[i] - {downstream_neighbor}
        discard cell
    else if type = ack and cell_color = red then
        discard cell
```

Fig. 3. State Machine for Bichromatic Algorithm

The use of timeouts to detect lost packets can delay retransmission unnecessarily, limiting overall performance. Frequently, it's possible for a receiver to detect that a packet has been lost and immediately send a negative acknowledgement to the sender, requesting a retransmission. (In a typical sliding window protocol operating over an "order-preserving" network, the arrival of a packet with a sequence number different from the "next" one in sequence indicates one or more lost packets.) When a packet is lost in a reliable multicast connection, all receivers downstream of the point where the loss occurs may detect the loss

```
else if status[i] = ack(1) or . . . or status[i] = ack(d-1) then
    if type = start then
        currslot = i
        currcolor = cell_color
        if currcolor = ews then
            forward cell to output_set - ackset[i]
        else
            forward cell to ackset[i]
    else if type = data or type = end then
        if currcolor = plus then
            forward cell to output_set - ackset[i]
        else
            forward cell to ackset[i]
    else if type = ack and cell_color = red and currcolor = red then
        ackset[i] = ackset[i] + {downstream_neighbor}
        if ackset[i] = output_set then
            forward ack to upstream_neighbor
        else
            discard cell
    else if type = ack and cell_sign = minus and currcolor = black then
        ackset[i] = ackset[i] - {downstream_neighbor}
        if ackset[i] = {} then
            forward ack to upstream_neighbor
        else
            discard cell
    else
        discard cell
```

Fig. 4. Bichromatic Algorithm (cont.)

and send a negative acknowledgement. To ensure scalability of reliable multicast protocols in the presence of negative acknowledgements, the network should return only the first negative acknowledgement for a particular lost packet. This requires that the switches keep track of whether a nack has been sent for a given packet, and if so to suppress forwarding of further nacks. This requires adding some additional state to the switch state machine.

In particular, for each transmission slot, the switch must keep an additional bit that is cleared when a new packet is sent using that slot and set when the first nack for that slot number is received. Start cells associated with retransmissions do not re-enable nack forwarding. Referring to the picture at the top of Figure 3, the nack bit would be cleared on a transition from $ack(d-1)$ to $ack(d)$ or on a transition from $ack(1)$ to $ack(0)$. If a negative acknowledgement is received when the nack bit is 0, the nack is forwarded upstream and the nack bit is set, but the state machine remains in the same state. Note that the correctness of the protocol still relies on the positive acknowledgements; nacks merely improve performance when packets are lost.

In [13], it is shown how these mechanisms can be used in combination with a conventional sliding window protocol to provide reliable one-to-many multicast. This requires that the number of transmission slots be set equal to the maximum window size (in packets) of the protocol.

3   Many-to-Many Multicast with Fully Ordered Delivery

In distributed computing applications, it is often desirable to have not just reliable one-to-many communication, but also reliable many-to-many communication, in which any member of a group can reliably send a packet to the other members. Moreover, in some cases it can be important for the packets to be ordered so as to provide consistent delivery order to all receivers. The most straightforward (and efficient) way to implement reliable many-to-many multicast is to have one end system act as a *relay node* receiving packets from all senders, ordering them and forwarding them on a reliable one-to-many connection to all receivers. In this section we describe mechanisms for implementing reliable multicast in this way. However, we also show, in the next section, how these mechanisms can be extended to provide reliable many-to-many multicast without use of a relay node.

The use of a relay node breaks the reliable multicast problem into a many-to-one problem and a one-to-many problem. Since the one-to-many problem has already been addressed, we focus here on the many-to-one problem. There are two issues that must be addressed in the many-to-one problem. First, we need a way to enable the receiver to identify cells coming from different senders that are sharing a single virtual circuit. Second, we need a mechanism to allow the receiver to acknowledge a packet sent by a particular sender, while using a single virtual circuit. Of course, one could simply address this problem using point-to-point virtual circuits between the senders and the receiver, but this leads scaling limits that we seek to avoid.

There are a variety of approaches one can take to sharing a single many-to-ome virtual circuit among multiple senders. The different options are discussed in some detail in [13]. We have concluded that the most attractive general approach to this problem is a contention based scheme in which switches observe the flow of packets from different senders and perform collision resolution at every point where packets from different senders come together. This allows senders to transmit packets without coordinating their transmissions. In the simplest variant of this scheme, the switches only allow one packet at a time to propagate through a "merge point." Unfortunately, this leads to unacceptably high collision probabilities unless the connection is very lightly loaded.

To get better performance using local collision resolution, we allow multiple packets to propagate through a merge point at the same time by implementing dynamically assigned *subchannels* within each virtual circuit. When the start cell of a packet arrives at a merge point, the packet is assigned an outgoing subchannel, a local mapping is created and subsequent cells in that packet are forwarded on the assigned subchannel. The outgoing subchannel is released when the end cell of the packet is received, or on expiration of a timeout. If all outgoing subchannels are in use when the start cell of a packet arrives, then the packet is discarded.

To implement subchannels, we need to add a subchannel identifier to every cell. Because the subchannel field is required in data cells as well as start and end cells, it needs to be kept small so as not to take away too many bits from other parts of the ATM cell header. Fortunately, it does not take a large number of subchannels to give good performance. If we have n sources in a many-to-one virtual circuit, h subchannels and an average of m busy sources, the probability of a burst being blocked due to the unavailability of any subchannels is approximately

$$\sum_{i=h}^{n-1} \binom{n-1}{i} p^i (1-p)^{(n-1)-i}$$

When $n = 1000$, $h = 15$ and $m = 1$ the probability of a burst being discarded is less than 10^{-12}. If we increase m to 4, this becomes .00002. For $m = 8$, it is .02. To accommodate applications in which we expect more simultaneously active sources, we can use multiple virtual circuits with sources randomly selecting a virtual circuit on which to transmit. While the subchannel remapping takes place only within each virtual circuit, the number of virtual circuits needed to give low collision probabilities is less than the average number of active sources.

With 15 subchannels, a subchannel number can be encoded in four bits, making it possible to use the GFC field of the ATM cell header to carry the subchannel number (we leave one value unused, as an idle subchannel indication). At each merge point, a switch must store the status of all the outgoing subchannels. This status information includes the incoming subchannel number of the burst using the given output subchannel (if no incoming burst is currently using the output subchannel, the stored value is the idle subchannel value), the incoming branch that the burst is coming in on and timing information used to determine when a given entry has been idle for more than the subchannel timeout period.

To make the reliable multicast mechanism useful in a general setting, it's important that there be some strategy for interoperability between switches that implement reliable multicast and those that don't. For the one-to-many mechanisms described in the previous section, interoperability is easy, since all that is required of switches that do not support the reliable multicast is that they be capable of forwarding the control cells and data on point-to-point virtual circuit segments. For the many-to-one case, the subchannel remapping mechanism can interfere with interoperability. For switches that propagate the GFC field without change along point-to-point virtual circuit segments, there is direct interoperability. However for switches that overwrite the GFC field (the usual case), some alternative approach is needed. The simplest way to address this is to allocate a block of consecutive virtual circuit identifiers on the link from a reliable multicast switch to a "standard" switch, and remap the virtual circuit subchannels to distinct virtual circuits. This is done by simply adding the subchannel number of forwarded cells to the first virtual circuit identifier in the allocated range. Similarly, when coming from a standard switch to a reliable multicast switch, distinct virtual circuits can be remapped to a single virtual circuit with subchannels. This mechanism for converting virtual circuit subchannels to consecutive virtual circuits is particularly useful in the context of delivery to end-systems, where the network interface circuitry will typically not be able to directly interpret the subchannel information. The use of distinct VCs at this point allows conventional network interface circuitry to properly demultiplex the arriving packets into separate buffers.

The collision resolution mechanism allows senders to transmit packets to the relay efficiently, but we still need a way for the relay to send acknowledgements back to the sender of a packet, without requiring a point-to-point virtual circuit for each sender. The most straightforward way we have found to do this is to implement a simple *trace-back* mechanism, that allows a cell sent in reply to a cell previously received on the many-to-one path to be returned to the same place. The trace-back mechanism requires a one-to-many virtual circuit that has the same branching structure as the many-to-one virtual circuit that it is used with. Control cells sent on the many-to-one path (i.e. start of packet cells) include a *trace field* that switches on the path can insert trace information into. The relay includes the same trace information in cells it sends on the upstream path back to the sender and each switch along the path uses this information to forward the cell to the proper upstream branch.

4 Many-to-Many Multicast Without a Relay

If one is not concerned with the provision of consistent delivery order to all receivers in a reliable multicast connection, it is possible to directly combine a many-to-one connection with a one-to-many connection, eliminating the intervening relay node. This requires extending the acknowledgement suppression mechanism to recognize different subchannels. The main cost of this extension is that for each of the 15 subchannels, the switch entry must keep track of which transmission slot the last start cell on that subchannel specified (so that the data cells for the subchannel can be forwarded to the proper downstream branches).

Now, because this allows multiple sources to send packets directly into the one-to-many part of the connection, sources that are sending information concurrently must use distinct transmission slot numbers. The end systems can handle this in a variety of different ways. One is to simply assign slot numbers to sources statically. This is a reasonable approach when the number of senders is small. The other option is for the senders to allocate transmission slot numbers dynamically, using any general distributed resource allocation algorithm.

The elimination of the relay node makes it possible to structure a multicast connection that does not funnel through some common point and then funnel out again to all the receivers. Instead we can have a more distributed situation in which data flows from senders through the multicast connection tree, branching at various points to reach the receivers.

5 Implementation in WU Gigabit Switch

The mechanisms described above are being implemented in the Washington University Gigabit Switch (WUGS). This section provides some of the implementation details. Readers are referred to [4] for background on the WUGS architecture and to [13] for a more detailed account of the reliable multicast mechanisms.

The WUGS architecture breaks large multicast connections into binary copy steps. For example, suppose we have a multicast connection in which each cell arriving at a given switch is to be forwarded to four outputs. In the WUGS architecture, we would select two ports of the switch to act as *recycling ports* for the connection, and send arriving cells, not directly to the output ports, but to the recycling ports, instead. Now, every output port of the switch has a direct data path back to its corresponding input port (that is, there is a data path from output i back to input i), allowing cells to be recycled. So, when the two copies of the cell in the example arrive at the recycling ports, they are sent back to the input side of the interconnection network, and sent through the network again with the four copies produced in this pass forwarded to the four required outputs. To accomplish this, a virtual circuit table lookup is performed at the input port where the cell first arrives and at each of the two recycling ports, before it is sent back through the interconnection network. The table entries, in each case, specify the pair of switch output ports that the cell is to be sent to next and the virtual circuit identifier that is to be used to access the next table entry.

The use of binary copying and recycling, together with the particular interconnection network design used in the WUGS architecture yields a system that has optimal scaling properties. Moreover, it makes the implementation of reliable multicast particularly straightforward. With binary copying, the one-to-many mechanism described in section 2 has $d = 2$, which means that for each transmission slot defined for a given virtual circuit, we need just two bits of state information for positive acknowledgements and a third bit to suppress negative acks as well. This allows one to implement one-to-many multicast connections supporting large end-to-end transmission windows without using much memory in the switch's virtual circuit tables. If one considers the overall reliable multicast connection, the memory required is 3 bits per transmission slot for every receiver in the reliable multicast. Since each end-system maintains buffers that consume far more memory than this, the overhead in the switches is acceptably modest.

Collision resolution is also handled most easily when the merging of data flows from different senders is done on a binary basis. The ability to recycle cells from outputs back to inputs, makes it possible to do this as well. With binary merging the subchannel mapping information can be kept quite small. In particular, for each of 15 outgoing subchannels we require 1 bit to specify the upstream branch using that outgoing subchannel, 4 bits to specify the input subchannel number and two bits of timer information, used to ensure that subchannels are eventually released, in the event of a lost end-of-packet cell.

There are several cell types that make up the reliable multicast protocol:

One-to-many

TYP=3,RC,CYC,CS,UD,SC,RCO,BR		UADR	
DADR			
DVXI1			BDI1
DVXI2			BDI2
UVXI			− − −
MAXSLOT		CURRSLOT	

ACKSET[0]..ACKSET[63]

⋮

Many−to−one/merge

TYP=5,RC,CYC,CS,UD,SC,RCO,BR	NSC	SCXT	
DADR			
DVXI			BDI

SCXT

Fig. 5. Virtual Path/Circuit Table Formats for Reliable Multicast

start cells, end cells, acknowledgement cells, negative acknowledgement cells, reject cells and data cells. The start, end, ack, nack and reject cells are all encoded using the ATM Resource Management cell type (PTI=110), with the first byte of the payload equal to the Reliable Multicast Protocol ID (123). The second byte of the payload contains a cell type field (0 for NOP, 1 for start, 2 for end, 3 for ack, 4 for nack and 5 for reject). The next two bytes contain the transmission slot number used for the one-to-many part of the protocol. The first bit of this two byte field is taken as the current color bit. The next eight bytes contain trace information, the subsequent eight bytes are reserved for future use, and the remainder of the payload is available for end-to-end information and is passed through by the switches without modification. In both data cells and control cells the GFC field of the standard ATM cell header is replaced by a subchannel field in which values 0–14 represent valid subchannels and 15 is reserved as an idle subchannel indicator.

There are several different virtual circuit table entry formats. Figure 5 shows the two key formats for reliable multicast. The first of these is used in a one-to-many connection, as described in section 2. The second is used in a many-to-one connection as described in section 3. The one-to-many format implements one node in a binary tree. UADR and UVXI identify its parent in the tree and DADR and DVXI1 and 2 identify its children in the tree. MAXSLOT is the maximum number of transmission slots that the connection can support and CURRSLOT is the current transmission slot number. Since different connections may require different numbers of transmission slots, we allow a given reliable multicast virtual circuit to use multiple consecutive table entries. The control software that sets up the virtual circuit is responsible for allocating these table entries. As shown in the figure, each entry contains six words of four bytes each, so each added table entry supports 64 transmission slots.

The many-to-one format implements one binary merge point in the many-to-one part of a connection. It stores a complete subchannel mapping table (tt SCXT) as shown in Figure 5. When a start cell is received on a connection, the VXT entry is read and an unused outgoing subchannel is selected from the SCXT stored in the VXT entry. The identity of the incoming branch and subchannel is stored in the entry. When data cells are received, their input branch and subchannel number are used to select the right entry from the SCXT. Their subchannel field is then modified appropriately and they are forwarded to the downstream node in the tree.

As discussed in section 3, start cells in a many-to-one connection acquire trace information to allow acknowledgement cells to be efficiently returned to the proper sender. This is done by adding one bit of trace information to the trace field of the start cell as it passes through a binary merge point. Acknowledgement cells flow back on a separate one-to-many connection with the same branching structure as the one-to-many connection and are routed using the trace information.

The two virtual circuit table entry types described here are also used in general many-to-many connections. The complete implementation requires several other entry types which cannot be described here due to space limitations. A more complete description of the implementation can be found in [13].

6 Performance Analysis

If a packet is delivered to all receivers in a one-to-many connection the first time it is sent, the amount of work done by the sender is about the same as for sending a point-to-point packet. Similarly, for each of the receivers. Furthermore, no matter how many times a given packet is lost, the receivers who got it the first time need do no extra work on behalf of other receivers. In fact, the amount of work that a receiver must do per packet received is essentially the same as for point-to-point transmission, since the probability of any single receiver not receiving the packet is essentially the same as in a point-to-point connection (there can be some difference, since the multicast connection path length may be longer than would be used in a point-to-point connection). However, in large multicast connections, the sender may have to send packets multiple times before they are received at all receivers. This is true of any protcol in which the network elements do not buffer and retransmit lost packets. The remainder of this section assesses the magnitude of this effect on the scalability of the reliable multicast mechanism.

Consider a multicast connection with n receivers, a maximum sender-to-receiver path length of d links and a probability of packet loss of at most ϵ on any single link. Let x_i be the number of receivers that have not received a given packet following the i-th transmission (we assume that packet losses on different links and in different 'rounds' are independent). For any particular receiver, the probability that it fails to receive a packet when it is first transmitted is $\leq \epsilon d$, hence the expected value of x_1 is $\leq \epsilon dn$. Similarly, the expected value of x_2 is $\leq \epsilon dx_1 \leq (\epsilon d)^2 n$. Similarly, the expected value of $x_i \leq (\epsilon d)^i n$. Since x_i is a non-negative random variable, the probability that x_i is ≥ 1 is less than or equal to its expected value. Using this, one can show that for

$$i \geq \frac{\ln n + \ln 1/\epsilon}{\ln 1/\epsilon d}$$

the probability that $x_i \geq 1$ is at most ϵ. For $n = 1000$, $\epsilon = 10^{-5}$ and $d = 6$, this implies that with probability $1 - \epsilon$, all endpoints receive the packet after two transmissions. For $n = 10^6$, $\epsilon = 10^{-4}$ and $d = 10$, four transmissions are enough. For still larger connection sizes, it might be necessary to have some end systems act as repeaters, buffering packets for retransmission to smaller subsets. However, it's hard to imagine a real application that would require this.

7 Closing Remarks

We have shown that the mechanisms proposed for reliable one-to-many multicast are highly scalable. Indeed, it does not appear possible to do better unless the switches store packets and retransmit them when lost or unless the end systems play a more active role. For the many-to-one case, a single virtual circuit can support an arbitrary number of senders with uncoordinated bursty transmissions, so long as the average number of packets arriving concurrently at the receiver is small (ideally, an average of one or two). Since many-to-many multicast connections are naturally constrained by the ability of the recipients to sink data, we believe that even very large many-to-one connections will rarely have more than a few simultaneous senders.

This paper does not address the issues of flow control and congestion control, in the reliable multicast context. For a one-to-many reliable multicast, one can use adaptive windowing techniques like those used in point-to-point protocols to adapt the sender's rate to accommodate slow receivers and/or congested links. Similar techniques are applicable to a many-to-one connection. The use of flow/congestion control on a one-to-many multicast does have the effect of slowing the connection data rate to that of the slowest receiver or most congested link. For distributed computing applications, this may well be the right thing to do. For information distribution applications, it's not clear that this is an appropriate approach. Indeed, there may be no single approach that is really suitable for all applications, as argued in [6].

We have neglected the problem of dynamically updating a reliable multicast connection in progress. Adding a new endpoint requires proper initialization of the acknowledgement state information for the new branch. The most straightforward way to accomplish this is as follows. When requested to add a new endpoint, the network signaling system can allocate the appropriate resources for the new branch, clearing all the acknowledgement information, but not linking the new branch into the connection. It then asks the connection "owner" to inform it when it is safe to update the connection. When all outstanding packets have been acknowledged, the owner can signal to the network to perform the update. While the update is in progress, all senders must refrain from sending any new packets on the connection. If pausing a connection during updating is unacceptable, an alternative is to maintain two parallel connections, one for normal use and one for transitional purposes. When a new endpoint is to be added, it's first added to the second connection. After the new endpoint has been added to the second connection, the senders begins shifting transmission to the second connection. When there are no outstanding packets on the first connection, the owner signals to the network to add the new endpoint to that connection as well.

References

1. Armstrong, S. A. Freier and K. Marzullo. "Multicast Transport Protocol," RFC 1301, 2/92.
2. Braudes, R and S. Zabele, "Requirements for Multicast Protocols," RFC 1458, 5/93.
3. Chang, J. and N. Maxemchuk. "Reliable Broadcast Protocols," *ACM Transactions on Computer Systems*, 8/84.
4. Chaney, Tom, J. Andrew Fingerhut, Margaret Flucke and Jonathan S. Turner. "Design of a Gigabit ATM Switch," Washington University Computer Science Department, WUCS-96-07, 2/96.
5. Crowcroft, J. and K. Paliwoda. "A Multicast Transport Protocol," *Proceedings ACM SIGCOMM*, 1988.
6. Floyd, S., V. Jacobson, S. McCanne, L. Zhang, C. Liu. "A Reliable Multicast Framework for Light-weight Sessions and Application Level Framing," *Proceedings of ACM SIGCOMM*, 9/95.
7. Holbrook, H., S. Singhal and D. Cheriton. "Log-Based Receiver-Reliable Multicast for Distributed Interactive Simulation," *Proceedings of ACM SIGCOMM*, 9/95.
8. Papadopoulos, Christos and Guru Parulkar. "Error Control for Continuous Media and Multipoint Applications," Washington University Computer Science Department, WUCS-95-35, 12/95.
9. Pingali, S., D. Towsley and J. Kurose. "A Comparison of Sender-initiated and Receiver-initiated Reliable Multicast Protocols," *Proceedings of SIGMETRICS*, 1994.
10. Shacham, N. "The Design of a Heterogeneous Multicast System and its Implementation Over ATM," *Proceedings of the IEEE Workshop on Computer Communications*, 9/95.
11. Whetten, B., S. Kaplan and T. Montgomery. "A High Performance Totally Ordered Multicast Protocol," *Proceedings of Infocom*, 1995.
12. Turner, Jonathan S. "An Optimal Nonblocking Multicast Virtual Circuit Switch," *Proceedings of Infocom*, 6/94.
13. Turner, Jonathan S. "Extending ATM Networks for Efficient Reliable Multicast," Washington University Computer Science Department, WUCS-96-16, 11/96.

ATLAS I: A Single-Chip ATM Switch for NOWs

Manolis G.H. Katevenis   Panagiota Vatsolaki
Dimitrios Serpanos   Evangelos Markatos

Institute of Computer Science (ICS)
Foundation for Research & Technology – Hellas (FORTH)
P.O.Box 1385, Science and Technology Park,
Heraklio, Crete, GR-711-10 GREECE
markatos@ics.forth.gr
http://www.ics.forth.gr/proj/avg/asiccom.html

Abstract. Although ATM (Asynchronous Transfer Mode), is a widely accepted standard for WANs (Wide Area Networks), it has not yet been widely embraced by the NOW community, because (i) most current ATM switches (and interfaces) have high latency, and and (ii) they drop cells when (even short-term) congestion happens. In this paper, we present ATLAS I, a single-chip ATM switch with 20 Gbits/sec aggregate I/O throughput, that was designed to address the above concerns. ATLAS I provides sub-microsecond cut-through latency, and (optional) back-pressure (credit-based) flow control which *never* drops ATM cells. The architecture of ATLAS I has been fully specified and the design of the chip is well under progress. ATLAS I will be fabricated by SGS Thomson, Crolles, France, in 0.5 μm CMOS technology.

1 Introduction

Popular contemporary computing environments are comprised of powerful workstations connected via a high-speed network, giving rise to systems called *workstation clusters* or Networks of Workstations (NOWs) [1]. The availability of such computing and communication power gives rise to new applications like multimedia, high performance scientific computing, real-time applications, engineering design and simulation, and so on. Up to recently, only high performance parallel processors and supercomputers were able to satisfy the computing requirements that these applications need. Although recent networks of workstations have the aggregate computing power needed by these high-end applications, they usually lack the necessary communication capacity. Although there exist several high-speed interconnection networks specifically designed for NOWs, no one of them has clearly dominated (or is likely to dominate) the market yet [2, 15, 16].

Recently, ATM (Asynchronous Transfer Mode), a widely accepted standard for WANs (Wide Area Networks), gains increasing popularity in Local Area Communications as well. Although, ATM was initially developed for Telecommunications over Wide Area Networks, it can also be efficiently used for communications over LANs, for several reasons, including: (i) ATM provides fixed-size cells that make communication hardware simpler and faster, (ii) ATM cells are small allowing low latency, which is of utmost importance in LANs, and (iii) by using the same ATM equipment both for LANs and WANs, costs will be reduced through mass production.

Although several ATM-based NOWs are in everyday operation around the world, there are several concerns whether ATM is appropriate as an interconnection network for NOWs for the following reasons:

- *Most ATM switches (and interfaces) have high latency today*: In several cases, end-to-end application latency over ATM is similar to the latency observed over more traditional networks, like Ethernet. Thus, most applications that communicate using short messages, will not benefit from such ATM equipment of today significantly.

- *ATM switches drop cells when (even short-term) congestion happens*: ATM was originally developed for voice and image transmission over WANs. In such an environment, it is more important to deliver the information on time (even if it has to be slightly distorted), than to delay the information. For example, if short-term congestion happens during the transmission of live-video image, and some cells are dropped (as a result of the congestion), the human viewers of the video will at most see a short-term distortion in their image, if they notice it at all. However, dropping cells when data (e.g. text) is transferred over LANs is not acceptable. Dropping cells will result in incomplete messages that have to be retransmitted, which increases latency and wastes bandwidth.

In this paper, we present ATLAS I (ATm multi-LAne Switch I), a general-purpose, single-chip gigabit ATM switch, with credit-based flow control and other advanced architectural features. ATLAS I is being developed within the *ASICCOM* (Atm Switch for Integrated Communication, COmputation, and Monitoring) project[1]. ATLAS I was designed to address the above concerns. ATLAS I can be effectively used as a high-speed ATM switch for NOWs because:

- ATLAS I provides cut-through routing, and its latency is well under one microsecond.
- ATLAS I (optionally) provides multi-lane back-pressure (credit-based) flow control: i.e. it *never* drops cells. In back-pressure flow control, an ATM cell is transmitted to the next switch only if there is guaranteed buffer space to store it. Thus, data can be reliably transferred to their destination without wasting throughput and time for retransmissions.

The architecture of ATLAS I has been fully specified and the design of the chip is well under progress. ATLAS I will be fabricated by SGS Thomson, Crolles, France, in 0.5 μm CMOS technology.

---

[1] the "Gigabit Switching" task project of the European Union *ACTS* (Advanced Communication Technologies and Services) Programme.

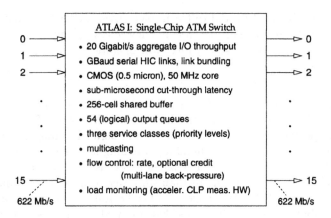

Fig. 1. ATLAS I chip overview

2 Description of ATLAS I

The ATLAS I chip is a building block for high speed ATM networks, for both wide and local areas. ATLAS I based systems can participate in general ATM WANs or LANs as nodes, or they can be used to build complete networks or subnetworks of larger ATM configurations. With appropriate interfaces, they can interoperate with third vendors' equipment that complies to the standards, and they offer the additional advantages of credit flow control when operating within appropriate environments. The ATLAS I chip is a full ATM switch, since it provides all necessary functionality required by the standards, except for management. Although management functions are not provided on-chip, ATLAS I includes the necessary support for a management processor to be either directly attached to it or accessed through the network itself; the resulting configuration provides full ATM switch functionality.

ATLAS I is a single-chip 16× 16 ATM switch, with unidirectional, point-to-point, serial links, running at 622.08 Megabits per second, each.

Figure 1 illustrates the main characteristics and features of this chip, which are explained below.

20 Gbps Aggregate I/O Throughput: the 16 incoming links can handle a sustained throughput of 16 × 622.08 Mb/s, i.e. an aggregate throughput of 9.95 Gigabits/second. The 16 outgoing links, operating in parallel with the incoming links, offer an aggregate output throughput of another 9.95 Gb/s.

Link Bundling: ATLAS I is configurable so that its links can operate either as individual independent links of 622 Mbps each, or as pairs of links operating at 1.25 Gbps (the pair), or as quadruples of links operating at 2.5 Gbps (the quad), or as octets of links operating at 5.0 Gbps (the octet). Furthermore, mixtures of the above configurations, for different links are acceptable.

CMOS Technology: ATLAS I will be implemented in CMOS technology which offers the advantages of high density and lower cost (compared to BiCMOS or GaAs). The high speed (serial) links will operate in CMOS, using BULL's "STRINGS" technology [25].

Low Latency: ATLAS I provides cut-through routing – the head of a cell can depart from the switch before its tail has entered the switch. Short latency is of crucial importance for several distributed and parallel computer applications running on NOWs, as well as in building switching fabrics that offer low overall delay. The ATLAS I cut-through latency is considerably shorter than one microsecond. This represents more than an order of magnitude improvement relative to today's ATM switch boxes. No valid comparison can be made to the latency of unbuffered crosspoint chips that are used to build switching fabrics, since, unlike ATLAS I, these chips are not complete ATM switches.

Cell Buffering, Shared Queueing: ATLAS I is not merely a crosspoint switching matrix -it contains much more than that, starting with an on-chip cell buffer for 256 ATM cells (110 Kbits). Within this shared space, 54 (logical) output queues are maintained; output queueing offers the best switching performance. Moreover, for non-backpressured traffic, memory space is shared among all lines, which is the queueing structure that gives the best utilization of the available buffer space.

Three Priority Levels / Service Classes: ATLAS I supports, via distinct queues, three service classes, at a different level of priority each. These distinct logical queues are also organized *per output*, thus eliminating head-of-line blocking; they all share the same physical buffer space – the shared cell buffer. The top two priorities are intended for policed traffic, while the low priority is intended for non-policed (flooding) traffic. The top priority is non-back-pressured, while the two bottom ones are (optionally) back-pressured – see discussion on flow control, below. The top priority class is designed for voice and other similar real-time traffic, where dropping cells is preferable over delaying cells during congestion periods. The middle-priority class is intended for policed data and other similar traffic, where we wish to offer certain performance guarantees to the user, and we also wish that cells are not dropped. The lowest priority class is appropriate for best-effort data.

Multicasting: Any entry in the translation table of ATLAS I can specify a mask of output links to which a corresponding incoming cell will be multicast. The VP and VC numbers of all outgoing cells, for a given incoming cell, are all identical to each other.

Flow Control: ATLAS I features advanced flow control capabilities. Besides ATM Forum standard EFCI, *optional* credit flow control is additionally provided.

Multi-lane (VP/VC-level) credit (back-pressure) flow control, like what ATLAS I offers, has many, important advantages over rate flow control – the current ATM Forum standard. Low priority traffic always "fills in" the available throughput, and cells are never dropped, resulting in full utilization of the (expensive) link capacity; transmission can start right away at top speed, being automatically throttled down to the correct level, and retransmissions are not needed, resulting in the minimum possible transmission time for a given message.

IEEE Standard 1355 "HIC" Links: The ATLAS I links run ATM on top of IEEE Std. 1355 HIC/HS as the physical layer. Although ATM today is most frequently run on top of SDH/SONET (STM1/STM4), ATM is a network-level protocol that is independent of physical layer; ATM has already been run on top of at least UTP-3, T1/T3, E1/E3, STM1/STM4, and FDDI-physical. HIC (IEEE 1355) is our link protocol of choice, because ATLAS I is optimized for short-distance links, as found inside large ATM switch boxes for WANs and in local and desktop area networks. Although HIC needs a higher signaling (Baud) rate than SDH/SONET for a given effective (data) bit rate, HIC is much simpler than SDH/SONET to implement in hardware; in fact, 16 SDH/SONET interface circuits would not fit on the single chip of ATLAS I. Second, all cells on an SDH/SONET link must be aligned on cell-time boundaries (idle periods last for an integer number of cell times), whereas cells on a HIC link can have arbitrary byte-aligned starting times. This reduces the average (cut-through) latency of the switch (under light load) by half a cell time (340 ns), which is important in local area applications. Third, for short distance links and correspondingly small buffer spaces, the transmission of a flow control credit cannot cost as much as an entire cell, neither can it be delayed until it gets bundled with other credits inside a cell; SDH/SONET leaves no room for credit transmission outside cells, while HIC/HS allows credits to be encoded in a straightforward way, on arbitrary byte-aligned times, using dedicated control character(s). To yield a net SONET/OC-12 rate of 622.08 Mb/s (1.4128 Mcells/s), HIC/HS uses a signaling rate between 0.91 and 1.05 GBaud (1.4128 Mcells/s × 54 to 62 characters/cell × 12 b/character), depending on whether single-lane and/or multi-lane back-pressure is enabled. This high data rate requirement results mainly from HIC/HS's encoding of each byte using 12 bits. The advantage of this encoding, however, is that no external crystals and no internal PLLs (expensive circuits) are needed for each incoming link of every ATLAS I chip; in this tradeoff situation, HIC/HS is clearly the option to be chosen, given the optimization of the switch chip for short links.

Load Monitoring: ATLAS I includes hardware support for the accelerated measurement of the cell loss probability (CLP) of its real traffic, for non-back-pressured classes of service. In order to accelerate the measurement, this hardware simulates a set of buffers of smaller size than the real chip buffer, loaded by a (different) subset of the real VCs each, and measures their (increased) CLP. The measurement is completed in software, by running a sophisticated extrapolation algorithm that computes the real CLP from the simulated CLP's [6].

3   Credit-Based Flow Control

In switch-based networks, contention for outgoing links of switches may lead to buffer overflows; these are handled in either of two ways. Some networks allow packets/cells to be dropped, and use *end-to-end* congestion control protocols [18, 26]. Other networks use *credit-based (back-pressure) flow control*, on a hop-by-hop basis, so as to never drop packets. ATLAS I supports both methods. In networks (or service classes) where cell dropping is allowed, ATLAS I provides ATM Forum standard EFCI [26]. In addition, ATLAS I implements optional, multi-lane credit flow control, which has many important advantages as explained below.

We believe that credit-based flow control will be mostly useful in high-performance applications running on top of a Network of Workstations. Parallel applications provide the underlying interconnection network with lots of bursty traffic. Many-to-one communication patterns that are very common in parallel programs, can easily lead to severe network contention. Although rate-based flow control has been proposed to regulate flow in ATM networks, it works at its best only when the traffic sources behave in a repeated predictable way (e.g. voice/image transmission). In the presence of unpredictable bursty data traffic, rate-based flow control algorithms drop cells leading to messages arriving incomplete. To ensure reliable data delivery, programmers are forced to use a high-level flow control protocol (e.g. TCP/IP) on top of the hardware-provided rate-based flow control. Unfortunately, such high level protocols take large amounts of CPU resources, require the expensive intervention of the operating system kernel, and may waste even more bandwidth by retransmitting a whole message even when a single ATM cell is dropped. This situation can soon lead to thrashing, since messages that arrived incomplete will be retransmitted, leading to more cell drops, which will lead to more message retransmissions, etc. On the contrary, credit-based flow control delivers all cells of a message reliably[2], relieving higher levels of the burden of implementing an expensive software flow control protocol. Thus, credit-based flow control reduces (even eliminates in some cases) the software intervention and all its associated overheads, while at the same time allows full utilization of the network's bandwidth.

Furthermore, credit-based flow control allows message transmission to start at maximum (available) transmission rate, being automatically throttled down to the correct level only if and when necessary. This results in minimum transmission time for a given message. On the contrary, rate-based flow control has an initial ramp-up delay (usually a few round-trip times) before it is able to achieve maximum transmission rate. Thus, a message transmitted using rate-based flow control will suffer some initial overhead, which is especially high for short messages. Given that traffic in NOWs consists mostly of unpredictable bursts of short messages, we can easily see that credit-based flow control is more appropriate for this kind of traffic than rate-based flow control.

---

[2] Except in case of line transmission noise, which is very rare in today's LAN technologies

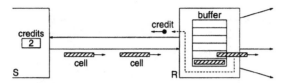

Fig. 2. Back-pressure (credit) flow control: the credit count says how much buffer space is available in the downstream switch.

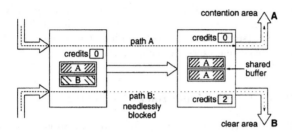

Fig. 3. Indiscriminate (single-lane) back-pressure and buffer sharing: a burst of cells destined to A has filled all available buffer space in the downstream switch, and was then stopped by back-pressure due to contention further down the path to A. As a result, a cell destined to B is needlessly blocked in the upstream switch; poor link utilization results.

3.1 Back-Pressure (Credit) Flow Control

Credit flow control, also called back-pressure, or hop-by-hop window, or virtual channel (circuit) flow control, dates back to Tymnet [27], GMDNET [14], and Transpac [29], in packet switched networks; see also the survey [13]. Under credit flow control, a cell is only transmitted to the downstream neighbor if the transmitter knows that buffer space is available for it at the receiver. This is implemented as illustrated in figure 2, using a count of available receiver buffer space. This "credit count" is decremented every time a cell departs and is incremented when a credit token is received; credits are sent back every time a unit of buffer space becomes available. For a given link peak throughput, the receiver buffer space that is necessary and sufficient is equal to this *throughput* times the *round-trip time* (RTT) of data and credits.

In the "single-lane" back-pressure described above, there is *no selectivity* of which cells (VCs) it is desirable to stop and which ones to let go. This creates a behavior similar to *head-of-line blocking* in input queueing [19], leading to performance degradation. Also, it is not possible to implement multiple levels of priority with single-lane back-pressure. An analogy in every-day life is single-lane streets (where the name came from): cars waiting to turn left block cars headed straight. If one uses the single-lane credit flow control described above, and *indiscriminate sharing* of buffer space, then bursty traffic creates the equivalent effect to head-of-line blocking, as illustrated in figure 3.

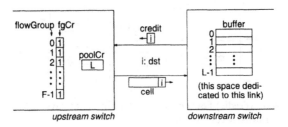

Fig. 4. ATLAS I back-pressure: F flow groups sharing L lanes on a link. A cell can only depart if it can get a pool credit (so as to ensure that there is buffer space for it at the other end) *and* the (single) credit of its flow group (so as to ensure that identically destined cells do not consume excessive buffer space).

3.2 The ATLAS I Multi-Lane Back-Pressure

Multi-lane (VP/VC-level) credit-based flow control solves the above performance problem by selectively allowing unblocked traffic to proceed, while preventing congested connections from occupying all available buffer space thus delaying all other traffic as well. In wormhole routing, multi-lane back-pressure was used to prevent deadlocks [9], or to improve performance [10]; multi-lane wormhole routing has been implemented in hardware in Torus [9] and iWarp [3]. For ATM, VC credit-based flow control extensions have been proposed and studied for long-distance (WAN) links; e.g. see [4, 24]. In case of contention, VC-level credits combined with round-robin servicing allow the fair sharing of the available network capacity among all competing flows [17, 20, 22]. DEC's GIGAswitch/ATM [30] is a commercial ATM switch that implements VC credit flow control. Our earlier switch, Telegraphos [23], also had a simple form of multi-lane back-pressure.

The credit flow control protocol of ATLAS I is reminiscent of, but simpler than those of [4] and [24], since the ATLAS I protocol is adapted to short links and single-chip hardware implementation. ATLAS I credits operate on the granularity of *flow groups*. A flow group is defined as a set of connections, sharing one or more links in their path through the network, whose cells need never or can never overtake each other, i.e. whose cell order is preserved over the length of their common path. Ideally, each flow group on each network link should consist of all connections whose destination is one, common, *single-threaded* device. When this definition leads to an impractically large number of flow groups, either a compromise is suggested (group together connections that go to nearby destinations), or a higher level of back-pressure signals may be employed to appropriately guide the multiplexing (selection) of cells at their point of entry into the flow group.

The ATLAS I chip is optimized for short-distance links; thus, each flow group can have at most 1 credit, for 1 cell's worth of buffer space. [3] Given that the

---

[3] Although each flow group can have only one ATM cell in each switch, each link may have several flow groups, and thus several cells in each switch.

round-trip time on links up to several meters long, including switch logic, is no more than one cell time (about 700 ns), one credit per flow group is enough. This restriction also simplifies queueing, since there is no need to remember cell order when at most one cell per VC can be present inside the switch at any given time. Figure 4 shows the ATLAS I credit protocol. For each link, the downstream switch (statically) allocates a buffer pool of size L. In order for this buffer space not to overflow, the upstream switch maintains a credit count (per output port), called *pool credit* (*poolCr*), corresponding to the available pool space at the receiver. This buffer is shared among cells according to their flow group. As shown in figure 4, separate credit counts, $fgCr$, are maintained for each flow group, initialized to 1. Since the buffer pool contains L cell slots, and since each flow group is allowed to occupy at most 1 of these slots, L of the flow groups can share this buffer pool at any given time; thus, L is the *number of lanes*.

A cell belonging to flow group i can depart if and only if $fgCr[i] > 0$ (i.e. $fgCr[i] == 1$) and $poolCr > 0$. When it departs, $fgCr[i]$ and $poolCr$ are decremented by 1, each (i.e. $fgCr[i]$ becomes 0). When that cell leaves the downstream switch, a credit carrying its flow group ID, i, is sent up-stream. When credit i is received, $fgCr[i]$ and $poolCr$ are incremented by 1, each (i.e. $fgCr[i]$ becomes 1). The pool credit counts of all upstream neighbors of a switch (for the links leading to this switch) are initialized to values whose sum does not exceed the total buffer space available in the switch.

3.3 Wormhole Routing and ATM

Several developers are skeptical about adopting ATM for network-based parallel computing, since several of its properties are fundamentally different from the familiar wormhole routing that has been successfully used in multiprocessors for several years. For example, wormhole routing usually employs variable size messages that propagate as a string of bits (worm) through the network, not allowing bits of different messages to get interleaved. On the contrary, ATM employs fixed-size cells that may be intermixed with other cells, since each of them carries identification information in its header.

We believe however, that ATM with back-pressure flow control (like that implemented in ATLAS I) is very similar to wormhole routing, and thus such ATM networks are more attractive for use NOWs and cluster-based computers: In wormhole routing, message packets may have variable sizes, but they are all a multiple of a fixed *flit* size. Although the flit size in early parallel processors was 1 byte long, flit sizes in recent wormhole-based interconnection networks range between eight [5, 28], sixteen [12], and thirty two [31] bytes. Extrapolating from this trend, flit sizes in the near future may easily reach up to 48 bytes (which is the size of an ATM cell). Current architecture trends push flit size to higher values for the following reasons:

- The control circuits of a switch must operate at the flit rate (especially if back-to-back single-flit packets are to be handled correctly). Clock rates increase by about 30% each year (see [7] section 1.2.2). Interconnection network throughput increases 45% each year ([8] page 8). Since network throughput increases faster than clock speed, if flit size remained constant, flit rate would increase faster than clock rate. Thus, the control circuits would have to operate at a rate faster than the clock rate, which would make them very complicated (if implementable at all). Increasing the flit size, decreases flit rate, which allows the switch circuits to operate at rates less or equal to the available clock rate.

- Switch developers prefer short flit sizes, in order to reduce buffer space requirements. However, there is no benefit from reducing flit size below (*round trip time*) × *Throughput*. Reducing flit size to that value reduces buffer space requirements; further reduction leaves buffer space unaffected, while increasing flit rate, hence control speed. For short low-bandwidth networks, (*round trip time*) × *Throughput* is a few bits long. For example, for a 100 Mb/sec link that is one meter long, the above value is close to 1 bit. For a modern 2.5 Gb/sec link that is ten meters long, this value is close to 32 bytes.

On the other hand, it is not desirable to increase flit size with no bound, since large flits imply long latencies. Most messages, especially in parallel applications, are short. For example, a cache line is 32-64 bytes long; a "remote write" message is a couple of words long. The prompt delivery and handling of short messages is critical for the completion time of the most applications [11]. Thus, the flit size in wormhole networks will not exceed a small value, probably in the neighborhood of 48 bytes. Thus, a packet in wormhole routing will be a sequence of 48-byte flits stored in switch buffers in the network. This is exactly what an ATLAS I ATM message is: a sequence of 48-byte cells (53 bytes including the header) stored in a sequence of switches from the source node to destination node.

Since latency is of critical importance for short messages, some wormhole networks provide multi-lane wormhole routing [10], which allows several messages to share the same physical link, as long as each of them gets its own *lane*. Thus, although some lanes may be blocked with long and slowly moving messages, some other lanes may be free and allow short messages to get routed to their destination rapidly. To provide similar properties in ATM networks, ATLAS I implements *multi-lane* back-pressured flow control. Each VC (or VP) can occupy at most a single lane; thus, slowly moving VC's (or VP's) leave the remaining lanes free to other traffic.

Although both multi-lane wormhole routing and multi-lane back-pressure ATM base flow control on credits and lanes, they use lanes differently, which is the reason for their significant performance differences. Wormhole dedicates each lane to a single packet until the end of that packet's transmission; if the packet gets blocked, so does the lane. Also, wormhole allows packets with the same destination to simultaneously occupy multiple lanes on the same link; while no advantage is gained relative to using a single lane, the remaining traffic is deprived of the additional lanes. In [21] we compared the performance of these two network architectures, using simulation. Our simulation results show that, for a same buffer size and number of lanes, ATM performs consistently better than wormhole –by a large margin in several cases. For ATM, saturation throughput approaches link capacity with buffer sizes as small as 4 or 8 cells per link (for 64-port networks), and stays high regardless of the number of lanes. On the other hand, multi-lane ATM switches provide much lower delay than single-lane ones when bursty or hot-spot traffic is present in the network. When the number of lanes is higher than the number of hot-spot destinations, non-hot-spot traffic remains virtually unaffected by the presence of hot spots. For wormhole routing, much larger buffer sizes and many lanes are needed in order to achieve high saturation throughput. When saturation throughput is low, delay characteristics suffer as well, because any given operating point of the network is closer to saturation. Bursty and hot-spot traffic negatively affects wormhole performance to a much larger degree than it does for ATM. [4]

4 Implementation Status

At the time of this writing (December 1996), the architecture of ATLAS I has been fully specified, and the design of the chip is under progress. ATLAS I will be fabricated by SGS Thomson, Crolles, France, in 0.5 μm CMOS technology. The majority of the chip blocks are synthesized using standard cell libraries and macrocell generators of the UNICAD SGS-Thomson design environment, while a few multi-port and CAM blocks are implemented in full-custom. The latter are basically the Free List, which contains 256 flip-flops and a priority encoder, and the Creditless Cell List, which contains a 2-port memory and a 3-port memory with 1 search port each, and a 2-port memory with 1 read-modify port.

The estimated area of the ATLAS I chip is 225 mm^2, as determined by the pre-existing pad frame to be used. The 16 bidirectional serial link interfaces occupy approximately 60 mm^2, and another 10 mm^2 are taken by the remaining pads. The core of the chip is estimated to occupy roughly 120 mm^2. Table 1 presents preliminary estimates of chip area; the largest block in the core is expected to be the shared data buffer, occupying about 25 mm^2 when implemented with compiler-generated memories.

5 Conclusions

Although ATM is a rapidly advancing standard both for voice/image and data communications, it has not been widely accepted by the LAN community yet, since most ATM switches suffer from *high latency*, and *data loss* under bursty traffic.

In this paper we briefly described the architecture of ATLAS I, a single chip ATM switch that is appropriate both for Local Area Networks (NOWs, DANs), and for Wide Area Networks, since it provides sub-microsecond latency and back-pressure flow control that avoid data loss. We have mostly focused on the novel aspects of ATLAS I, which are:

---

[4] More information ca be found in [21].

Part	Area Estimate: mm^2
16 Bidirectional Serial Link intf. & pads	60
Other pads	10
Elastic Buffers, etc.	20
Pipelined Shared Data Buffer	25
Queue Management (full-custom)	10
Credit Extraction, Queueing, Insertion	15
Routing/Translation Table	15
Credit Table	15
Control & Monitoring, other logic	20
Total chip (determined by pad frame)	225

Table 1. Area estimates of the ATLAS-I ATM switch

- *Sub-microsecond latency:* ATLAS I provides cut-through routing –the head of a cell can depart from the switch before its tail has entered the switch. Short latency is of crucial importance for several distributed and parallel computer applications running on gigabit ATM LANs, The sub-microsecond latency of ATLAS I represents more than an order of magnitude improvement relative to today's ATM switch boxes.

- *Back-pressure (credit-based) flow control:* Most ATM manufacturers are reluctant to adopt credit-based flow control, since they believe that it requires large amounts of memory to store ATM cells. Although this is true in WANs, back-pressure requires very little additional memory when used in LAN environments. In this paper we present a novel (but simple) credit-based flow control algorithm, and show that it is feasible to implement it within the limited silicon area of a CMOS single-chip ATM switch.

- *Single-Chip implementation:* Although there exist several single-chip ATM "switches", most of them provide little functionality, and operate mostly as unbuffered crosspoint matrices, or as buffered switches with rather primitive buffer organizations. ATLAS I is the first single-chip ATM switch to provide back-pressure flow control, shared buffering, VP/VC translation, and cut-through capabilities at the same time.

Based on our experience in designing and building ATLAS I, we believe that it is an appropriate switch for Local Area Network configurations, including Networks of Workstations (NOWs), Clusters of Workstations (COWs), and System (Desktop) Area Networks (SANs or DANs). At the same time, by being an ATM switch, ATLAS I is an appropriate building block for large scale ATM Wide Area Networks.

Acknowledgements

ATLAS I is being developed within the "ASICCOM" project, funded by the Commission of the European Union, in the framework of the ACTS Programme. This is a collective effort, with many individuals making valuable contributions. We would like to thank all of them, and in particular Vagelis Chalkiadakis, Christoforos Kozyrakis, Chara Xanthaki, George Kalokerinos, George Dimitriadis, Yannis Papaefstathiou, George Kornaros, Costas Courcoubetis, Luis Merayo, Roland Marbot, Helge Rustad, Vassilios Siris, Kostas Kassapakis, Bjorn Olav Bakka, Geir Horn, and Jorgen Norendal.

References

1. T.E. Anderson, D.E. Culler, and D.A. Patterson. A Case for NOW (Networks of Workstations). *IEEE Micro*, 15(1):54–64, February 1995.
2. N.J. Boden, D. Cohen, and W.-K. Su. Myrinet: A Gigabit-per-Second Local Area Network. *IEEE Micro*, 15(1):29, February 1995.
3. S. Borkar and e.a. Supporting Systolic and Memory Communication in iWarp. In *Proc. 17-th International Symposium on Comp. Arch.*, pages 70–81, 1990.
4. G. Varghese C. Ozveren, R. Simcoe. Reliable and Efficient Hop-by-Hop Flow Control. *IEEE Journal on Selected Areas in Communications*, 13(4):642–650, May 1995.
5. J. Carbonaro and F. Verhoorn. Cavallino: The TeraFlops Router and NIC. In *Proceedings of the Hot Interconnects IV Symposium*, pages 157–160, 1996.
6. C. Courcoubetis, G. Fouskas, and R. Weber. An On-Line Estimation Procedure for Cell-Loss Probabilities in ATM links. In *Proceedings of the 3rd IFIP Workshop on Performance Modelling and Evaluation of ATM Networks*, July 1995.
7. D. Culler, J.P. Singh, and A. Gupta. *Parallel Computer Architecture*. Morgan Kaufmann, 1996.
8. M.D. Dahlin. *Serverless Network File Systems*. PhD thesis, University of California at Berkeley, 1996.
9. W. J. Dally and C. L. Seitz. Deadlock-Free Message Routing in Multiprocessor Interconnection Networks. *IEEE Transactions on Computers*, C-36:547–53, May 1987.
10. W.J. Dally. Virtual-Channel Flow Control. In *Proceedings of the 17th Int. Symposium on Computer Architecture*, pages 60–68, May 1990.
11. T. von Eicken, D. E. Culler, S. C. Goldstein, and K. E. Schauser. Active Messages: A Mechanism for Integrated Communication and Computation. In *Proc. 19-th International Symposium on Comp. Arch.*, pages 256–266, Gold Coast, Australia, May 1992.
12. M. Galles. The SGI SPIDER Chip. In *Proceedings of the Hot Interconnects IV Symposium*, pages 141–146, 1996.
13. M. Gerla and L. Kleinrock. Flow Control: A Comparative Survey. *IEEE Trans. on Communications*, 28(4):553–574, 1980.
14. A. Giessler and e.a. Free Buffer Allocation - An Investigation by Simulation. *Comput. Networks*, 2:191–208, 1978.
15. R. Gillett. Memory Channel Network for PCI. *IEEE Micro*, 16(1):12, February 1996.

16. D. B. Gustavson. The Scalable Coherent Interface and Related Standards Projects. *IEEE Micro*, 12(2):10–22, February 1992.

17. E. Hahne and R. Gallager. Round Robin Scheduling for Fair Flow Control in Data Communication Networks. In *Proc. IEEE Int. Conf. on Commun.*, pages 103–107, 1986.

18. V. Jacobson. Congestion Avoidance and Control. In *Proceedings of the ACM SIGCOMM '88 Conference*, pages 314–329, 1988.

19. M. Karol, M. Hluchyj, and S. Morgan. Input versus Output Queueing on a Space-Division Packet Switch. *IEEE Trans. on Communications*, COM-35(12):1347–1356, December 1987.

20. M. Katevenis. Fast Switching and Fair Control of Congested Flow in Broad-Band Networks. *IEEE Journal on Selected Areas in Communications*, SAC-5(8):1315–1326, October 1987.

21. M. Katevenis, D. Serpanos, and E. Spyridakis. Credit-Flow-Controlled ATM versus Wormhole Routing. Technical Report 171, ICS-FORTH, Heraklio, Crete, Greece, July 1996. URL: file://ftp.ics.forth.gr/tech-reports/1996/1996.TR171.ATM_vs_Wormhole.ps.gz.

22. M. Katevenis, S. Sidiropoulos, and C. Courcoubetis. Weighted Round-Robin Cell Multiplexing in a General-Purpose ATM Switch Chip. *IEEE Journal on Selected Areas in Communications*, 9(8):1265–1279, October 1991.

23. M. Katevenis, P. Vatsolaki, A. Efthymiou, and M. Stratakis. VC-level Flow Control and Centralized Buffering. In *Proceedings of the Hot Interconnects III Symposium*, August 1995. URL: file://ftp.ics.forth.gr/tech-reports/1995/1995.HOTI.VCflowCtrlTeleSwitch.ps.gz.

24. H.T. Kung, T. Blackwell, and A. Chapman. Credit-Based Flow Control for ATM Networks: Credit Update Protocol, Adaptive Credit Allocation, and Statistical Multiplexing. In *Proceedings of the ACM SIGCOMM '94 Conference*, pages 101–114, 1994.

25. R. Marbot, A. Cofler, J-C. Lebihan, and R. Nezamzadeh. Integration of Multiple Bidirectional Point-to-Point Serial Links in the Gigabits per Second Range. In *Proceedings of the Hot Interconnects I Symposium*, 1993.

26. H. Ohsaki and e.a. Rate-Based Congestion Control for ATM Networks. In *Proceedings of the ACM SIGCOMM '95 Conference*, pages 60–72, 1995.

27. J. Rinde. Routing and Control in a Centrally Directed Network. In *Proc. Nat. Comput. Conf.*, 1977.

28. S. Scott and G. Thorson. The Cray T3E Network: Adaptive Routing in a High Performance 3D Torus. In *Proceedings of the Hot Interconnects IV Symposium*, pages 147–156, 1996.

29. J. Simon and A. Danet. Controle des Ressources et Principes du Routage dans le Reseau Transpac. In *Proc. Int. Symp. on Flow Control in Comp. Networks*, pages 63–75, February 1979. as reported in: L. Pouzin: "Methods, Tools, and Observations on Flow Control in Packet-Switched Data Networks", IEEE Transactions on Communications, Vol. COM-29, No. 4, April 1981, p. 422.

30. R. Souza, P. Krishnakumar, C. Ozveren, R. Simcoe, B. Spinney, R. Thomas, and R. Walsh. GIGAswitch System: A High-Performance Packet-Switching Platform. *Digital Technical Journal*, 1(6):9–22, 1994.

31. B. Zerrouk, V. Reibaldi, F. Potter, A. Greiner, and A. Derieux. RCube: A Gigabit Serial Links Low Latency Adaptive Router. In *Proceedings of the Hot Interconnects IV Symposium*, pages 13–18, 1996.

Arachne: A Portable Threads Library Supporting Migrant Threads on Heterogeneous Network Farms

Bozhidar Dimitrov and Vernon Rego

Department of Computer Sciences, Purdue University, West Lafayette, IN 47907

Abstract. We describe the design of an efficient and portable threads system that supports multi-threaded distributed computations on heterogeneous networks. The system enables threads to migrate between processes that run on different hardware platforms. We present a complete implementation of the design in ANSI C++. This implementation consists of a code preprocessor and a runtime library, and supports applications developed in C or C++. The runtime environment is capable of supporting tens to hundreds of thousands of threads. We also present some performance measurements on the costs of basic thread operations and thread migration.

1 Introduction

Threads enable cheap and highly effective forms of system- and user-level concurrency in software executions. Despite programming complexities induced by concurrency, it is our experience that the potential benefits of threads amply justify the extra care required in their use. The creation and manipulation of user-space threads is cheap; a thread can be initialized via an invocation of its associated *thread-function*. With user-space threads, control information (i.e., id, arguments, program counter, stack pointer) can be kept in a protected area, and many threads may run within a single process, sharing its CPU time-slice. There is a general acceptance that threads can enhance application development in various ways. For example, process-oriented simulations (e.g., CSIM [14], Si [11]) which are known to offer the simplest simulation programming model [1], are surprisingly easy to construct using threads [13].

There are two factors that significantly impact upon the runtime performance of large distributed systems: *load-imbalance* and *non-local data access*. Threads are a simple remedy to performance problems caused by both factors. If threads are free to migrate (i.e., move their data and computation state) from one processor to another, threads from densely populated processors may migrate to less densely populated processors with the aim of balancing loads. For example, on shared-memory multiprocessors the Ariadne threads system [8, 7] sees balanced loads as a direct result of placing runnable threads in a shared queue. If threads on one processor require frequent access to data on remote processors, these threads may migrate to their respective data hosts so that subsequent data accesses become local. With appropriate layering and support for locating objects [8], thread migration can be made transparent to end-users. This approach has proven very useful in the ParaSol parallel simulation system [6, 4, 9].

In this effort, we focus on the design of a threads system that enables threads to migrate between heterogeneous hosts. Because contexts and stacks are meaningless across distinct architectures, the formidable problems of context and stack translation make thread migration on heterogeneous systems a real challenge. To accommodate heterogeneity, we take a transformation-oriented approach to migration and other threads operations. Our system builds upon and removes significant limitations of an earlier work, namely, the Ythreads [12] system.

Very few user-space threads systems support thread migration, and these are almost exclusively runtime-only systems supporting migration across *homogeneous* platforms. These tend to implement context-switch actions using either the C-library setjmp() and longjmp() primitives [8, 2] or assembly [10]. Because transforming migrant stacks at runtime is prohibitively expensive, we advocate a solution based on the use of a preprocessor [12] for C/C++. With such a setup, the user writes programs in that language, preprocesses the code, and finally compiles with a conventional compiler.

A related effort has been reported in [15], where a group of researchers developed a heterogeneous compiler for the Emerald programming language [3]. This compiler inserts instructions that encode the function's state, thus enabling threads and objects to freely migrate between the four supported architectures: Sun 3, Sun SPARC, VAX, and HP. While very powerful, this approach has disadvantages. Adding a fifth architecture requires porting the entire compiler, integrating Emerald threads and objects with software that already relies on some threads library is difficult, and finally, performance may be poor. It was found that the heterogeneous compiler takes 60% longer to migrate and subsequently invoke a function in comparison to its homogeneous counterpart.

The outline of the rest of the paper is as follows. Section 2 contains some basics on Arachne's functionality, and Section 3 addresses difficulties a designer faces in providing support for heterogeneous thread migration. The program transformation methodology is briefly described in Section 4, and the architecture of the basic runtime and thread migration system is described in Section 5. We give some performance results in Section 6 and conclude briefly in Section 7.

2 The Arachne System

Functionality

Without actually introducing a new language, Arachne provides a library-based approach to implementing user-space threads. Moreover, it provides for a hardware-independent thread-migration functionality, in addition to standard thread operations. Arachne consists of a code preprocessor, **app**, which transforms application code developed in a slightly extended C++ style into ANSI C++ output. The preprocessed code is then compiled and linked with the runtime library libarachne.a on every machine that will participate in the program's execution. Because Arachne, its output, and libarachne.a all conform to ANSI C++, the system is readily portable to different environments.

The idea behind our design has its origins in work done by Malloy and Soffa [5]. By augmenting Pascal with certain Simula control structures, the authors defined a language called SimCal. They then developed a preprocessor that accepts SimCal as input and produces Pascal as output. While similar, the SimCal preprocessor's duties are a small subset of app's duties.

Because threads are lightweight and can execute in a shared address space with low management costs and high efficiency, they are preferable to their heavyweight process counterparts (e.g., Unix processes). But threads require explicit creation, suspension, context-switching, migration, and destruction. To enable thread-manipulations to occur even within nested function calls, and to further reduce overheads, we introduce the notion of migratable functions, or *strands*. Like functions, strands have no ids and cannot be created or destroyed, but they are merely invoked. They have persistent contexts, however, and are free to migrate.

Given an input file, app facilitates context-switching and migration by preprocessing threads and strands in a special manner, leaving ANSI C++ functions untouched. The keywords **thread** and **strand** enable this selective preprocessing. As will be seen in Section 4, Arachne performs a series of actions before every strand invocation. To enable this, each statement containing a strand invocation must be preceded by the keyword **call**. These are the only changes to ANSI C++, and since they are so minimal, we call this augmented language "the extended C++ language".

A direct consequence of preprocessing is the extraction of all thread functions' local variables and the creation of corresponding global **structs** allocated on the heap. In a sense, these **structs** are like activation records that Arachne manages in its own data-structure—a stack of **struct** pointers. We call this the *A-stack*.

Arachne threads may be created with any number and order of integer and float parameters[1]. There is complete support for recursion and migration of arbitrarily deep activation stacks. The latter point is of great significance since a thread may, for example, invoke a strand s1() which in turn invokes a strand s2() that subsequently requests migration. While this scenario is prohibited by Ythreads [12] and SimCal [5], Arachne packages the entire activation stack, ships it to the remote machine, and continues to compute.

We should point out that while Arachne supports programs written in C or C++, Arachne threads (currently) can only execute C-type functions and not class methods, as for example Java threads do.

Context-Switching

All functions exported by libarachne.a that can potentially cause a transfer of CPU control are called *primitives*. These are a_create(), a_destroy(),

[1] Characters and floats cannot be used due to a limitation in the C and C++ implementation of variable arguments.

a_migrate(), a_resume(), a_set_prio(), a_suicide(), a_suspend(), a_yield, and a_yield_to(). Threads may transfer control to one another or to the scheduler only at well-defined points in their execution sequences, also called *suspension points*. A thread may effect a transfer of control in one of two ways: via an explicit invocation of an Arachne primitive, or by invoking a strand which in turn invokes a primitive. Because of this, each primitive or strand invocation is followed by a suspension point.

The main program makes the scheduler loop until the termination condition is met (described in Section 5.2). The body of this loop simply invokes the thread function corresponding to the thread identified by the global variable next_thread. Upon a call to a primitive, the system determines if a context-switch is to occur, and if so, it identifies the next thread to be run and loads next_thread with the appropriate thread id. Then it sets the value of did_yield to true, and returns control to the (still) current thread. Through the intervention of the Arachne preprocessor, all calls to primitives are followed by an if-statement that forces the execution of a return statement to the scheduler if did_yield is true.

By executing a return statement, thread functions unload their machine activation records from the machine stack. If thread functions invoked one-another directly, the machine stack would eventually overflow, thus forcing the program to terminate.

3 The Challenge of Thread Migration

Architectural Dependencies

Migration under heterogeneity poses certain problems that the Arachne system must solve. The run-time stack is machine-dependent, the size of machine words may differ between architectures, the representation of the base types may use a different number of words, and byte ordering may either be big endian or little endian. Further, some architectures require that data be aligned on even addresses or some other word-multiple, conventions for function-calling and return-value handling may differ, and besides instruction sets, the number and sizes of CPU registers may differ across hardware platforms. Finally, compilers on different machines may produce different code or be capable of yielding different levels of optimization.

Arachne solves these problems by preprocessing all thread and strand functions in user code. With the help of any one of a number of suitable communication libraries[2], Arachne produces a machine-independent representation of the A-stack. Just before the system enables a thread to migrate, Arachne encodes that stack and forces all active thread and strand functions to return. When a migrant thread's context arrives at a remote machine, Arachne recreates the

---

[2] Arachne provides an interface through which it can exploit different communication libraries. The current implementation uses PVM.

A-stack and invokes the appropriate thread and strand functions. This effectively solves the problems related to function invocation and parameter passing. All code that Arachne emits is ANSI C++, and each machine's compiler is responsible for dealing with the different instruction sets, register allocation and optimizations.

Address Space

In heterogeneous environments, a mechanism is needed for correcting the values of all function pointers after migration. App outputs an array of pointers to all thread-functions, and each runtime thread context contains an integer field, holding the index of the thread's corresponding function. When a thread is initialized, the function index is properly set, and after migration the runtime environment reassigns the function pointer using the index (which is guaranteed to be correct at all times).

4 Program Transformations

To illustrate the app's manipulations, consider the thread function t1(), defined as shown in Figure 1.

```
thread void t1 (int i)
{
  char ch = '+';
  unsigned long l;

  a_migrate (procs[0]);
  call s1 (i, l);
}
```

Fig. 1. A simple thread function definition.

Variable and Parameter Manipulation

When a thread relinquishes control of the CPU, its state must be preserved. But in our implementation, a thread that relinquishes control of the CPU does so by performing a **return**, causing the loss of local variable values. As previously explained, app converts all thread function local variables into the fields of a global struct. For example, t1()'s activation record structure is shown in Figure 2.

Observe that the activation record structure contains two extra fields: i and state. The field i is present because the function t1() has a parameter i. The field **state** is automatically inserted by app in every activation record. This is used to resume execution of a ready thread at the point where it last relinquished CPU control.

```
struct t1_ar {
  short state;
  int i;
  char ch;
  unsigned long l;
};
```

Fig. 2. Definition of t1()'s activation record, t1_ar.

Packing and Unpacking Thread-contexts

The preprocessor **app** has knowledge of the types of all variables on the A-stack, and is able to represent these variables in a machine-independent format whenever a thread needs to migrate. When parsing a thread or a strand function, say f(), **app** generates and outputs the functions f_pack() and f_unpack(). These are responsible for packing and unpacking f()'s activation record before and after migration. These functions make calls to the underlying communications substrate. Figure 3 shows the code generated for packing of t1()'s activation-record.

Variables whose structure and sizes are known at compile time ("stack" variables and static arrays) are correctly handled by Arachne. For example, in an XDR manner, for a static array of n elements, code will be produced for handling each element and will be executed n times. However, there is no elegant solution for dynamically allocated arrays. Since their size and stricture are usually unknown, the programmer must manually edit the packing and unpacking routines.

We have not agreed on the semantics of a function that can migrate and that can access variables outside its scope. A thread executing such a function will be migrated with only its local variables, and after migration, it will be accessing the values of "global" variables inside its new host process. In this context, "global" means within a given process and not among all Arachne processes. At the present, there are no global variables that are synchronized between the distinct processes.

Thread- and Strand-Function Manipulations

In Figure 4 can be seen the preprocessed version of the thread function t1(). Although the code manipulations may appear overwhelming at first glance, they can be grouped into only a few categories: removal of the keywords **thread** or **strand**; removal of all function arguments; extraction of all local variable declarations; preservation of "local" variable initializations; modification of accesses to "local" variables; declaration and setting of the value of a pointer to a thread's or strand's context; insertion of a series of jump labels; insertion of a series of statements just before and just after calls to primitives and calls to strands;

```
int t1_pack (ar_p act_rec)
{
  struct t1_ar *ar = (struct t1_ar *)(act_rec->ar);

  (ar->state)++;
  if (pvm_pkshort (&(ar->state), 1, 1) < 0)
    return FALSE;
  if (pvm_pkint (&(ar->i), 1, 1) < 0)
    return FALSE;
  if (pvm_pkbyte (&(ar->ch), 1, 1) < 0)
    return FALSE;
  if (pvm_pku long (&(ar->l), 1, 1) < 0)
    return FALSE;

  return TRUE;
}
```

Fig. 3. Code for packing the contents of the activation record of thread function t1().

insertion of a **switch** statement to determine entry points; and insertion of a call to the primitive a_suicide().

To preserve the semantics of parameter passing, thread function parameters must be evaluated only once, and not every time the thread-function is invoked. Thread parameters are added as fields of the thread's activation record, their values are passed along when a thread is created, and the code (part of libarachne.a) for thread creation assigns these values directly to the corresponding fields.

While extracting local variables and making them fields of a global **struct**, app notes local variable declarations that contain initializations (e.g., the variable ch in t1()), and leaves the initialization in the body of the preprocessed function.

In a preprocessed thread- or strand-function, all accesses to "local" variables become accesses to the corresponding field of cur_ar->ar, the pointer to the activation record. Just before a particular thread-function is invoked, the runtime environment sets the value of the global pointer cur_ar to the address of this function's context. Thus through the statement

struct t1_ar *ar = (struct t1_ar *) (cur_ar->ar);

inserted at the beginning of every preprocessed function, **ar** gets the correct type and value.

Preserving the program counter, to indicate just how far a function's execution has progressed, is just as important as preserving the values of all its local variables. The value of the program counter, however, is machine-dependent. Therefore after **app** determines all suspension points, it inserts jump labels immediately after each of them. In this way, a **goto** statement can be used to *logically* set the value of the program counter to point to the address where

```
void t1 (void)
{
  struct t1_ar *ar = (struct t1_ar *) (cur_ar->ar);

  _did_yield = 0;
  switch (ar->state)
   {
    case 0: goto t1_state_0;
    case 1: goto t1_state_1;
    case 2: goto t1_state_2;
    case 3: goto t1_state_3;
   }

t1_state_0:
  ar->ch = '+';

  a_migrate (procs[0]);
  (ar->state)++;
  if (_did_yield)
    return;

t1_state_1:
  pushAR ();

t1_state_2:
  cur_ar = cur_ar->next;
  s1 ((ar->i), (ar->l));
  cur_ar = cur_ar->prev;
  (ar->state)++;
  if (_did_yield)
    return;
  else
    popAR ();

t1_state_3:
  a_suicide ();
}
```

Fig. 4. Code for the preprocessed version of thread t1().

execution must resume. In addition to the jump labels, **app** inserts statements that increment the value of the field **state** in the activation record. Thus, at all times, the value of **state** is equal to the current jump label. The last part of the mechanism that manipulates the program counter is a **switch** statement located at the beginning of the preprocessed-function's body. Depending on the value of the field **state**, a **goto** statement moves control to the corresponding jump label.

5 The Runtime Support Subsystem

Arachne applications run as a system of distributed (UNIX) processes. Each process has the ability to create, destroy, migrate and manipulate threads in any way that suits the application. Arachne relies on a communication library to provide facilities for messaging and distributed process management.

While a thread is alive, its context is located in a *thread context area* (TCA). Migrating a thread is equivalent to transferring its TCA to a receiving process, and restarting the thread's computation there. A graphical representation of a TCA is shown in Figure 5. The TCA contains all information that is useful in scheduling a thread—its id, state, priority, and a pointer to its thread-function as well as the thread activation stack (implemented as a doubly-linked list of context wrappers).

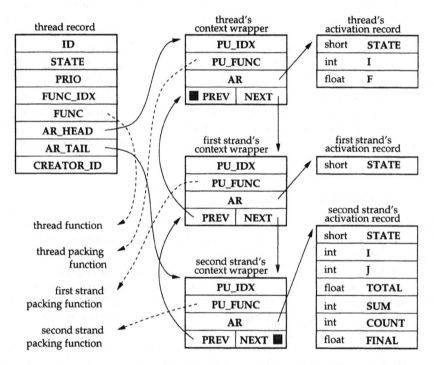

Fig. 5. A thread context area (TCA) containing two strands. A TCA consists of a fixed-size thread record and an expandable thread activation stack—a doubly-linked list of context wrappers.

5.1 Thread Migration

The TCA of the current thread is equivalent to the A-stack. The minimal TCA contains one thread context, but while executing, strand contexts can be added and removed. Thus migrating a thread involves the following four steps: converting a thread's state into a machine-independent representation, sending the representation to a remote machine, receiving and reconstructing the thread's TCA from the machine-independent representation, and finally performing a context-switch so the immigrant thread may resume execution.

The context wrappers within a TCA are similar to C++ objects in that they contain data, as well as functions to operate on this data (the packing and unpacking functions). When invoked, a_migrate() initializes the network buffer, packs the thread record (whose fields are well-defined and fixed for all TCAs), then traverses the linked list of context wrappers and invokes their corresponding packing functions. Finally, it flags the end of the message by inserting the integer -1.

After a TCA is converted into a machine-independent form and copied into a buffer, the communications substrate constructs a message containing the TCA and sends the message to a remote machine. At the receiving end, the communications substrate probes for incoming messages from the network and places them in a buffer. If the buffer is found to contain one or more thread-migration messages, the scheduler invokes an unpacking driver that performs the packing actions in reverse: it unpacks the thread record (the fixed part of a TCA), extracts the function index of the unpacking function and then invokes that function. The procedure is repeated until it encounters the terminator -1. After all thread reconstruction work is performed, the "new" thread(s) are inserted in the ready queue, and the scheduler locates the highest priority thread to give it CPU control.

5.2   Distributed Termination

There is difficulty in detecting Arachne's termination conditions, primarily because all processes may be idle but messages that can potentially reactivate the system might be in transit. To cope with this problem, in Arachne a process is either *active* or *inactive*. Each thread created by a process is an *offspring* of that process. A process is said to be *active* if at least one of its offspring is active, or if it currently hosts at least one offspring of another process. If both conditions are false, a process is *inactive*. Each time a process changes its status from active to inactive it sends messages to all other processes with the corresponding number of offspring that it destroyed. It also sends a message to process zero each time it makes a state transition. When process zero finds no active processes in the system, it sends termination messages to all processes. Upon receipt of such a message, each process performs all necessary cleanup operations and exits.

6   Performance Results

We report Arachne's performance as measured on three machines: a Sun Sparc 5 (with a 70 MHz CPU), a Sun Sparc 20 (with four 50 MHz CPUs), and a Silicon Graphics Indy (with a 132 MHz CPU). We also compare Arachne's performance with that of the SunOS 5.3 multi-threads (Sun-MT) and Ariadne threads systems, all operating on the Sun Sparc 20. The performance numbers for the latter two systems are those reported in [8]. For each run, the average time required to execute an operation is obtained by dividing the run time (as measured by Unix's clock(3C)) by the total number of operation invocations. To account for variability, we report an average over ten independent runs. Table 1 summarizes the results for the basic thread operations, and Table 2 reports timings for thread migration.

Operation	Sun Sparc 5	Sun Sparc 20			SGI
	Arachne	Arachne	Ariadne	Sun-MT	Arachne
Thread Create	18	14	35	1000	13
Null Thread	35	24	40	1130	19
Context-Switch(0)	22	13	15	12.5	11
Context-Switch(1)	27	16	15	12.5	14
Context-Switch(2)	30	18	15	12.5	16

Table 1. Run-times (in μsec) for performing thread operations. Note that Arachne exhibits competitive run-times, even though context-switching cost grows as a function of stack depth).

Operation	Same Subnet	Across Subnets
Migrate (12 byte ar)	4304	4412
Migrate (128 byte ar)	4896	4900

Table 2. Run-times (in μsec) for performing migration.

Comparing Arachne and Ariadne to Sun-MT threads is somewhat unfair, as the latter is a kernel-level preemptive system. One the other hand, the results reveal some of the advantages of user-level threads.

To get a rough idea of the Arachne-induced preprocessor overheads on the user code, we measured the time taken by two programs to compute the sum of all positive integers smaller than 10^7. One program computed without threads or strands and the other program performed the summation within a strand function. The result was an overhead of 61%, due mainly to the indirect addressing of local variables in the A-stack.

7 Conclusions and Future Work

In designing and implementing Arachne, our main goal was to develop a threads system (in a short time) that supports efficient thread migration on heterogeneous networks of machines. Having completed a prototype, we plan on some immediate performance enhancements, such as the inclusion of Ariadne's `setjmp()` and `longjmp()` context-switching mechanisms, to eliminate Arachne's context-switching overheads in deeply nested situations. This will enable Arachne to provide constant low-context switching overhead, while leaving its powerful heterogeneous-migration framework intact. We also plan on using our current framework to support object-migration by building global **structs** that are specific to every class definition. The **app** preprocessor builds **struct** definitions corresponding to every thread- and strand-function by extracting all local variable declarations and converting them into **struct** fields. But because variables from all function scopes are mapped into a single **struct** scope, **app** cannot handle identical variable names even though they may be declared in nested scopes. Our solution is to build a more appropriate **struct**, which maintains information not only on variable names and types, but also on scope.

Currently, Arachne is meant as a threads library used by a process-oriented heterogeneous simulation system. As such, there is no need for shared-memory operations or synchronization primitives. However, we recognize the need for including such features if Arachne is to be used as a general threads system. In particular, threads are capable of doing I/O, but there is no way of ordering these accesses other than by controlling scheduling.

We also plan to reduce the 61 registers and by performing additional optimizations. However we feel that Arachne's strongest point is its heterogeneous capability, and the fact that the user can run distributed computations over a multitude of machines with different architectures partially offsets the computation overhead.

References

1. J. Banks and J. Carson. Process interaction simulation languages. *Simulation*, 44(5):225–235, May 1985.
2. IEEE. Information Technology—Portable Operating System Interface (POSIX)—Part 1: System Application Program Interface (API) [C Language]. Std. 1003.1c-1995, 1995.
3. E. Jul, H. Levy, N. Hutchinson, and A. Black. Fine-Grained Mobility in the Emerald System. *ACM Transactions on Computer Systems*, 6(1):109–133, 1988.
4. F. Knop. *Software Architectures for Fault-Tolerant Replications and Multithreaded Decompositions: Experiments with Practical Parallel Simulation*. PhD thesis, Purdue University, August 1996.
5. B. Malloy and M. Soffa. Conversion of Simulation Processes to Pascal Constructs. *Software: Practice and Experience*, 202(2):191–207, February 1990.
6. E. Mascarenhas, F. Knop, and V. Rego. ParaSol: A Multi-threaded System for Parallel Simulation Based on Mobile Threads. In *Proceedings of the Winter Simulation Conference*, pages 690–697, December 1995.

7. E. Mascarenhas and V. Rego. Migrant Threads on Process Farms: Parallel Programming with Ariadne. Technical Report TR 95-081, Department of Computer Sciences, Purdue University, December 1995.

8. E. Mascarenhas and V. Rego. Ariadne: Architecture of a Portable Threads System Supporting Thread Migration. *Software Practice and Experience*, 26(3):327–357, March 1996.

9. E. Masceranhas. *A System for Multithreaded Parallel Simulation and Computation with Migrant Threads and Objects*. PhD thesis, Purdue University, August 1996.

10. J. Sang, F. Knop, V. Rego, J. Lee, and C. King. The Xthreads Library: Design, Implementation and Applications. In *Proceedings of the 17th Annual Computer Software and Applications Conference (COMPSAC '93)*, November 1993.

11. J. Sang, E. Mascarenhas, and V. Rego. Mobile-Process Based Parallel Simulation. *Journal of Parallel & Distributed Computing*, 33(1):12–23, February 1996.

12. J. Sang, G. Peters, and V. Rego. Thread Migration on Heterogeneous Systems via Compile-Time Transformations. In *Proceedings of the International Conference on Parallel and Distributed Systems - ICPADS*, pages 634–639, 1994.

13. J. Sang and V. Rego. A Simulation Testbed based on Lightweight Processes. *Software, Practice & Experience*, 24(5):485–505, May 1994.

14. H. D. Schwetman. Using CSIM to model complex systems. In *Proceedings of the Winter Simulation Conference*, pages 246–253, 1988.

15. B. Steensgaard and E. Jul. Object and native code thread mobility among heterogeneous computers. In *Proceedings of the ACM Symposium on Operating Systems Principles*, pages 68–78, 1995.

Transparent Treatment of Remote Pointers Using IPC Primitive in RPC Systems

Shik Kim[1], Muyong Hyun[2] and Sangjo Lee[3]

[1] Department of Computer Science, Semyung University, Korea
[2] Department of Computer Science, Daewon Junior College, Korea
[3] Department of Computer Engineering, Kyungpook National University, Korea

Abstract. The practicality of Remote Procedure Call(RPC) systems is well recognized and used as the basis for many experimental and commercial distributed systems. However, compared with an ordinary procedure call, conventional RPC systems have a crucial restriction: pointers cannot be used as the arguments of remote procedure without explicit and nontrivial programming efforts. This paper describes the design and implementation of method that eliminates this restriction in current computing environments without extra hardware support. The method enables transparent treatment of pointers in RPC based on caching techniques using shared memory manipulation, pointer swizzling, and coherency protocol. To validate the usefulness of the proposed method, an experimental RPC system was implemented on Linux-based workstations connected to a 10 Mbps Ethernet network. Compared to conventional methods, experiments show that the method provides performance that is proportional to the access ratio of the remotely referenced data.

1 Introduction

Recent widespread use of distributed computing environment is confronting us with the need to increase productivity in the development of distributed application. RPC's are a key technique for building distributed systems and applications[1, 2, 3, 4, 5]. No message passing or I/O at all is visible to the programmer. They provide message-passing semantics for the procedure calls found in most programming languages. The practicality of this approach is well recognized, and used as the basis for many experimental and commercial distributed systems. DCE is based on client/server model. Clients request services by making remote procedure calls(RPC) to distant servers. The RPC system can automatically handle data type conversion between the client and the server in the DCE[6]. In ODBMS client/server implementations, Two basic approaches for splitting the application between ODBMS clients and servers are the object server and the page server. However, references across databases require the use of RPC's or remote functions[7].

Conventional RPC systems have a crucial restriction: only certain data types can be used as the arguments of a remote procedure. For example, pointers or higher-order functions cannot be used directly as arguments. In ordinary programming languages, it is common for programmers to pass pointers(addresses) to subroutines as arguments, but in the conventional RPC systems, it is either not permitted at all or must be controlled by the programmer. To circumvent this limitation, the programmer should, for example, write callback routines to dereference remote pointers or to call remote functions passed as arguments.

This paper describes a method for transparent support of remote pointers in RPC. It allows remote pointers to be used in the same way as local pointers without assuming any linguistic support and describes a solution to the potentially great source of overhead in RPC. The method gives programmers the illusion that pointers can refer freely to data in other address spaces. The illusion is not restricted to the source code level; once a remote data is referenced, it is cached in the local address space and the runtime cost to access it is exactly the same as the cost to access ordinary local data, except for the cost to write back the modified cached data. The key issues to realize the transparent treatment of remote pointers are threefold:

- efficient detection of dereferencing of remote data,
- transparent treatment of remote pointers, and
- guarantee of the coherency of address spaces.

To deal with these, we incorporated three techniques into the RPC; shared memory manipulation, pointer swizzling, and coherency protocol. Shared memory manipulation in IPC takes advantage of the sharing of memory segments widely available in current computing environments without any extra hardware supports. Modern operating system kernels such as SVR4 and BSD versions provide primitives for user-level program control of segment access to shared memory and segment-fault handling[8, 9]. This enables efficient and transparent detection of the first request to access remote data without modification of the operating system kernels. The other advantage is the fastest form of IPC because the data does not need to be copied between the client and server.

Pointer swizzling is an address translation technique that has been used for persistent objects and persistent programming languages[10, 11, 12]. Our method applies pointer swizzling to allow programmers to describe the manipulation of remote pointers in the same way as local pointers. The scheme for supporting huge address spaces and pointer swizzling with no extra hardware was first proposed by Paul Wilson[14] as an efficient method of implementing larger address spaces than the word size of the available hardware in distributed environment. The method described in this paper took up his method extensively to deal with distributed and heterogeneous address spaces.

To make the semantics of RPCs as close as those of the ordinary procedure calls, the method includes a runtime protocol that guarantees coherency among the address spaces involved in an RPC session. When the transferred remote data is modified in an address space(including memory allocation and release operations), the runtime system properly reflects the modifications in the original data, which may be in another address space. The rest of this paper is organized as follows. Section 2 addresses the problems involved in implementing transparent treatment of pointers in RPC. Section 3 describes our method. Section 4 presents experimental results on the proposed method and compares the method with related work. Section 5 concludes the paper.

2 Problems in Conventional Message Passing Semantics

Before presenting our approach, let us survey the problems posed by handling pointers with the conventional RPC techniques. One straightforward way to pass a pointer to a remote procedure is to take the closure of the pointer on the caller side and pass it to the remote procedure as an input RPC argument. This method is eager in the sense that the data is transferred prior to the request to access it in the remote procedure body. The strong point of the eager method is that stub generation for the method is not complicated. Most dynamic data structures that use pointers have recursive structures in their type definitions, so the generator simply generates the programs that recursively call one another. Indeed, Sun Microsystems' rpcgen system[13] passes recursive data structures such as lists or trees in this way. This is useful if the data pointed to is relatively small. However, consider the case that a large body of data is organized as an array or a binary tree, and access to only some portion of the data is required by the remote procedure. This method has the drawback that the execution overhead occurs when marshalling the whole tree and sending it to the remote procedure.

Another approach to passing pointers as arguments in RPC's is to use the callback mechanism supported by many RPC systems. Callback means that a callee remotely calls its caller. Whenever a remote pointer must be dereferenced during the execution of a callee program, the callee calls back the caller with a request to pass the contents of the pointer. In this way, the pointer contents are passed by the on-demand or lazy method. This method is suitable when a relatively small portion of a large amount of data is accessed in a remote procedure. When a relatively large portion of the data is accessed, the method is less attractive, since the increased number of callbacks reduces execution performance. Also, a naive implementation of this approach might perform callbacks whenever a pointer is dereferenced, even if the pointer has already been dereferenced.

3 Development of Caching Method

The solution suggested in the paper for the above-mentioned drawbacks is to "cache" a remote data. The referenced data is transferred from the caller to the callee when the data is first requested. The callee reuses the transferred data each time it must be accessed. The caching effect will probably reduce execution time because the callee accesses the locally cached data and remote data accesses the locally cached data and remote data access is minimized. This approach is attractive, however, significant problems posed when it is implemented are as below:

-- How can the first access to remote data be distinguished from subsequent accesses with low overhead ?

- Can distribution transparency on the source code level be accomplished in a higher degree ?
- When the callee requires modification of the cached data, how can the coherency between the cache and the original data be maintained ?

3.1 Basic Techniques for Caching Method

In conventional RPC execution model, a program is executed by a thread in an address space. The execution sequence is the following steps when a thread calls a remote procedure.

1. The execution of the thread is blocked until the output arguments are returned from the remote procedure.
2. A thread is initiated on the callee site to execute the called remote procedure.
3. The initiated thread on the callee terminates when it returns the output arguments to the caller.
4. Only a single thread is active in an RPC session, even when several sites participate in the session.

Our method is a fairly sophisticated one; it incorporates the eager, lazy and caching techniques into an RPC system. For ease of description, we first mention the lazy portion of the method with caching, and then discuss the eager portion. To concentrate pointers, we describe the case where a pointer that references data on the caller side is passed from the caller to the callee. Then we mention the general case where pointers are passed freely.

We begin by introducing some notions. Generally, in a single address space, a pointer can designate a location valid only in the address space. To allow the passing of pointers beyond the boundaries of an address space, pointer definition must be extended to the entire distributed system. Thus, we introduce the concept of a long-format pointer (long pointer for short). We then term the non-long format pointer an ordinary pointer. A long pointer is composed of three elements:

- an address space identifier defined in the distributed environment(typically a pair consisting of a site ID and a process ID in the site),
- an address valid within the address space, and
- a data type specifier that specifies the type of the data referenced by the pointer.

To locate a data in a distributed environment, we require an address space identifier and an address valid within the address space. Additionally, a data type specifier is necessary for the system to be heterogeneous. Data type is essential to interchange of internal data representations, among different architectures. We assume that the system can obtain an actual data structure from a data type specifier by querying a database that serves as a network name server. All data referenced by long pointers are assumed to be located in the heap area under the system control.

Since generally-available hardware only deal with ordinary pointers, long pointers must be translated into ordinary pointers, at least until the hardware uses them. We call the translation from a long pointer into the corresponding ordinary pointer swizzling , and we call the reverse translation pointer unswizzling . When a remote pointer is passed as an argument of a remote procedure, the pointer is unswizzled on the caller side. This translation is coded in the caller stub for the remote procedure. On the other hand, the callee stub for the remote procedure includes the code that swizzles the pointer.

Here, a question arises how the system distinguish between ordinary pointers and long pointers in the callee side. Ordinary pointers in the callee address space can only reference addresses within that address space, but referenced data exists only on the caller side at this time. The solution is that when the callee receives a long pointer from the caller, the callee allocates for the referenced data a protected segment area. Protected segment area means that the area is protected from access(including read or write) by the segment-protection mechanism of the shared memory among the IPC primitives. The allocation determines the location to which the referenced data will be copied if the protected segment area must be accessed. The determined location is used as the address into which the long pointer is swizzled. Note that the segment contains no data at this time. The data to fill the segment are transferred when the callee tries to access the segment as described below.

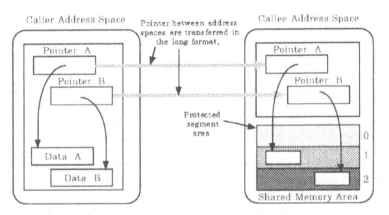

Fig. 1. Just after pointers A and B are swizzled in the callee address space

The above situation is illustrated in Fig. 1, where two pointers, A and B, are transferred from the caller to the callee. One protected segment can include several sets of referenced remote data. In the figure, two sets of data are allocated to the protected segment. The data allocated to a protected segment area is transferred later when necessary.

The segment-protection mechanism supported by the shared memory cannot detect the first access to data allocated to a protected segment, since it provides the read-only access permission. The method in the paper suggests that the swizzled address be not attached to the shared memory segment until the first access to data has occurred in the callee side. The operating system kernel detects the first access to the data allocated to the protected segment, and raises an access-violation exception. Catching the exception, the handler determines at which location the exception was raised and attaches the swizzled address to the shared memory segment. The requested data is transferred from the caller's address space to the callee's at this time. All of the other data allocated to the segment must be transferred at this time, because once the access protection of the segment is released, the first access to the other data in the segment can no longer be detected.

The runtime system maintains a data allocation map that records what data should be transferred from remote address spaces. The entries of the map are the segment number, the offset within the segment, and a long pointer. for the example shown in Fig. 1, the data allocation map would be like Table 1. The runtime systems refers to the data allocation map and then communicates with the other runtime systems that manage the original data to request the sending of the data.

Table 1. Data allocation map

segment #	offset	long pointer
1	$offset_1$	A
2	$offset_2$	B

Fig. 2 illustrates the data transfers for this example. After the data transfer, the runtime system directs the operating system kernel to release the access protection of the segment. The runtime system then resumes the thread that caused the access-violation exception. Since the transferred data is cached in the segment, the subsequent accesses to the data are the same as accesses to local data.

On the data transfers, data representations must be encoded and decoded to preserve their data types in a heterogeneous environment. We can use the standard methods except for the case of pointers, which must be unswizzled and swizzled as described above when the transferred data structures include them.

3.2 Eagerness in the Method and Nested RPCs

Until now we have concentrated our description on the lazy portion of the method. Next we describe how eagerness is incorporated. As mentioned in Section 2, eagerness concerns the timing of the transfer of data referenced by remote pointers. Generally, a remote pointer can be considered as a capability to access

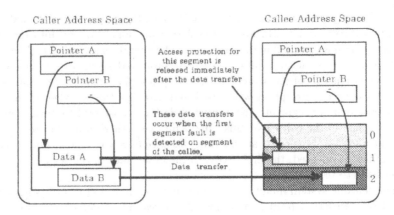

Fig. 2. When a protected segment is accessed, all the data allocated to the segment are transferred with their representations properly translated

the data referenced by it; the data might, or might not be accessed in the address space that received the pointer. We can expect eager data transfer to provide better execution performance than lazy transfer, when most of the remotely referenced data is accessed, since fewer communications are required.

We introduce eagerness to the method by transferring a certain depth of the transitive closure of a pointer when the pointer is transferred to a remote address space. On the transfer, of course, proper encoding, decoding, unswizzling, and swizzling must be done according to the data types in a way similar to the lazy case described above. There are several alternative algorithms and parameters for taking a certain depth of transitive closure. Our current implementation uses the breadth-first traverse algorithm with the maximum amount of the traversed data explicitly specified by the user.

Above, we have described mainly the case where pointers are passed between two distinct address spaces. The explained method works well even when RPCs are nested -that is, a program calls a remote procedure P1 and in its execution P1 calls another remote procedure P2, and so on. That is made possible by the long pointers and the data allocation map; whenever required, and an ordinary pointer can be translated into and from a long pointer by reference to the data allocation map. Therefore, pointers can be freely passed in the same way as described above, even when RPCs are nested, by the combination of unswizzling and swizzling.

3.3 Coherency Protocol

In general, all the caching techniques that permit update operations inherently have the problem of coherency between original data and their copies. In our method, the system must maintain the coherency of cached data in all address spaces that participate in an RPC. To maintain coherency of the cached data in all address spaces, we take advantage of a virtue of RPC, synchronous communication. In an RPC session, even when the session includes nested RPCs, there is only one active thread of control. Even though some people might say that this is a limitation of RPC, this work concentrates on the issue of eliminating the restriction on the treatment of pointers. Therefore, coherency of cached data must be guaranteed only for the execution of the active thread.

Our coherency protocol forces the runtime system to send all the "dirty" data in the cache when the activity of threads moves beyond address spaces-that is, when input arguments are passed to a remote procedure and output arguments are passed back to the caller. When a thread issues an RPC and the address space of the thread has dirty caches, the protocol transfers all the cached data allocated to dirty cache segments to the caller. The reason why the protocol works well with the method described hitherto is that the protocol can be seen as a case of the eager data transfer described in Section 3.3; the protocol tells the runtime system to send eagerly the data in the dirty cache segments when the input arguments of the RPC are sent.

To efficiently detect data modification, we make use of the access-permission mode in the shared memory primitive. Once remote data are copied in the cache area of an address space, the runtime system sets read-only access permission to the segments. When a thread tries to modify one of the write-protected segments, the operating system kernel raises an access-violation exception, and lets the runtime system know which segment is being modified.

When a nested RPC occurs, the protocol forces all the data in all the dirty segments to be passed between address spaces. (Note that dirtiness can be detected by segment-grain.) Those dirty segments, which we call modified data set, must be written back to the original location. Otherwise, it would continue to increase monotonically, decreasing the runtime performance. When should the modified data set be written-back ? We assume that there would be a "working set" in distributed computation as well as centralized computation, and use the concept of an RPC session to determine that working set. Each site involved in the RPC session keeps all the cached data until the ground thread declares the end of the session. Up to the end of the session, the modified data set is passed among the address spaces with the transition of thread activation. Thus, each address space in the session can always see the correct working set with minimum segment transferring cost. At the end of the session, the runtime system managing the address space of the ground thread performs the following two tasks:

- Examine the modified data set, and write back each modified segment to the original address space.
- Multicasts a message to the address spaces concerning the RPC session to invalidate all the cached data.

3.4 Remote Memory Allocation and Release Primitives

The system supports transparent remote memory allocation and release operations to another site, and provides the following two primitives used the notation of ANSI C:

– void *remote_malloc(address_space_ID, data_type_ID)

This primitive allocates a memory area in the address space specified by address_space_ID to store data whose type is specified by data_type_ID. It returns a swizzled pointer valid in the address space in which it is issued.

– void *remote_free(void* p)

This primitive releases the memory area allocated for the data referenced by pointer p. Note that p may reference data whose original location is not in the address space in which it is issued.

When a thread issues these primitives, the runtime systems of the address space of the thread performs the required memory allocation or release operation on the cached memory area in the address space. The operation must be reflected in the data allocation map in the address space. Also, the data area must be allocated or released in the original address space specified by address_space_ID. One straightforward timing for allocation and release of the data in the original space is upon each issuing of the allocate and release primitives. However, this would degrade the runtime performance terribly, considering that remote allocation and release of hundreds of data sets may be requested consecutively. Our solution to this problem is that the runtime system batches the memory allocation and release cooperation requests to the original address spaces. The batch operations are performed when the activity of the thread moves to another address space. This restrains the runtime overhead, since the number of communications is reduced; a single message to an address space can include multiple requests of data allocations and releases to the address space.

3.5 Related Work

The proposed method and distributed shared memory (DSM) systems have some common properties. First, both techniques enable access to remote data as if they were local data. Second, both techniques use a virtual memory manipulation techniques as a central part[15]. It might be said that the proposed method is subsumed by the (heterogeneous) DSM systems, since the proposed method was designed for RPC's-a typical synchronous communication pattern. The proposed method, however, has the following several remarkable features lacked by the DSM systems.

The proposed method takes advantage of the synchronous nature of RPCs in the design of the coherency protocol. The protocol of the proposed method does not have concurrency control, since at any time there is only one active thread in an RPC session. This makes the coherency protocol of the proposed method lighter than that of the DSM systems. Thus, if an application is satisfied by RPC communications, it can enjoy faster execution by using the proposed method. Second, heterogeneity dealt with in the heterogeneous DSM systems is restricted.

For example, Mermaid[16], one of the most recently designed heterogeneous DSM systems, has the following limitations.

All processors must use the largest main-memory word alignment. For instance, if one machine has a 64-bit CPU and the rest have 32-bit CPUs, all the data on the DSM must be aligned with 64-bits words. Every compiler must use the same data format. For instance, the usage map for a record type must be the same in every machine. These limitations originate from the fact that the heterogeneous DSM systems physically share distributed memory. In contrast, the proposed method does not share distributed memory; it shares only the logical type of the shared data. Therefore, the proposed method does not have the above limitations.

4 Experimental Results and Analysis

To validate the usefulness of the proposed method, an RPC system with the proposed method was implemented. The system was created on Linux(kernel version 2.0.0) running on Pentium-based(75 MHz) workstations. The stations with 40 Mbytes of main memory are connected by a 10Mbps Ethernet network. The system uses the TCP/IP network protocol and specifies the TCP_NODELAY option in the socket system call so that small packets are sent as soon as possible. As a canonical data representation, the system uses XDR(eXternal Data Representation) which guarantees the transformation of basic data types such as integers, floating point numbers, and strings between CPUs with different architectures. We used the XDR library provided with the Linux[17]. Although the experimented system consists of only a few Pentium-based stations, the system was carefully implemented so as to deal with heterogeneity. Therefore, the experimental results reflect the heterogeneity overhead, such as data representation conversion.

Although several reports show that only System V has supported the three forms of IPC - message queues, semaphores, and shared memory, most vendors derived from BSD version have also supported these three IPC's[9]. Shared memory is the fastest form of IPC because the data does not need to be copied between the client and server. However, it has the limitation of maximum number, maximum size and minimum size in manipulation of segment. It is observed that the maximum number is 128, maximum and minimum size is 131 Kbytes and 1 byte respectively in Linux-based systems. The limitation of shared memory usually depends on the Unix vendors.

5 Comparison and Consideration

Here, we compare the performance of our method and the eager and lazy methods described in Section 2, which we call respectively fully eager and fully lazy methods. The experimental subject was a search of a complete binary tree. Each node of the tree has 16 bytes(two 4-byte pointers and 8-byte data). Initially, a

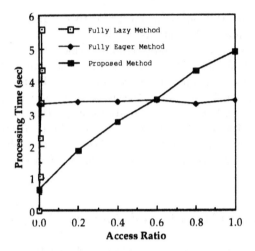

Fig. 3. Comparison of the three methods. X-axis: (number of nodes accessed in the callee)/(total number of nodes); Y-axis: processing time(sec)

complete binary tree of 32,767 nodes was created in the caller address space. We measured the average time required to process one remote procedure call that retrieves the tree, varying the number of nodes were retrieved in the callee. The gettimeofday function in the Unix system was used to measure the average time. The nodes of the tree were visited in a depth-first manner until the ratios of the number of nodes retrieved in the callee. The nodes of the tree were visited in a depth-first manner until the ratios of the number of visited nodes to the total number of the nodes reached the ratio indicated by X-axis in Fig. 3. The tree was not sent back to the caller since no modification was performed. The RPCs were performed by the following three methods.

- With the fully eager method, the caller sent the whole tree(524,272 bytes) to the callee, which accessed the tree locally.
- With the fully lazy method, the caller sent to the callee a pointer to the root of the tree, and the callee retrieved the tree by performing callbacks for each dereferencing of the pointers in the tree.
- With the proposed method, the callee received a pointer to the root of the tree and retrieved the tree as if it were in the callee's address space. When a dereferencing request to a pointer caused a segment fault in the callee, the transitive closure of the pointer was retrieved in a breadth-first manner in the caller. We set the closure size to 11 Kbytes in this experiment.

Fig. 3 shows the experimental results. With the fully eager method, The processing time is nearly constant, because the whole tree was sent once just before the execution of the remote procedure body. With the fully lazy method, the processing time is obviously bad. This is because of the increased number of callbacks. Fig. 4 is the same as Fig. 3 except that the Y-axis designates the number of callbacks. By comparing Fig. 3 and Fig. 4. we can see that the number of callbacks, which take much time, dominates the processing time of the fully lazy method. In this method, the data transfer granularity was too fine to fully utilize the network bandwidth. The fully lazy method is expected to show good performance when a small portion of the large data is accessed (for example, retrieval of a hash table).

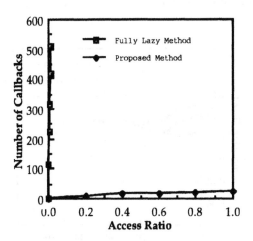

Fig. 4. Comparison between the lazy method and the proposed method. X-axis: (number of nodes accessed in the callee)/(total number of nodes); Y-axis: number of callbacks

The proposed method provides the best processing time of the three methods for access ratios between 0.0 and 0.6. This owes to the combined effects of the lazy, eager and caching techniques. With the proposed method, only limited portions of the tree were sent to the callee, as is clearly observed in Fig. 4. The improved performance relative to the fully eager method was obtained because relatively small portions of the remote data (tree) were transferred. When relatively large portions of the data were accessed(access ratio > 0.6), the increase in the number of communications rendered the proposed method disadvantageous.

5.1 Degree of Transitive Closures

In the proposed method, the closure size parameter, which specifies the degree of transitive closures, plays an important role. When the parameter is set to zero, the behavior is similar to the fully lazy method, When set to infinity, the behavior resembles the fully eager method. We did an experiment using almost the same experimental subject to determine how the parameter affected execution performance. In the experiment a complete binary tree created on a caller was remotely searched in a callee. We measured the average time to process only one remote procedure call in which the nodes of the tree were remotely visited from the root to the leaves 16 times. The reason for repeating searches is to increase the effect of caching; nodes in the upper level will be reused in the subsequent searches. Fig. 5 shows the results. The performance is not good when the closure size is too small. In the experiment the optimal closure sizes are relatively small: respectively 6, 11 and 22 Kbytes for 16383, 32767 and 65535 nodes. This is because of the nature of the experimental subject. As the number of nodes in the tree increases exponentially, the larger closure could not effectively carry the retrieved data.

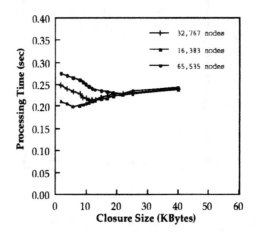

Fig. 5. Relationship between the closure size and processing time

5.2 Restoring the Updated Data

Finally we examined how update operations on the data referenced by remote pointers affected the system performance. The experimental subject used was the same as that in subsection 4.1; a complete binary tree residing on a caller was remotely accessed in a callee. We set the closure size parameter to 11 Kbytes. In Fig. 6, the solid line represents the case where the data in the tree were updated in the ratio indicated by the X-axis, while the dotted line represents the case where the data were not updated, but patterns in both cases were the same except for updates so that we could measure overheads incurred by two reasons. First, the increase in the processing time for the updated case is proportional to the update ratio. Second, each processing time for the update case is just twice of that of the not-updated case. This is reasonable, since the update in the remote procedure body requires at least two segment accesses: one for reading and the other for writing-back the updated data.

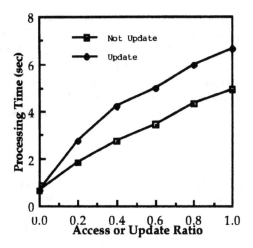

Fig. 6. Update performance. X-axis: (number nodes updated in the callee)/(total number of nodes) in the not updated case; Y-axis: processing time(sec)

6 Conclusion

Transparency generally refers to the concealment of particular details from the user or application programmer. A distributed system may try to conceal the fact that it is distributed and aim to provide the same interface as a single-node system. We have developed a method for treating pointers in RPCs in a transparent way. The method suggested in the paper combines three key techniques: shared memory manipulation, pointer swizzling, and coherency protocol. Shared memory manipulation is used to detect requests to access the data remotely referenced by pointers. Additionally, it contributes to automatic caching of the transferred referenced data. The pointer swizzling technique gives the programmers the illusion that the address space boundary does not exist in a distributed system; the programmers see that an ordinary pointer can be passed to any address space, and the dereferencing of the pointer works precisely the same way as when pointers are passed between procedures within a single address space. So as not to limit the data referenced by a remote pointer to read-only, we developed a coherency protocol for the RPC session. The protocol can effectively find modified data using shared memory manipulation. The synchronous communication nature of RPC contributes to free the protocol from complicated and heavy concurrency controls.

The experiment demonstrates the usefulness of the proposed method in that it takes less processing time than that of the eager and lazy method for access ratios between 0.0 and 0.6. It owes this to the combined effects of these methods and caching techniques.

There still remains an interesting research issue concerning treatment of remote pointers in the proposed method; the method does not support a remote pointer to a function. This limitation might not be negligible, since passing a pointer that references a function to remote procedure is one of the strongest motivations for using remote pointers and performing callbacks in the conventional RPC programming style. We are currently working on developing an RPC system supporting a remote pointer to a function.

The authors would like to thank Dohak Lee, who is a reasearch assistant in Semyung Univ., for his valuable efforts on installations of Linux versions and various implementation issues on RPC with the Pentium-based machines.

References

1. Batlivala, N., Gleeson,B., and etc.: Experience with SVR4 Over Chorus. Proc. USENIX Workshop on Microkernels and Other Kernel Architectures. USENIX. (1992) 223-241
2. Boykin, J. Kirschen, D, and etc.: Programming Under Mach, Reading, MA. Addison-Wesley. (1993)
3. Bershad, B.N., Anderson, T.E., and etc.: Lightweight Remote Procedure Call. ACM Trans. on Computer Systems. **8** Feb. (1990) 37-55
4. Bever, M., Geihs, K., and etc.: "Distributed Systems, OSF DCE, and Beyond" in DCE-The OSF Distributed Computing Environment. A. Schill(ed.). Berlin: Springer-Verlag. (1993) 1-20
5. Shirley J.: Guide to Writing DCE Applications. O'Reilley & Associates (1993)
6. Tannenbaum A. S.: Distributed Operating Systems. Prentice Hall (1995) 68-86
7. Orfali, R., Harkey, D., Edwards, J.: The Essential Distributed Objects Survival Guide. Wiley (1996)
8. O'Reilley & Associates: Guide to OSF/1 A Technical Synopsis (1991)
9. Stevens W. R.: Advanced Programming in the UNIX Environment. Addison-Wesley Publishing Company (1992) 463-470
10. Cattell R G G.: Object Data Management—Object-Oriented and Extended Relational Database Systems. Addison-Wesley (1991)
11. Moss J E B.: Working with persistent objects: to swizzle or not to swizzle. IEEE Trans. Software Engineering. **18(8)** Aug (1991) 657-673
12. Hagimont, D., chevalier, P. and etc.: Persistent Shared Object Support in the Guide System. OOPSLA '94 Conf. Proc. Oct. (1994) 129-144
13. Sun Microsystems: SUN OS Reference Manual. (1988)
14. Wilson P.: Pointer swizzling at page fault time: efficiently supporting huge address spaces on standard hardware. ACM Computer Architecture News. Jun (1991) 6-13
15. Hermannson, G., and Wittie, L.: Optimistic Synchronization in Distributed Shared Memory. In Proc. 14th Int. Conf. on Distributed Computing System. (1994) 345-354
16. Zhou S, Stumm M, Li K, and Wortman D.: Heterogeneous distributed shared memory. IEEE Trans. Software Engineering. **3(5)** Sep. (1992) 540-554
17. Boutell T., Wirzenius L.: Linux Software Map <URL:http://www.boutell.com /lsm/lsmbyid.ogi/000963>. Feb. (1996)

An Operating System Support to Low-Overhead Communications in NOW Clusters

P. Marenzoni, G. Rimassa, M. Vignali, M. Bertozzi, G. Conte[1] and P. Rossi[2]

[1] Dipartimento di Ingegneria dell'Informazione,
Università di Parma, Viale delle Scienze
I-43100 Parma, Italy
[2] SMART S.r.l., Via dell'Artigianato 31/2,
I-40057 Granarolo Emilia (BO), Italy

Abstract. This paper describes an Operating System approach to the problem of delivering low latency high bandwidth communications for PC clusters running a public domain OS like Linux and connected by standard, off-the-shelf networks like Fast-Ethernet. The $PARMA^2$ project has the main goal of designing the new light-weight protocol suite PRP, in order to drastically reduce the software overhead introduced by TCP/IP. PRP wants to offer at high level a stream socket oriented interface and at low level compatibility with any device driver. High level compatibility is crucial in facilitating the porting on PRP of existing applications or message passing packages. Moreover, an optimized version of MPI, based on PRP and evolution of the widespread MPICH implementation, is under development, allowing for a very effective reduction of the communication latencies in synchronous communications, compared to the TCP/IP-based MPI.

1 Introduction

Today the use of workstation or PC clusters as platforms for parallel processing is widely spreading [1], often adopting off-the-shelf network solutions. Significant experiences have born recently regarding both the implementation of high performance computing applications on PC or workstation networks [2, 3, 4] and the development of hardware/software components dedicated to speedup communications at the performance level achieved by the parallel machines with special purpose networks [5, 6, 7]. The least effort implementation of a NOW cluster as a parallel computing platform relies on OS services such as the TCP/IP protocol. This has an obvious disadvantage, mainly the high latency associated to the requirements that TCP enforces in order to work in almost all conditions across highly heterogeneous platforms and WANs. The great advantage is that one is automatically endowed of a truly multi user, reliable programming environment.

At the onset of our PARMA PARallel MAchine ($PARMA^2$ in the following) project we decided that the multi user environment had to be preserved by all means, but we did not think necessary to maintain every feature needed by a platform with heterogeneous nodes or by wide area networks with different data link level protocols. In fact, $PARMA^2$ is meant to be a homogeneous PC cluster connected by Fast-Ethernet and running a standard operating system as Linux, whose source code availability allows kernel-level interventions to be made.

Within these goals the first thing to assess is the viability of the idea, that is whether it is possible to design a protocol with a sufficiently low latency to make the project meaningful. This is the primary scope of PaRma Protocol (PRP). The requirement of multi user imposes a heavy burden on PRP, that is to be seamlessly integrated with OS kernel and to cope with overheads associated to interrupt handling, memory management and so on. On the other hand, having limited $PARMA^2$ scope to a homogeneous LAN, we can conceivably design a greatly simplified protocol with respect to TCP/IP.

The solution we propose for integrating PRP within the kernel is the standard one for all network protocols under Unix, that is insertion between socket layer and physical layer (i.e. device driver). This solution offers immediately the added advantage that all of the parallel computing paradigms, developed on socket interfaces, will be effortlessly ported to PRP. In its first implementation PRP has to assess what level of latency is attainable while fulfilling simultaneously all the design constraints. To achieve this goal we realized a stripped down solution, with no mechanism associated to flow control, data recovery etc. (that could be introduced in a light form into the final protocol). The results obtained are extremely encouraging given that we halved TCP/IP latencies and substantially improved bandwidths.

Despite the fact that current PRP release is by no means a complete protocol, in practical applications we observed very few situations where it delivers incorrect results. This validates our optimistic protocol implementation that limits itself to error detection: in fact the tests on real applications described in this paper are performed in this fashion.

Moreover, since the typical discrepancy between latencies visible at higher level (MPI or PVM) are about one order of magnitude greater in NOW or PC cluster environments than in MPP machines with dedicated communication libraries, $PARMA^2$ aims at developing an optimized version of MPI (MPIPR) finely tuned for an homogeneous local NOW cluster running PRP and based on the MPICH implementation by Argonne National Laboratory.

The current $PARMA^2$ implementation is based on a set of PCs connected by a Fast-Ethernet 100 Mbps LAN. Each node comprises an Intel Pentium 100 MHz CPU, equipped with a PCI mother board, 512 KB of secondary cache and 32 MB RAM. The Fast-Ethernet network adapter is a 3COM 3C595-TX. Each PC runs Linux version 2.0 and supports the gcc and g77 GNU compilers.

2   The *PRP* protocol of *$PARMA^2$*

UNIX computing environments are characterized by pervasive, smoothly integrated networking capabilities [9]. Many application interfaces (i.e. many sets of *system calls*) have been devised and built, and BSD sockets are nowadays probably the most successful and popular among them, besides being the only one actually implemented in Linux. They support both client/server model (using connect()/accept() pair) and peer-to-peer model (using read(), write(), recvfrom() and sendto() system calls) and have a plethora of ready-to-run applications based upon them. Programmers can select a socket address family using a special parameter when invoking socket() and bind() system calls. They use AF_INET when setting up network wide, TCP/IP based, internet domain sockets. Subsequent system calls will be automatically redirected to the correct handler, thus providing a uniform and consistent programming interface to interprocess and interprocessor communications. Focusing only on interprocessor communications, which give birth to real networking, one finds network protocol as the software layer immediately under socket address family (by the way, socket domains can be seen as a demultiplexer which routes messages to the proper protocol): Linux, as a UNIX OS, ships along with the complete IP suite support but, as a PC-hosted OS, also has Novell's IPX and Apple's Appletalk capabilities.

The main purpose of PRP project is maximum compatibility with all socket-based Unix applications and message passing interfaces, preserving ordinary Linux functionalities and avoiding the oversized TCP/IP protocol suite [10]. Therefore, a new "light-weight" protocol suite has been inserted in the existing Linux architecture, resulting in two new independent software layers (corresponding to standard network and transport OSI layers). Thus, the OS can continue to perform its functionalities and coordinate the processor activity in a multitasking environment.

2.1 The Linux network architecture

Network protocols are seen by Linux OS as homogeneous subsystems which are supposed to coexist painlessly and can even be added or removed dynamically during normal operations, much in the same way as device drivers and filesystems are (this is accomplished by installable modules, ordinary object files that can be linked in by the kernel without the need to reboot the computer). To ease this task Linux provides well defined hooks and interfaces to the system programmer.

Linux networking structure is composed by a unified application interface, that is socket family, by a set of independent network protocols, by a generic device driver interface and finally by several device drivers for the network adapters present in the system. Since a network operation involves every system layer, each of them maintains a suitable data structure representing its own view of the same data: the structures that accomplish this are, starting from top to bottom, struct socket, struct sock and struct sk_buff. The first two elements describe the connection at socket family and network protocol levels, whereas the third one is an abstraction for a data packet. In particular, struct sk_buff must be directly handled by device drivers, so it must reside in a contiguous memory area. Therefore, various functions are provided to insert and remove data at the start or at the end of the buffer, which is allocated all at once.

A kernel level implementation must deal with several facets of the operating system: among them we recall asynchronous events, such as interrupts and context switches, and memory protection with multiple address spaces. When it comes to networking, Linux OS must deal with three address spaces: the network adapter I/O space, the kernel and the user address spaces. Two predefined functions exist to copy data across different address spaces, namely `memcpy_fromfs()` and `memcpy_tofs()`. To obtain maximum performance it would be nice to directly copy messages between user and network card spaces. This approach has been successfully employed in [8]. While this is theoretically possible during send phase, it is not feasible in the callback phase as long as PRP approach not to interfere with process scheduling is maintained. The callback must be regarded as an interrupt handler which cannot assume that the destination process is running and cannot access its user memory. Furthermore, to be completely hardware independent, a network protocol must deliver to device drivers a regular buffer in kernel space. All these considerations have brought to following implementation solutions:

- use of the predefined memory management functions to move data between user and kernel space;
- delegation to network device drivers of the actual copy to and from the I/O space;
- exclusive usage of the `struct socket`, `struct sock` and `struct sk_buff` structures to hold the information about the connection, so that it can be exploited in the callback phase and the protocol code is completely reentrant.

2.2 *PRP* characteristics

The PRP protocol implementation relies on the basic assumption that the *local* homogeneous interconnection network assures correct delivery of the packets. In other words, we assume that the percentage of packets incorrectly delivered is negligible and the software layer dedicated to error recovery can be discarded. While TCP/IP implements both flow control mechanisms and error control coding, PRP only worries about lost packets, because Ethernet cards automatically discard corrupted packets, exploiting Ethernet CRC field. This way a corrupted packet is turned into a missing one and error detection falls into lost packet detection, verifying whether segments arrive at the destination in exact order and returning an error message when appropriate. This choice has been strengthened by the fact that all common user-level MPI-based applications typically running in our cluster never caused protocol failures. Only intensively communicating custom tests have detected problems related to packet loss.

Therefore, typical flow control mechanisms and acknowledge-retransmission schemes needed by a general purpose, WAN oriented protocol as is TCP/IP are currently not present inside PRP. However, we are studying the impact on performance of some simple packet loss recovery implementations (go-back n vs. selective repeat), which we plan to insert into PRP's next releases. The complex reliable three-way handshake phase present inside TCP/IP has been simplified too, resulting in a straightforward two-way connection setup phase. Besides, PRP can be installed as a module inside all Linux kernels starting from 2.0.0 version.

2.3 The *PRP* Socket Interface

The protocol is implemented as a new family for the high level socket interface and can be called by setting the socket family parameters in the system calls to AF_PRPF. The whole set of system calls available in a standard Unix environment for networking and socket management has been implemented from scratch also for PRP. The new structure sockaddr_prp, available in the suitable prp.h header file, is equivalent (with the family, address, and port fields) to standard sockaddr_in structure which supports AF_INET sockets. PRP supports up to 1024 port numbers, that can be automatically assigned by the OS. The sockaddr_prp structure is defined as:

```
struct sockaddr_prp {
    short int           sprp_family;    /* Address family  */
    unsigned short int  sprp_port;      /* Port number     */
    unsigned short int  sprp_addr;      /* PRP address     */
};
```

In a cluster supporting PRP, machine nodes are numbered with logical addresses from 1 to N_p, in such a way that IP addresses are unknown from inside the new protocol family. In PRP, besides logical node numbers, only Ethernet addresses are needed. The prphosts configuration file placed in the /etc directory contains the mapping between logical and hardware addresses. The network layer, responsible for converting addresses from logical to Ethernet back and forth, allows us to support any possible routing scheme the user wants to impose to machine configuration. Since PRP layers are completely independent of underlying ones, the protocol must know the device ethx, which packets are to be delivered to and collected from. This information also is stored in the configuration file.

The main socket features and parameters seen at application level and the state of the socket in use are stored, as done by other protocol suites in Linux, in the struct socket.

2.4 *PRP* Transport Layer

The PRP transport layer is responsible for performing packet segmentation, allocating and deallocating buffers to be sent or that have been received, coding and decoding header flags, copying data to/from user space from/to kernel space. Finally, being the last software level (starting from the application) knowing about both user processes and kernel buffers, PRP transport layer must identify the destination socket (if any) during the callback phase and wake up the receiving process when it's time to do so. Due to the absence of flow control and error recovery this layer does not implement retransmission timeouts nor packet queuing during send phase.

The very light-weight structure of PRP also results in a socket AF_PRPF to have only four states named PRP_CLOSE, PRP_CONN_WAIT, PRP_LISTEN, and PRP_ESTABLISHED. The two-way handshake phase taking place upon starting a connection is as follows: the client requesting the connection sends a special packet to the server, which in turn responds sending a final acknowledge packet. After a listen()/accept() system call pair server's socket goes from PRP_CLOSE to PRP_LISTEN state. On the other side, the socket requesting the connection goes to PRP_CONN_WAIT. After this simple handshake phase, both sides move to PRP_ESTABLISHED state.

The tl_prp_sendmsg() function applies a segmentation on user buffer using up to the maximum Ethernet size (1484 bytes of data) for each segment; for each packet a suitable socket buffer sk_buff is allocated. The header added to each segment contains information on source and destination ports (coded in 16 bit integers), the sequence number of the segment (coded in 16 bits), the packet length (taking other 16 bits), and finally the flags (32 bits). Flags identify a condition of *connection request* when a process makes a connect() system call, a *connection acknowledge* by the server side when establishing the connection, an *end of message* when sending the last packet of a sequence, and the *end of connection* request. After adding the header, we are ready to append user data to kernel buffer, through the memcpy_fromfs() function, and finally to forward the packet to network layer.

During callback phase the tl_prp_rcv() is the last function executed. It must extract the header information and, on the basis of the port number, identify the destination sock which must handle the packet. The header flags are checked and different routes are taken according to socket state and flag values. For example a data packet arriving in a PRP_ESTABLISHED condition is enqueued to the list of received buffers. An out-of-sequence data packet, instead, is automatically discarded, in agreement with our error detection policy. The last task the callback must accomplish is the wake-up of the processes waiting for the message. The tl_prp_recvmsg() function (called by socket family layer in a read() system call) is held responsible for dequeuing received packets from socket list and copy data from sk_buff to user supplied buffer, with a memcpy_tofs() call.

2.5 *PRP* Network Layer

During send phase the PRP network layer must identify Ethernet addresses and devices to which packets must be delivered. On the other hand, during callback, it must verify if the local node is the destination of the arriving packet, otherwise it must redirect the packet to another device for a new destination (that is packet routing).

The nl_prp_send() function adds its own (very simple) header to the buffer coming from upper levels. This header is made by two 16 bit integers storing source and destination logical addresses of the connection endpoints. A suitable kernel routing table structure stores the mapping between logical and Ethernet addresses and the device associated to each destination node. After that, the network layer function is ready to deliver the **sk_buff** to the lower level generic interface of the corresponding **ethx** device, filling Ethernet address fields.

3   The dedicated MPI implementation

Almost every parallel architecture supports a custom MPI version, developed directly on the basis of the hardware/software machine specifics, with the main purpose of achieving maximum efficiency. Therefore, one among the main goals of $PARMA^2$ project is to develop also a dedicated version of MPI, evolution of the MPICH implementation. MPIPR library is mainly devoted to greatly simplify the internal protocol used by the MPI **ch_p4** device [17], in order to dramatically decrease software latencies. Until now only *synchronous* MPIPR primitives have been implemented, as they mainly affect the performance of distributed applications.

The MPICH implementation of MPI adopts a useful layered approach [18]. The *channel interface* is responsible for providing all "high level" data transfer operations and relies by default on the **ch_p4** device layer, which in turn exploits the standard Unix socket facilities. The interface implements its own data exchange protocols and data management mechanisms. Messages are sent in two parts. The control message stores the information about message tag, length, etc. The data part stores user message actual data. Specific routines are designed to send and receive the two message parts, and to check the presence of incoming messages. In case of small user messages sending two packets can determine a substantial latency overhead. Therefore, packets with size below a preset cut-off are sent together with the control part. The default cut-off value is 1024 bytes. The **ch_p4** device derives from the preexisting **p4** parallel programming system [17], developed at Argonne National Laboratory too. Its protocol imposes that, during a send operation, a suitable 40 byte header is built, with all necessary information (source, destination, message-type, length, etc.) and sent apart from data message, in a separate socket **write()** system call. This protocol assures the correct buffer allocation strategy at the receiver side, since message characteristics are available before real data arrives, but on the other hand it doubles the overheads.

Our intervention has concerned the substitution of this layered structure with a single interface, with its own internal protocol, the main purpose being the elimination of duplicate communication latencies, at least for small packets. The new internal protocol assembles the 48 bytes message header needed to store all necessary information and then sends the whole packet (header and data) to the destination. At receiver's side standard stream socket features are exploited in order to correctly scan incoming message headers until the one matching requested criteria is found. Stream socket allow in fact to read only the header packet portion, apart of the rest of the message. This permits to allocate a suitable buffer and then to read remaining message data. The new MPIPR layer relies of course upon the PRP protocol instead of the standard TCP/IP family.

We are also completing the implementation of an optimized version of asynchronous MPI primitives, in order to realize a self-consistent PRP-based MPI version.

4 Performance measurements

A key experimental ingredient, when evaluating quantities as small as latency times (expected to be 10^{-4} seconds or less), is an accurate timing measurement. This is accomplished by means of the TSC Pentium register, which is incremented every clock tick. By reading TSC content before and after the execution of a piece of code we are able to measure the exact execution time of that code with a 10 nanoseconds resolution (on a Pentium 100 CPU).

Latency and bandwidth are parameters commonly used to characterize communication performance [11, 12]. Despite the fact that bandwidth is a much heralded feature of interconnection networks, from a minimal experience in the application field it results, quite obviously, that most of the damage is caused by latency. Almost any reasonable bandwidth turns out to be quite acceptable, while latency can be and often is an unbearable bottleneck. Besides, bandwidth is pretty much bounded by hardware features of the system at hand, while latency is given by a complex interplay of software and hardware to the point that becomes handy to distinguish between network hardware contribution, software overhead introduced by the CPU to perform a network operation, and CPU hardware contribution, in turn made up by memory to memory copies and back and forth memory to device copies. The sum of the various types of overhead is the meaning of latency we like to endorse, in order to relate it to the cost we pay in executing real application code, that is the overhead related to memory to memory delivery of a zero length message.

It must be pointed out that Ethernet allows frame sizes ranging from 60 bytes to 1514 bytes, so that every packet smaller than 60 bytes (including headers) is actually padded by the network card, resulting in a constant network hardware overhead for a data size from 0 to 34 bytes. Let then N_{min} be the data size resulting in a 60 byte frame and be N_{max} the data size giving a frame of 1514 bytes; let also a be the overall constant communication overhead (i.e. a is the sum of the three terms independent of data size, each referring to a different latency contribution). Finally, let $1/B_N$ be the coefficient of the linear part (i.e. the one proportional to data size) arising from network hardware and let $1/B_{CPU}$ be the same for CPU hardware and software contributions. If we want to parameterize communication time T versus message size N we cannot use a single formula for the whole range, since network contribution has different expressions for data size greater or lesser than N_{min}:

$$T = a + \frac{N_{min}}{B_N} + \frac{N}{B_{CPU}} = L + \frac{N}{B_0} \quad 0 \leq N \leq N_{min}, \tag{1}$$

$$T = a + \frac{N}{B_N} + \frac{N}{B_{CPU}} = L' + \frac{N}{B_1} \quad N_{min} \leq N \leq N_{max}, \tag{2}$$

where $L = a + N_{min}/B_N$, $B_0 = B_{CPU}$, $L' = a$ and $1/B_1 = 1/B_N + 1/B_{CPU}$ are the resulting parameters for the model.

	Latency (μs)	Bandwidth (MB/s)
PRP	74	6.6
TCP/IP	146	5.5

Table 1. Latency and bandwidth for the ping-pong operation.

The usual "ping-pong" application is employed to carry out our measurements. A standard socket-based implementation is adopted for ping-pong experimental setup with both TCP/IP and PRP, the only difference being AF_PRPF sockets used instead of AF_INET sockets. Experiments performed with very large messages give a measure of effective bandwidth, whereas relevant latency, as previously defined, is clearly L, measured through experiments conducted with message length going to zero. The ping-pong results taken on 100 MHz Pentium processors with Fast-Ethernet are reported in Table 1. PRP shows half overall latency overheads, if compared to TCP/IP, while the improvement of effective bandwidth is about 20%.

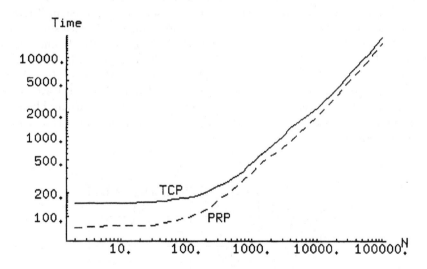

Fig. 1. Delay as a function of the message length N.

The behavior of transmission delay T as a function of message length N on a wide range of values (from 0 to 200 KB) is drawn in Fig. 1 for TCP/IP and PRP. Despite the significant difference between the two curves near the origin, measuring the difference in latency of the two protocols, we notice that they tend to narrow the gap asymptotically, offering further support to the fact that bandwidth is not much affected by TCP/IP. In order to address $PARMA^2$ scaling problem measurements have been carried out with increasing numbers of nodes (up to 16): as expected from a bus-based topology, a remarkable decrease in available bandwidth has been observed for ping-pong applications with eight or more PCs. In this heavy load conditions both PRP and TCP/IP performed equally, being the physical channel the main system bottleneck.

An usual countermeasure is breaking out network traffic using switches; since they work directly with Ethernet frames, they support every higher level protocol without distinctions. Alternatively, network topologies exclusively composed by point to point links (an hypercube is a typical example) are a feasible way to overcome scaling problems and are indeed supported by means of PRP static routing scheme.

5 $PARMA^2$ applications

Preliminary results allowed by MPIPR have been measured, in order to compare them with other assessed MPI implementations (the standard MPI, based on TCP/IP, and the MPI version simply adapted to PRP). The test is a ping-pong experiment, implemented using `MPI_Isend()` and `MPI_Recv()` primitives. Comparative results on two Pentium 100 processors are reported in Table 2, that report also commercial MPP platform results [13, 14, 15] with some available message passing libraries. On Cray T3D ping-pong results obtained using the *shared memory* configuration are also reported, giving much better results. Latencies with MPIPR are 2.2 times smaller than with MPI plus TCP/IP, allowing our environment to be competitive with parallel machines, at least within a factor of four or five, using only standard low-cost hardware and suitably modified public domain software. In particular, we are only two times slower than the CM-5, at the same application level.

	Latency (μs)	Bandwidth (MB/s)
CM-5 CMMD	93.7	8.3
T3D MPI	43.3	29.6
T3D SHMEM	1.5	58.5
SP2 MPI	44.6	33.9
MPI + TCP/IP	401.5	4.51
MPI + PRP	256	5.37
MPIPR	181.5	5.37

Table 2. Latency and bandwidth for the ping-pong operation using the three MPI versions available on the $PARMA^2$ platform.

The availability of the MPI interfaces, with TCP/IP and PRP, and the MPIPR dedicated version, allows us to measure how user applications can benefit from improvements obtained in communication latencies. We have chosen a common and widely used regular lattice problem [16], based on the Cellular Neural Network (CNN) computational paradigm, in order to implement a test where communication latencies can play a very important role.

CNNs [19] [20] are defined on discrete regular N-dimensional spaces. The basic element of the paradigm is the *unit* (or *cell*), corresponding to a point in the grid. Cells are characterized by an *internal state variable*. The main characteristic of CNN is the *locality* of the connections among the units: the most important difference between CNN and other Neural Network paradigms is the fact that information is directly exchanged only between neighboring units. From another point of view, it is possible to consider the CNN paradigm as an evolution of the Cellular Automata paradigm. A formal description of the discrete time CNN model is:

$$x_j(t_{n+1}) = I_j + \sum_{k \in N_r(j)} A_j[y_k(t_n), P_j^A] + \sum_{k \in N_s(j)} B_j[u_k(t_n), P_j^B] \qquad (3)$$

$$y_j(t_n) = \phi[x_j(t_n)], \qquad (4)$$

where x_j is the internal state of a cell, y_j is its output, u_j is its external (*control*) input and I_j is a local value (e.g. a threshold) called *bias*. A_j and B_j are two generic parametric functionals, P_j^A and P_j^B are the corresponding parameter arrays (typically the inter-cell connection weights). The y and u values are collected from the cells of the neighborhood N_r (for the functional A) and N_s (for the functional B). A and B are also called *templates*. The *activation function* ϕ, which generates the output from the internal state, can be typically a linear with saturation, a sigmoidal, a step, a quantizer or a Gaussian [19]. All data are represented as 32-bit floating-point numbers.

At each iteration, and for each lattice point, the CNN must perform the collection of the u and y neighbor values of the previous iteration, compute the A and B templates, then x is determined adding to I the A and B results. Finally, the activation function is applied to x to obtain the new value of the output y. For our purposes only the *linear* template subset of 2-D CNN is considered. Moreover, only periodic boundary conditions are implemented, as usually happens in many physics and engineering problems. In all tests a linear with saturation activation function ϕ has been used. In spite of its simplicity, the CNN formalism may express many complex problems or applications, for example in Image Processing, Field-Dynamics, and Theoretical Physics. An exhaustive list of many CNN applications can be found in [19].

The overall computational times required to execute 100 complete CNN iterations have been measured on $L \times L$ square lattices. Fig. 2 reports the overall performance (in M-Flop/s) measured with four $PARMA^2$ nodes (Pentium 100), as a function of L, using the general MPI version with TCP/IP and PRP and the dedicated MPIPR version. The graph emphasizes the significant performance

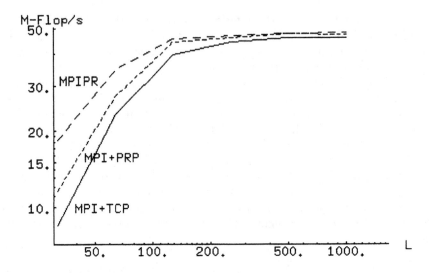

Fig. 2. Performance (in M-Flop/s) on four PCs for the CNN application, with the standard MPI version with TCP/IP and PRP, and the dedicated MPIPR version, as a function of the 2-D $L \times L$ lattices.

improvement (more than a factor of two) allowed by MPIPR on a real synchronous application when communications become a bottleneck, that is when frequently exchanging small packets. The difference with respect to the standard TCP/IP-based MPI version becomes asymptotically negligible, the application being computation bounded at this regime.

6 Lessons learned and future work

In this work a development suite supporting fast communications in PC clusters running Linux was presented. The PRP network protocol realized with the purpose of preserving complete OS functionality and maintaining the high level socket interface, although very simple, showed remarkable latency improvements with respect to TCP/IP. Moreover, the MPI custom implementation (MPIPR) furtherly encourages the $PARMA^2$ approach of comprehensive interventions in both OS kernel and user-level libraries.

Several annotations arose during software development. First of all, when operating with modern and fast networks the major latency contributions come from system and software overheads. In particular, every system component (i.e. device drivers, virtual memory management, and to a lesser extent - 33% - PRP code itself) yields a non negligible percentage of total communication time when sending very small packets, as is explained in Fig. 3. Furthermore, the effective bandwidth allowed by system hardware (bus architecture, cache memory hierarchy, CPU speed) is still far (53%) from Fast-Ethernet theoretical peak

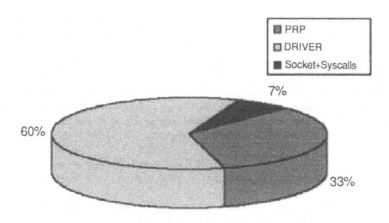

Fig. 3. Contributions to PRP latency.

performance. Having implemented a minimal protocol, it results quite evident that for both performance aspects a crucial role is played by the complex interaction between device driver and system bus. Therefore, future investigations and enhancements will concern on one hand testing improved device drivers, and, on the other hand, adding error control features to PRP protocol.

Finally, all performance advantages of PRP over TCP/IP measured with custom tests are gradually reduced by successive software layers (common socket interface and MPI library); in order to avoid masking out kernel level improvements it is necessary to extend upward software optimizations. This is another main direction in our future developments: completion of the dedicated MPIPR implementation and integration of enhanced higher level programming paradigms on top of MPI, like HPF as compiled by ADAPTOR.

Acknowledgments

The authors warmly thank Prof. G. Chiola and Dr. G. Ciaccio of Università di Genova for the helpful discussions had during early phases of their research.

References

1. G. Bell: 1995 Observations on Supercomputing Alternatives: Did the MPP Bandwagon Lead to a Cul-de-Sac ? Communications of the ACM **Vol 30** No. 3 (1996)
2. L. Colombet and L. Desbat: Speedup and efficiency of large size applications on heterogeneous networks. Proc. EURO-PAR96 (1996)
3. C. C. Lim and J. P. Ang: Experience on Optimization and Parallelization of Existing Scientific Applications on Network of Workstations. Proc. PDPTA96 (1996)

4. R. van Drunen, C. van Teylingen and M. Kroontje: The Amfisbaena: A Parallel Supercomputer System Based on i860 as a Generic Platform for Molecular Dynamics Simulations. Proc. PDPTA96 (1996)

5. M.A.Blumrich, K.Li, R.Alpert, C.Dubnicki, E.W.Felten, and J.Sandberg: Virtual Memory Mapped Network Interface for the SHRIMP Multicomputer. Proc. "International Symposium on Computer Architecture" ISCA94 (1994) 142–153.

6. T. Sterling, D. Savarese, B. Fryxell, K. Olson, and D. J. Becker: Communication Overhead for Space Science Applications on the Beowulf Parallel Workstation. Proc. "High Performance Distributed Computing" HPDC95 Pentagon City Virginia USA (1995)

7. H. Lu, S. Dwarkadas, A. L. Cox and W. Zwaenepoel: Message Passing Versus Distributed Shared Memory on Networks of Workstations. Proc. Supercomputing95 (1995)

8. G. Chiola and G. Ciaccio: GAMMA: a Low-cost Network of Workstations Based on Active Messages. Proc. "5th EUROMICRO workshop on Parallel and Distributed Processing PDP'97" London UK (1997)

9. W. R. Stevens: Unix Network Programming. Prentice Hall New Jersey (1990)

10. D. E. Comer and D. L. Stevens: Internetworking with TCP/IP. Prentice Hall New Jersey (1991)

11. Z. Xu and K. Hwang: Modeling Communication Overhead: MPI and MPL Performance on the IBM SP2. IEEE Parallel & Distributed Technology **Vol. 4** No. 1 (1996) 25–42

12. R. W. Hockney: The Communication Challenge for MPP: Intel Paragon and Meiko CS-2. Parallel Computing **Vol. 6** No. 3 (1994) 389–398

13. J. J. Dongarra and T. Dunigan: Message-Passing Performance of Various Computers. Tec. Report ORNL/TM-13006 Oak Ridge National Laboratory (1996)

14. P. Marenzoni: Performance Analysis of Cray T3D and Connection Machine CM-5: a Comparison. Proc. Int. Conf. "High-Performance Computing and Networking HPCN95" Milan Italy Springer-Verlag LNCS **919** (1995) 110–117

15. P. Marenzoni and P. Rossi, Benchmark Kernels as a Tool for Performance Evaluation of MPP's,
    Concurrency Practice and Experience, 1997, in press, John Wiley & Sons.

16. G. Destri and P. Marenzoni: Cellular Neural Networks as a General Massively Parallel Computational Paradigm. Special Issue on Cellular Neural Networks of "International Journal of Circuits Theory and Application" **Vol. 24** No. 3 (1996) 397–408

17. R. M. Butler and E. L. Lusk: Monitors, Messages, and Clusters: The p4 Parallel Programming System. Parallel Computing **Vol. 20** (1994) 547–564

18. W. Gropp and E. L. Lusk: MPICH Working Note: Creating a New MPICH Device Using the Channel Interface. Tec. Report Argonne National Laboratory

19. L.O. Chua and T. Roska: The CNN Paradigm. IEEE Trans. on Circuit and Systems - I **Vol. 40** (1993) 147–155

20. L.O. Chua and L. Yang: Cellular Neural Network: Theory. IEEE Trans. on Circuit and Systems **Vol. 35** (1988) 1257–1272

Distributed Hardware Support for Process Synchronization in NSM Workstation Clusters[1]

Jordan Bonney, Ranga Ramanujan, Atiq Ahamad,
Siddhartha Takkella, and Kenneth Thurber

Architecture Technology Corporation
P.O. Box 24344
Minneapolis, MN 55424

Abstract. In this paper we present a method for providing shared binary semaphores for small- to medium-sized workstation clusters. Each semaphore is represented by a single bit in a slotted ring of bits. The ring is implemented by dedicated high-speed I/O adapters called ring controllers; every node in a workstation cluster contains one ring controller. The dedicated nature of the ring controllers provides a method for implementing shared binary semaphores that is significantly more efficient than implementing semaphores with software and existing interconnection networks.

1 Introduction

Network Shared Memory is a method for workstation clustering that uses a dedicated, high-speed network to replicate shared memory among the constituent nodes of the cluster and maintain sequential consistency among the shared memory. Details of the NSM approach can be found in [1,2]. In addition to providing sequentially consistent shared memory, the NSM approach also provides hardware-based locks, or shared binary semaphores, similar to those found in shared-memory multiprocessors. The implementation of NSM shared binary semaphores is the focus of this paper.

In an NSM environment, the individual nodes of the workstation cluster are arranged in a ring topology using high-speed, point-to-point serial links. Two rings are implemented in an NSM cluster: the data ring, which transfers shared memory between the nodes and is described in [1], and the synchronization ring, which is used to implement the shared binary semaphores for process synchronization, the focus of this paper. Figure 1, below, illustrates the two rings in a three-node NSM cluster:

---

[1] This material is based upon work supported by NSF's Small Business Innovative Research (SBIR) program under award number DMI-9509060. Any opinions, findings, and conclusions or recommendations expressed in this publication are those of the authors and do not necessarily reflect the views of NSF.

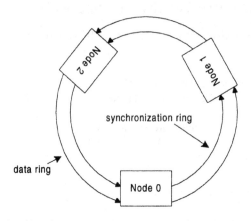

Fig. 1. NSM cluster with data and synchronization rings.

In order to realize the advantages of an NSM cluster, the serial links that comprise the ring must have throughput on the order of the local workstations' local memory throughput. Until recently, the disparity between memory-access speeds and serial-communications speeds prevented NSM from being realized. The availability of low-cost serial controllers operating in excess of 1 Gbps has enabled us to begin prototyping an NSM cluster that contains hardware support for process synchronization in the form of shared binary semaphores.

Clearly, shared binary semaphores are either provided by or can be constructed within parallel-programming environments such as p4 or PVM. However the low-speed communications networks, transport-protocol overhead, and message-passing overhead often used to implement these parallel environments severely curtail semaphore-operation performance. The performance problems do not stem from any shortcoming of p4 or PVM, but rather from implementation-dependent details. In fact, the goal of our research is to construct a prototype NSM cluster that is capable of running existing parallel codes and to compare the NSM cluster's performance to that of other types of workstation clusters. As such, we plan to implement both the p4 macros and PVM on the hardware we are currently developing. In addition to shared-memory performance gains, we expect significant improvements in semaphore-operation performance.

In the following sections we present the overall approach to NSM semaphore implementation, our current prototyping efforts, proposed refinements and open issues, related research, and the conclusions and status of the on-going research effort.

2 NSM Approach to Binary-Semaphore Implementation

In an NSM cluster, binary semaphores are represented by a constantly circulating ring of bits (we will interchangeably use the terms binary semaphore, lock, and synchronization bit). Each workstation in the NSM cluster contains a synchronization controller that is fixed at a particular ring position; the synchronization controller observes the circulating bits as they pass by the controller's ring position. Each bit spends a fixed hold time at each position before proceeding to its next downstream position; this hold time is long enough for the synchronization controller to observe, and possibly modify, a bit. The hold time is actually implemented by the synchronization controllers as they receive bits from their upstream neighbors and forward bits to their downstream neighbors. As all the synchronization controllers are simultaneously operational, the bits circulate around the ring. The synchronization ring and associated bits of a three-node NSM cluster are illustrated in Figure 2.

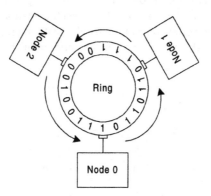

Fig. 2. A carousel of synchronization bits.

The synchronization ring is a slotted ring, i.e., the data that traverses the ring is broken into fixed-size slots. This also implies that the slots present on the ring are contiguously numbered from 0 through n-1, where n is the total number of slots. If we think of the synchronization ring's slot size as being one bit, then in addition to observing and modifying any passing bit, the synchronization controller also knows the bit's ring position, or address. With the ability to uniquely identify each bit on the ring and the ability to modify any passing bit, we can define a set of unique semaphores and operations on these semaphores. The available semaphore operations are as follows:

Test-and-set: a.) save current value of bit
                      b.) set the bit and forward it on the ring
                      c.) return the bit's previous value

Clear: a.) verify that the node requesting the clear operation originally set
                          the bit
                          b.) clear the bit and forward it on the ring

To minimize round-trip latency, the ring is expected to operate in excess of a gigabit per second. Even so, each node in the cluster introduces additional round-trip latency as it must inspect, possibly modify, and forward each passing bit. We realize this is a limitation of the NSM approach, but, as described in [1], the overall cluster size is never expected to exceed 100 nodes, and the round-trip latency is therefore acceptable.

While we can think of the synchronization ring as a carousel of bits as shown in Figure 2, the real-world implementation deviates slightly from this conceptual model. Most serial transmitters feature a parallel data interface and provide serialization, encoding, and transmission of the parallel data; most serial receivers recover a serial data stream, decode the data, and output the recovered data as a parallel word. Therefore, the slot size of the synchronization ring grows to the size defined by the selected serial controller's parallel data interface. Consequently, the control logic at each node must manipulate an entire multi-bit slot at once, as shown in Figure 3:

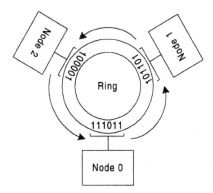

Fig. 3. Synchronization locks allocated to fixed-size slots.

Performing bitwise operations on a multi-bit slot is not difficult; however, it does require the control logic to keep track of each bit's offset within a slot. As shown in Figure 3, each synchronization controller implements a latch corresponding to one slot of the ring. Incoming data is latched, possibly modified, and forwarded to the downstream node. Bit-wise operations on these latches are easy to implement with programmable logic devices.

All NSM semaphore operations and control logic are implemented in hardware by the synchronization controller. The software interface to the synchronization controller is a C-language function call that provides user-level access to the test-

and-set and clear operations. As part of the NSM environment, the synchronization ring is initialized before any parallel applications are executed on the cluster. This initialization sequence ensures that all bits are set to zero and all synchronization controllers are operational before any parallel applications are loaded an run on the NSM cluster.

3 Prototype Implementation

The implementation of the NSM synchronization controller required an I/O-bus interface to the software, a high-speed serial controller to implement the synchronization ring, and a programmable device that can simultaneously operate the ring and service requests from the software. We chose a PCI-bus I/O interface, Hewlett-Packard serial controllers, and Altera FPGAs to implement the necessary control logic. A block diagram of the controller is provided in Figure 4.

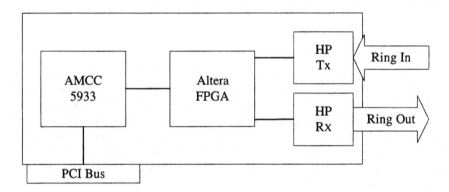

Fig. 4. PCI adapter conceptual layout.

3.1 PCI Interface

In order to expedite the implementation of the synchronization controller, we used an off-the-shelf ASIC for implementing the PCI interface. AMCC's 5933 controller can operate at the maximum 33-MHz rate of most current PCI buses, and it provides a simple mailbox interface that can be accessed in port-mapped or memory-mapped modes [3]. Each mailbox is a 32-bit register, and there are four incoming mailboxes and four outgoing mailboxes. The AMCC PCI interface can be programmed to generate interrupts to both the add-on hardware or the PCI bus when a byte is written to an incoming or outgoing mailbox. The synchronization controller only requires one incoming mailbox and one outgoing mailbox.

Because of the mailbox interface and the 5933's interrupting scheme, we encoded our test-and-set operations in a single mailbox. We reserved 8 bits for an opcode, of which only one bit is used for synchronization; the remaining bits are used to encode operations for the NSM's data ring. We reserve the remaining 24 bits for the address of the semaphore on which the operation is to be performed. After an opcode and address are written by the software to the mailbox, the 5933 asserts an interrupt line, referred to as IRQn, which will signal the programmable logic of a requested semaphore operation.

While the AMCC 5933 is a good choice for quickly getting up and running on Intel-based PCI systems, it does have some drawbacks, as can be expected with a general-purpose ASIC. The problems are a byproduct of the mailbox interface. After detecting the assertion of IRQn, another clock cycle is used by the FPGA to read the contents of the mailbox. Also, writing the previous value of a lock back to a mailbox and deasserting IRQn cannot be performed in a single operation. The result is that the FPGA wastes at least three clock cycles for AMCC overhead. We suggest PCI interface improvements later in this document.

3.2 HP G-Link Serial Controllers

The Hewlett-Packard G-Link chipset consists of the HDMP-1012 Transmitter and HDMP-1014 Receiver [4]. The chipset provides a 16- or 20-bit interface and isolates the user from the complexity of data serialization, encoding, and transmission. The chipset operates at a clock rate of between 7.5 and 75 MHz. An internal PLL multiplies the input clock and uses the PLL output for serial data transmission with throughput of between 120 Mbps and 1.2 Gbps in 16-bit mode. The HDMP-1014 Receiver recovers the clock of the transmitter that sends data and has no external clock input itself.

We operate the chipset in a 16-bit mode in order to minimize I/O pin counts on the control device, which are always at a premium. The chipset is also operated in a simplex mode wherein the only indicators of new data on a receiver are the assertion of the data available (DAVn) and recovered transmitter clock (STRBOUT) signals. Since the transmitter and FPGA of a particular synchronization controller run off the same clock, and since the receiver is in effect clocked by the upstream transmitter, it is necessary to provide asynchronous latching and buffering of the data recovered by the receiver. This latching and buffering are taken care of by the FPGA, as explained later.

The benefits of the G-Link chipset include its ability to run over coaxial cable, its relatively low price, and its obvious performance benefits. The largest single drawback to this point has been the fact the chipset uses ECL inputs and outputs. This has significantly complicated the PCB design of the synchronization controller because of the need for three separate power planes (+5, -5, and -2v), ground-plane isolation, and ECL-TTL translators. Additionally, the additional latency incurred from the transmitter and receiver running off of separate clocks could add an additional clock cycle to the receive-and-forward process. However, the chipset's low point-to-point latency and high transmission speed mitigates this problem.

3.3 Programmable Logic

A programmable logic device is required to interface to the AMCC PCI ASIC and to control the HP G-Link controllers. We chose Altera FLEX 8000 family of FPGA's for our implementation.

The FPGA is responsible for detecting the assertion of the IRQn signal from the AMCC 5933, reading the 5933's mailbox register that contains the opcode and lock number, decoding the operation to be performed, determining the slot containing the desired semaphore, modifying the corresponding bit after the slot is recovered by the receiver, and sending the data out on the transmitter.

Functionally, the ring-interface and PCI-interface logic are implemented in separate modules with a comparator situated between the two. The comparator takes as inputs the number of the incoming slot (maintained by the ring-interface logic) and the slot number of the semaphore to be operated upon (the high-order 20 bits received from the mailbox and maintained by the PCI-interface logic). The comparator manipulates the select line of a MUX; if there is no match between the desired semaphores's slot number and the received slot's number, the received data is simply passed through to the transmit send buffer. If, on the other hand there is a match, the comparator enables the appropriate semaphore modification to be propagated to the transmit send buffer by selecting the PCI-interface input to the MUX. Figure 5 shows the layout of the two logic modules, the comparator, and the output MUX.

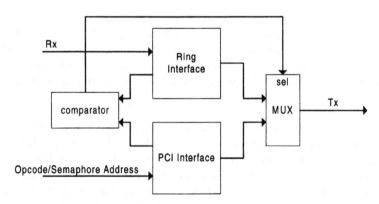

Fig. 5. Logical organization of synchronization controller.

Additional control lines to the transmitter and receiver are provided by the ring-interface logic. These control lines indicate when new slots arrive and control the sending of data by the transmitter. With the exception of the initialization sequence, no ring interface will never transmit unless data exists in the receive buffer. This is necessary because of the separate clocks maintained by each synchronization controller. Even though all the clocks run at the same speed, they have some amount of drift. Over time it is possible to encounter a situation where a transmitter is able to send a slot, but no new slot has yet been received. We discuss the issue further in a later section.

Since the receiver and transmitter run off of different clocks, it is necessary to asynchronously latch and buffer data from the receiver; a latching buffer is implemented within the FPGA and is operated by control lines that emanate from the receiver. The existence of data in this receive buffer determines whether or not the transmitter is enabled on the rising edge of the FPGA/transmitter clock.

The PCI-interface logic also implements the test-and-set and clear operations. A single bit of the 8-bit opcode received from the 32-bit incoming mailbox is dedicated to the synchronization operations. Therefore, if the lowest-order bit in the opcode is a '0', a clear operation is performed; if the lowest-order bit in the opcode is a '1', a test-and-set operation is performed. The lowest-order opcode bit is actually passed through the output MUX to effect the change in the passing ring slot.

The PCI-interface logic is also responsible for maintaining a table of all semaphores and which of the semaphores has been set by this synchronization controller. If an request is made by the software to clear a semaphore that this controller has not set, an error code is returned; only the controller who sets a semaphore can clear that semaphore.

We have successfully run the ring controller on an EPF8282 device at 15 MHz and our development tools indicate it is currently able to operate in excess of 45 MHz with the same device. Simulating for larger and faster FLEX 8000 devices shows potential increases to over 50 MHz, which translates to ring throughput of 800 Mbps.

The biggest drawback to the Altera devices has been shortage of I/O pins as the design grows and we attempt to include other NSM functionality. When implementing the data ring logic as well as the synchronization logic, there are immediately 64 pins to be considered for the serial controllers, plus an additional 32 I/O pins for the PCI interface. We have mitigated this problem somewhat by multiplexing the receive and transmit lines in the prototype, but would ideally like to use a larger device and remove the multiplexed I/O lines.

3.4 Timing Issues

The most difficult aspect of the synchronization controllers is the fact that each controller's transmitter and receiver are driven by separate clock. Moreover, the FPGA logic and the transmitter *are* driven by the same clock. While all the clocks in the cluster operate at nominally the same rate, the discrepancies between the separate synchronization controllers can lead to problems. Even if there were no clock-drift problems, all the clocks would likely be out of phase by some amount. As a result, it is necessary to asynchronously buffer incoming data and ensure that the transmitter does not send data if the receive buffer is empty.

To understand the effect of clock drifts on the ring speed we first need to understand some timing issues. Assume t_l as the time required to latch data. Figure 6 shows the local clock for some node A. For data to be transmitted on rising edge 2, the node should receive the data in the range shown as t_r. This ensures that there is sufficient time to latch incoming data. If there is a drift in the clocks in such a way that data is received at time t_{0+}, then the earliest time it can be transmitted is on rising edge 3. Hence the maximum possible delay is 1 clock cycle. This is true for each node. The two extreme effect f the clock's drift are, 1.) when all the clocks in the cluster drift constructively to minimize the delay of each node (the best case), and, 2.) when all the clocks drift destructively to maximize the delay at each node (the worst case). The conditions under which each occurs is described below.

Best case:
The best case scenario occurs when each node receives at time t_{0-}, in which case each node can transmit the incoming data in minimum time.

Worst case:
The worst case situation is when all the nodes receive at time t_{0+}, which is n cycles slower than the best case as each node has to wait an additional clock cycle, where n is the number of nodes.

The probability of the best and the worst cases diminishes rapidly as the number of nodes increases and it is reasonable to average the effect of clock drifts.

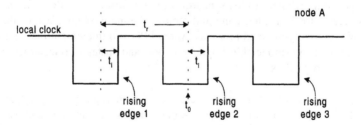

Fig. 6. Clock-skew considerations.

3.5 Initialization

There is a single exception to the send-after-receive rule, and this exception occurs during initialization. A single initialization node generates $(n+1)$ empty packets (i.e., a packet containing all 0's), which are successively forwarded to the downstream neighbor. Since additional initialization logic present in the NSM cluster guarantees that all nodes are operational when the synchronization-ring initialization sequence begins, we are assured that the ring has been set in motion after the initialization node generates $(n+1)$ empty packets. Following the packet-generation sequence, the initialization node behaves like all other nodes.

3.6 Software

Our current software implementation is a C-language function that makes a BIOS call to the PCI adapter and sends the opcode and semaphore number as a single 32-bit quantity to the synchronization controller. The functions are to be linked in with parallel applications in a completed prototype environment. The function prototypes are :

```
int ts_sem(int semaphore_num);
int clr_sem(int semaphore_num);
```

Error codes are returned by the functions and should be inspected by the invoking procedure.

4 Refinements and Open Issues

As we are currently working on the prototype versions of the synchronization controllers, we have had to make compromises in the design, but have at the same time identified ways to improve the next-generation controllers.

4.1 Improved PCI Interface

The biggest improvement to the synchronization controllers would be to use a more flexible device for PCI interfacing and remove the mailbox interface of the AMCC 5933. We originally planned to use an Altera FPGA to implement the interface, but instead chose to postpone this implementation and instead concentrate on issues with the ring controllers.

However, using an FPGA to implement the PCI interface has key advantages; it would be possible to map every semaphore to a unique address in the synchronization controller's PCI address space. In addition, the type of the operation could be encoded by the PCI bus's command (C/BE#) lines. As a result, no data would need to be sent across the PCI bus to the synchronization controller.

Instead, only the address of the appropriate lock and the type of operation (clear or test-and-set) to be performed would need to traverse the PCI bus, and this could be accomplished in a single PCI clock cycle. The synchronization controller would respond to a memory reference in the semaphore address space simply by performing the appropriate operation and subsequently writing the result back to a response buffer. Furthermore, no IRQn signal would be needed as the synchronization controller would immediately be interrupted by a read or write access to an address within the semaphore address space, and not time would be needed to reset the IRQn signal.

4.2 Serial Controller Improvements

The major improvement to be made to the G-link chips is the eradication of the ECL I/O. HP is currently developing a TTL version of this chipset that would significantly simplify our PCB design. However, with the exception of translation-buffer propagation delay, no improved performance would be realized. Buffer delay has not been an issue up to this point.

4.3 Improve FPGA Performance

While we are pleased with the projected 50-MHz operating speed of our logic devices (and the associated speed of the ring), we would still like to drive the ring faster. With the devices we are currently using, this may not be easy. We plan to try to hand-optimize for the Altera devices or alternatively port our HDL design to another vendor's devices. Our goal is to operate the logic device at the maximum G-Link operating speed in order to realize the 1.2-Gbps ring speed.

4.4 Open Questions

While we have identified that high-speed semaphore operations are important in NSM clusters, we have not investigated how many locks are sufficient for the environment. Since the G-Link hardware uses 16-bit packets and we provide an input and output buffer for each node, we currently provide $32n$ locks, where n is the number of nodes in the cluster.

With on-board RAM available in the FPGA devices, buffering additional slots on a synchronization controller is a simple matter. However, each buffered slot adds additional latency to the synchronization ring. Clearly, there is a tradeoff between optimal semaphore-operation speed and the appropriate number of locks. We plan to investigate this matter in order to determine the maximum buffer size required by each synchronization controller.

In order to maintain our focus on the fundamental hardware/software development issues, our software currently provides direct user-level access to the synchronization hardware. This is possible since we assume that no node is running more than one parallel application at a time. In the future we plan implement the software as a kernel-level process that is capable of supporting multiple parallel applications on s single cluster.

Thus far, we have not considered error handling on the ring. While the G-Link chipset has a low BER (10^{-14}), we have provided no method for error detection. Furthermore, even simple parity checks for each slot would reduce the number of available semaphores that are being transferred and further reduce ring throughput. We plan to analyze the tradeoffs between various error detection and correction methods and their impact on synchronization-ring performance.

5 Related Research

Over the past decade, several systems have been developed to provide a shared memory abstraction in a physically distributed environment. In these systems the solution to the distributed shared memory (DSM) problem has been implemented in both hardware and software.

Apollo Domain [5] is one of the earliest systems that employs the DSM paradigm to assure consistency of shared objects in a LAN environment. To assure consistency of replicated copies of an object, a two-level approach is adopted. The lower level detects concurrence violations using a time-stamp based version-number scheme for each object. The higher level provides an object locking mechanism. Several types of lock modes are provided including a multiple-readers/single-writer lock. Lock and unlock requests for remote objects are always sent to the home node. A lock request that is granted returns the current version number of the lock. This information is used to remove stale pages from the requesting node's main memory . The unlock operation forces modified pages back to the home node before the lock is released. In Domain, lock requests are not queued; if the lock is currently in use, then the requester is denied access to the lock and must retry later.

Clouds [6] is a distributed operating system using a DSM Controller (DSMC) at each node. The DSMC owns and maintains the segments that are created in the node, provides a set of primitives for segment access and transport, and is responsible for preserving the consistency of the segments that it owns. DSMC uses a lock-based protocol for coherence maintenance that unifies data synchronization and transport. It supports both exclusive (read- write) locks as well as shared (read-only) locks for segment access. Upon lock request, the owner DSMC encloses the requested segment in the message that grants the lock request, thus providing synchronization for free. A segment may be requested by a thread in one of the four modes: read-only, read-write, weak-read, and none. Read-only mode provides a non-exclusive lock on the segment while read-write mode provides an exclusive lock on the segment. Mode none gives exclusive access to the segment without locking the segment, i.e., any new request would result in the segment being yanked away to service the request. These three modes provide sequentially consistent memory semantics for the nodes accessing the segments.

Agora [7] is a system that is built on top of Mach [8] with the specific intent of providing shared memory semantics in a loosely-coupled system. The Agora system allows processes to share structured data, e.g., abstract data types across heterogeneous architectures over a LAN. It also provides simple locks to synchronize access to shared data. To provide sharing across the network, the shared data structures are stored in the shared memory of the process that created the data structure. The system expects that synchronization is implemented orthogonally using semaphores to guard against stale accesses.

Memnet [9] is a shared token-ring network. It provides loose coupling to the processors of a distributed multiprocessor system. There are three distinctive features of this project: first, it allows a granularity of access (32-byte chunks) finer than a page; second, it employs dedicated hardware (Memnet device) to service remote memory accesses; third, it exploits the features of a special-purpose token ring network to implement a write-invalidate-style cache protocol. Given that there is an appreciable software overhead for remote access, dedicated hardware is almost a necessity to assure acceptable performance in DSM systems.

Systran Corporation's SCRAMNet [10] and VMIC's Reflective Memory Network [11] are examples of commercial products that provide shared memory to a workstation cluster. However, both of these products are aimed at applications where strong memory consistency is not required, and as such, do not provide low-level locking mechanisms.

We expect the NSM approach to hardware-lock implementation to outperform the aforementioned approaches. The previous approaches are either too software intensive, run over a general-purpose LAN with large overhead, or both. By minimizing software interaction and communications overhead, NSM semaphore operations are hoped to be nearly as fast as semaphore operations on shared-memory multi-processors.

6 Conclusion

In this paper we have presented a method for implementing shared binary semaphores in an NSM environment. The fundamental idea of the approach is to circulate the semaphores, each represented by a bit, around a continuously operating high-speed communications ring. Any node in the NSM cluster can modify a particular bit as that bit passes the node. Because of the dedicated nature of the approach, and the high-speed operation of the ring, this approach is significantly faster than using message-passing software on top of lower-speed, higher-overhead communications networks.

We have discussed the operation of the individual components of the synchronization controller and have offered refinements. Currently, we are completing the details of prototype PCB layout of the NSM controllers which contain the synchronization controllers. We have used readily available commercial components to implement the controllers, and hope to port the p4 macros and PVM to an NSM cluster within the next year.

References

1. Architecture Technology Corporation, "Parallel Processing with Clustered Workstations," SBIR Phase I Technical Report for NSF Award No. DMI-9360753, Nov. 15, 1994.

2. S. Ramanujan, J. Bonney, and K. Thurber, "Network Shared Memory: A New Approach for Clustering Workstations for Parallel Processing," Proc. of the Fourth IEEE International Symposium on High-Performance Distributed Computing, Aug. 1995.

3. AMCC S5933 Data Book.. Applied Micro Circuits Corporation, 1996.

4. "Low Cost gigabit Rate Transmit/Receive Chip Set." HDMP-1012/HDMP-1014 Data Book.

5. Leach, et al, "The Architecture of an Integrated Local Network." *IEEE Journal on Selected Areas in Communications*, 1(5):842-857, November 1983.

6. Dasgupta, R. LeBlanc, M. Ahamad, U. Ramachandran. "The Clouds Distributed Operating System." *IEEE Computer* , April 1991.

7. Bisiani, A. Forin. "Multilingual Parallel Programming of Heterogeneous Machines." *IEEE Transactions on Computers*, 37(0):930-945, August 1988.

8. Rashid, et al. "Machine-Independent Virtual Memory Management for Paged Uniprocessor and Multiprocessor Architectures." *Proceedings of the Second International Conference on Architectural Support for Programming Languages and Operating Systems* , pages 31-39, 1987.

9. Delp, A. Sethi, D. Farber. "An Analysis of Memnet: An Experiment in High-Speed Shared-Memory Local Networking." *Computer Communication Review*, volume 18, pp. 165-174, Stanford, California, August 1988. ACM SIGCOMM.

10. Systran Corporation, http://www.systran.com/scramnet.htm

11. VME Microsystems International Corporation, "Reflective Memory Network," October, 1995. Corporate White Paper.

Synchronization Support
in I/O Adapter Based SCI Clusters

Knut Omang

Department of Informatics,
University of Oslo, Norway
Email: knuto@ifi.uio.no

Abstract. This paper examines synchronization support of two generations of SCI adapters from Dolphin Interconnect Solutions and compares the functionality to similar support on Digital's Memory Channel. Memory Channel enforces sequential consistency across the interconnect, while SCI allows store reordering. This gives SCI a potential performance payoff by allowing more flexible pipelining of data through the interconnect. The lower number of ordering constraints also reduces hardware complexity, but moves the complexity to software. For a straightforward implementation of message passing this overhead is significant. A new software algorithm, the valid flag algorithm, is introduced to improve this situation. A new hardware lock support mechanism is proposed to facilitate efficient locks in absence of lock support on the I/O bus. Performance of the simple message passing protocol is compared to the suggested valid flag protocol. The valid flag protocol reduces latency of a small message by 50% and also increases throughput for pipelined, small messages significantly.

1 Introduction

SCI (Scalable Coherent Interface[20]) is an IEEE standard for high speed communication over short distances. The SCI protocol supports implementation of hardware supported distributed shared memory, and is with its (optional) cache coherence support originally intended as an extension to the system bus.

The SCI interfaces discussed in this paper are connected to the I/O bus of each node in the cluster and provides *uncached* SCI accesses, (denoted non-coherent read/writes in the SCI standard). Neither the I/O bus nor the SCI to I/O bus interface has support for the SCI cache coherence protocol. This limits the usefulness of shared memory regions for traditional shared memory applications, since individual accesses to shared locations physically allocated in remote memory are much slower than accesses to the local memory or cache.

Dolphin Interconnect Solutions has SCI interfaces for the Sbus[5] and PCI[19] I/O buses. The interface boards are implemented around an internal bus, the B-link, which separates the host interface from the interface to SCI (see figure 1). Both cards use the same SCI interface, the LinkController (LC-1) chip, but have very different host interfaces. Low level performance of the Sbus/SCI board is presented in [17].

Digital Equipment Corporation has announced Memory Channel[7] as a high speed interconnect for the PCI bus. Both SCI and Memory Channel differ from standard network technologies like Ethernet and ATM and from most other off-the-shelf network

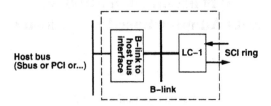

Fig. 1. An SCI interface board.

adapters by the support for direct access to remote memory through ordinary load and store instructions. Operating system support for memory mapped I/O makes it possible to export memory between user programs running on different hosts in the network. Once mappings are set up, user level programs can communicate across the interconnect without the overhead of operating system calls. Such communication can take place with much lower latencies than possible with ordinary network protocol stacks.

To prevent race conditions and inconsistency, processors sharing memory regions must coordinate their access to shared locations. Typically, underlying hardware features are hidden by an additional level of abstraction through a set of library functions. This paper investigates different implementations of two such abstractions on SCI:

- A basic message passing protocol between two uniquely identified parties, a sender and a receiver.
- Mutual exclusion locks that guarantees exclusive access to shared resources.

The paper is divided into two parts. In the first part two peer-to-peer message passing protocols are detailed, a simple remote write push algorithm (denoted Algorithm 1) and a new protocol (Algorithm 2), an algorithm for faster message passing in SCI shared memory in presence of store reordering. Interconnect error semantics and implementation of the algorithms on UltraSparc are investigated. The second part discusses implementation of mutual exclusion with and without special hardware support. A proposal for a hardware extension to support mutual exclusion locks on I/O buses without support for read/modify/write cycles is presented. Memory Channel is chosen for comparison as a technology with similar support for shared memory and which is reasonably well documented in other work.

2 Synchronization for Message Passing

A simple protocol for exchanging messages using direct memory accesses from remote nodes can be implemented by the following algorithm:

Algorithm 1 *Remote write push. Messages are queued in a ring buffer structure in the receiver's memory. A single read and write pointer is updated by the reader and writer respectively:*

1. *The writer writes a message into the next available buffer in the receiver's memory. The write pointer is located in the reader's memory for efficiency.*
2. *The writer updates the remote write pointer telling the remote node that a message has arrived.*
3. *The reader will if necessary spin on the write pointer (with some backoff strategy to avoid wasting too many CPU cycles) until the notification arrives through the pointer update.*
4. *The reader now have the message in local memory and can decide to pass a pointer to the application or to copy the message to a user buffer.*
5. *When the processing of the message is completed the reader updates the read pointer by issuing a remote store, notifying the writer that this buffer is available for reuse. The read pointer is located in the writer's memory.*

The invariant that makes this work without any race conditions is the fact that only one processor updates the write pointer and only one processor updates the read pointer.

2.1 Algorithm 1 on Sbus/SCI

SCI allows writes to arrive in another order than they were submitted. This is possible because a receiver on the SCI link may not be able to receive an SCI packet at a particular moment. If so, the sender link controller gets a busy notification and will automatically retransmit the packet. This feature is called busy retry in the SCI standard. In the meantime a later write may have successfully arrived. Another possible cause of reordering is that SCI also allows multiple routes to the same destination. During normal operation packets are never lost.

If Algorithm 1 were implemented naively for Sbus/SCI, there is a chance that whole or parts of the message would arrive after the pointer is updated. In this case, to guarantee consistency, a store barrier is needed between the writes for the message and the write needed to update the pointer. On Sbus/SCI store barrier semantics are offered through remote read operations, which are guaranteed to stall until all previous writes from the same node have completed. The implementation is pictured in figure 2a. The length of each bar in figure 2 denotes the latency for this operation to complete. These latencies are schematic and are for comparison made relative to the latency of minimal stores on the different interconnects. Measured 4 byte remote store latencies are presented in section 2.5.

A drawback with the store barrier semantics of reads is that even unrelated reads will have to stall the processor for all issued writes to complete. This makes remote reads very expensive in terms of CPU usage. The read transaction will not be issued across the B-link (see figure 1) until responses from all the write requests have arrived.

2.2 Algorithm 1 on PCI/SCI

The SCI/PCI interface introduces a concept of special *streams* in the PCI interface. The PCI interface has a set of dedicated write streams and read streams that can be configured for different modes of operation. A write stream is a 64 byte buffer in the host interface that can gather up to 64 bytes of data to enable sending only a single 64 byte

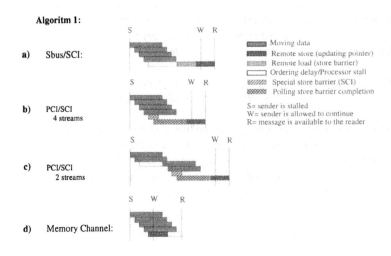

Fig. 2. Message passing in shared memory, Algorithm 1

SCI transaction as a result of multiple smaller transfers. The stream's operation is based on the addresses of the data to be sent. If the address is next to and within the same 64 byte aligned 64 byte address block as the previous request, the data is gathered in the stream, otherwise the stream will flush and generate SCI transactions of appropriate size(s) for the gathered data.

A stream will never have more than a single outstanding SCI transaction. This has the cost that stores through the same stream do not get pipelined. Thus, to get performance, the SCI/PCI interface includes an option to multiplex writes to several streams in a round-robin fashion based on the target addresses. The stream to be used for a particular address is handled by the hardware once setup. Figure 2b and 2c shows the situation using 4 and 2 streams respectively. In figure 2b the four data transfers can arrive in any order. In figure 2c a data transfer may only get reordered with respect to ongoing transfers from the other stream. Thus even in presence of multiple simultaneous users of the same stream sequential consistency[6] will be maintained for stores through a particular stream. Although writes from the same stream arrive in order, writes from *different* streams at the sender can arrive reordered. Thus, the PCI/SCI interface implements a solution that provides better pipelining than with total ordering, yet a stricter store ordering than in the Sbus/SCI case. The streams concept is also described in [19].

A special store barrier operation is available through writes to a specific register. This register will keep track of all outstanding writes at the time of the issue of the store barrier. The sender can then poll the barrier to see when all writes are completed, at which time the write pointer can be updated. This saves the application the delay of one SCI transaction compared to the Sbus/SCI case (the remote load) and provides an option for optimizing by utilizing cycles on the sender side to do other work.

2.3   Algorithm 1 on Memory Channel

Memory Channel has enforced a sequentially consistent memory model, so Algorithm 1 can be implemented directly. All operations can take advantage of pipelining, and the sending processor does not have to wait for any remote operations to complete. On the receiver side, due to enforcement of sequential consistency, completion of the last write will be delayed until the previous (possibly larger) write has completed. See figure 2d. Algorithm 1 adapted for Sbus/SCI is significantly slower (and more CPU demanding) than the plain version for Memory Channel. This is not counting the store barrier effects of remote loads issued by unrelated processes on the sender node. The situation is somewhat better for PCI/SCI, but still the full latency of the final remote store contributes to the latency of the message passing. On Memory Channel the hardware enforces ordering of stores through the interconnect while still maintaining a fair degree of pipelining (see [8] for details). Thus Algorithm 1 will perform significantly better on Memory Channel than on any of the SCI versions.

2.4   Algorithm 2: Reducing SCI Latency by Using a Valid flag

Low latency of minimal short messages is very important to many applications. A typical citation for interconnects are the minimal MPI[14] send/receive latency. In the SCI case the write ordering semantics makes getting performance close to the hardware latency limits harder, but not impossible.

An algorithm that gives Sbus/SCI similar minimal latency for MPI message passing as Memory Channel (relative to the minimal latency and pipelining capability) can be formulated at the cost of using 1 byte of each 64 byte of message as a valid flag:

Algorithm 2 *Message passing in shared memory optimized to work with store reordering:*

1. *The last byte of each 64 byte buffer is initially set to zero by the reader corresponding to the fact that the data in the buffer is invalid.*
2. *The message is written, in case of 64 byte stores the message can be no longer than 63 bytes, the last byte being the valid flag. The valid flag is set to 1 in the same remote store operation.*
3. *The reader will spin on the next unused message location and discover that a message has arrived when the flag value becomes 1.*

This concept is easily generalized to larger messages by using a flag for each 63 byte submessage. This has the additional cost of a valid flag and some assembling and reassembling of each 63 byte submessage. The behavior of Algorithm 2 is depicted in figure 3. Algorithm 2 is also useful in the PCI/SCI case but at a different granularity. Due to the sequential consistency of stores originating from the same stream, a message in an N stream setup can be viewed as N logical submessages that consist of 64 byte blocks strided $(N - 1) * 64$ bytes, each traveling over a a single stream. To ensure consistency, only the last 64 bytes of each submessage will need a valid flag.

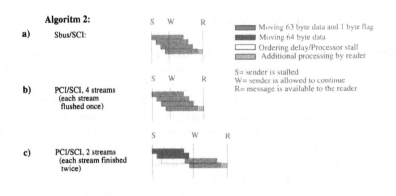

Fig. 3. Message passing in shared memory, Algorithm 2

2.5 Performance

Table 1 shows a 8.9μs latency of an implementation of the trivial 63 byte case of Algorithm 2. This represents the achievable latency for an optimized implementation of a message passing library like MPI. A similar 7 byte message case takes 6.9μs. The result for Algorithm 1 is obtained using 64 byte stores from/to aligned addresses. From the improved 2.6μs latency of 4 byte stores, the latency of a 63 byte message using Algorithm 2 should be expected to get below 6.9μs for PCI/SCI.

Algorithm 2 has been implemented for 7, 63, 126 and 189 byte messages. Achievable throughput of pipelined messages for the two protocols for the Sbus interface for different message sizes are presented in figure 4. The figure clearly demonstrates the positive effect the removal of the remote load (store barrier) has on achieved pipelining.

2.6 Implementation for Sbus/SCI on the UltraSparc Architecture

The UltraSparc facilitates 64 byte operations by an instruction set extension for block stores, the stda instruction[15, 23]. Block loads (ldda instruction) and stores bypasses the caches by loading and storing directly to/from 8 doubleword floating point registers simultaneously. The instructions requires data to be aligned to a 64 byte boundary and the doubleword registers to be a continuous sequence starting on an 8-register boundary. An UltraSparc extension for memory realignment (the alignaddress and faligndata instructions) can be utilized to allow copying from an arbitrary alignment to a different alignment without any additional copying (data is realigned inside registers).

Implementing Algorithm 2 requires an encoding of the valid flag for each 63 byte of data in the sender and a decoding (realigning) again in the receiver. Alignment in the sender can be done in the same copy operation as is needed anyway to copy data out on the I/O bus. On the receiver side extra overhead to reassemble the 63 byte messages with flags into a continuous message is needed. If user buffers and alignments are given by the user, in general the receiver end copying is needed anyway, and can then be combined

Platform	Interconnect	Protocol	msg.size	Latency(μs)
167 Mhz Ultra-1	Dolphin Sbus-2	rem.store	4	3.9
133 Mhz Pentium	Dolphin PCI [19]	rem.store	4	2.6
167 Mhz Ultra-1	Dolphin Sbus-2	alg.1	64	17.2
167 Mhz Ultra-1	Dolphin Sbus-2	alg.2	63	8.9
167 Mhz Ultra-1	Dolphin Sbus-2	alg.2	7	6.9
AlphaServer 4100	Memory Channel [8]	rem.store	4	2.9
AlphaServer 4100	Memory Channel [8]	MPI	?	6.9

Table 1. Latencies of remote stores compared to a full message passing algorithm

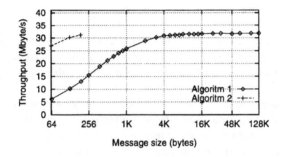

Fig. 4. Throughput of pipelining many messages for Algorithm 1 and 2 for Sbus/SCI.

with the reassembling. Thus, for these cases the extra CPU overhead by the valid flag algorithm is minimal.

Implementing a fully optimized version for Sbus of all cases of different alignment in receiver and sender requires a significant amount of assembly programming. The UltraSparc block load and store instructions are non-blocking, and two block loads and two stores can be pipelined. To move data at full speed, the program must work on three sets of 8 registers at the same time. This comes in addition to all the special cases of alignment and skewed register usage and creates a large number of corner cases at startup and finish.

The implementation of both algorithms uses a single level of copying (in addition to the necessary copying across the interconnect) and allows completely asynchronous operation as long as there is more to receive for the receiver and more available buffer space for the sender. The implementation is poll based and executes completely in user space. It also supports an arbitrary number of simultaneous connections operating in parallel. Both implementations have been tested with multiple reader and writer light weight processes, with thread yield as "backoff" strategy for each individual thread.

2.7 The Impact of Error Semantics for the Interconnects

Both SCI and Memory Channel guarantees either no delivery or correct delivery of each programmed I/O operation, and errors are very infrequent. For SCI errors will typically be due to an improperly connected cable or broken hardware.

In case of a remote store failure on SCI, due to possible store reordering it might be that subsequent, correct stores actually gets through SCI before an error is discovered. The Sbus/SCI implementation has a single error counter that gets incremented upon failures. In order to guarantee complete delivery of the whole sequence of stores, the message passing algorithm would have to check the local error counter before starting transmission, and then recheck the counter after transmission is completed. If any errors have occurred it might be the case that this error occurred in this process' writes (but it might as well has been in someone else's transmission). The PCI/SCI streams concept allows for separate error checking for each stream, giving a more fine grained error handling support.

In both the SCI cases errors can be discovered by software at the sender side as soon as the SCI write response messages for all the involved message parts have arrived. In order to be able to let the *reader* take action upon failure, either signaling or a timeout will be needed.

Algorithm 2 turns out to be very well suited for implementing a recovery scheme for interconnect fault tolerance on Sbus/SCI. Fault tolerance can easily be implemented in a system with two separate interconnects (two adapters in each node). The sender can periodically check the error counter, and at the same time save the current value of the read pointer, that is, commit the stores. In cases of errors (the error counter has changed since last check) the sender can just switch to the backup interconnect, check the read pointer and retransmit the messages sent, but still not processed by the reader. Even though parts of this information may already have arrived correctly and in the meantime been processed, no harm is done as long as the reader is not allowed to reuse the buffers (nil out the valid flags) before those stores are committed. In this way no out-of-band communication is needed at all, in fact the reader does not even have to know that anything went wrong. This simplifies the reader semantics and also reduces recovery time.

Upon errors on Memory Channel, the hardware will guarantee that no subsequent stores will arrive at all. This is easy accomplishable since Memory Channel already guarantees sequential consistency, disabling further operation until the connection is reset by software. Errors are discovered by software at the reader side and will then have to be communicated explicitly back to the sender. Thus, in all cases errors can be discovered quickly, but since errors are discovered on the reader side on Memory Channel, out-of-band communication between the two parties to communicate the errors back to the sender will make Memory Channel recovery somewhat more expensive.

3 Synchronization by Mutual Exclusion

Global synchronization is needed when multiple nodes can access the same shared memory area simultaneously. To avoid data races mutual exclusion is necessary. The modern

	Sbus-1	Sbus-2
lock:	write b[i]	write b[i]
	write x	write x
	read y	read y
	write y	write y
	read x	read x
unlock:	write y	write y
		read dummy
	write b[i]	write b[i]
		read dummy

Table 2. Necessary access pattern for Lamports algorithm to acquire/release a lock on two version of Sbus/SCI adapters for node i when no contention.

way of getting to a lock primitive is by using hardware supplied special atomic memory operations like for instance compare/swap. Sbus/SCI does not provide any such support. PCI/SCI provides hardware support based on PCI locks, which unfortunately is a part of the PCI standard that many PCI implementations do not support. This problem can be avoided with a minor hardware change which is suggested later in this section.

3.1 Mutual Exclusion in Absence of Hardware Support

In the Sbus/SCI case the adapter provides no hardware atomic synchronization support. Thus, in order to get mutual exclusion either some mutual exclusion algorithm based on only load/stores or on message passing with a lock server must be used. On the first version of the Sbus/SCI card, this approach was examined and different schemes evaluated. Results including code for both algorithms are presented in [16], and concludes that for this early version of the SCI adapter card (Sbus-1) it was possible to achieve mutual exclusion in the non-contending case in about 1/8th of the time needed to accomplish the same synchronization using message passing and a lock server. For the scalable algorithm, Lamports algorithm[11–13], it took a total of 7 remote stores/loads to acquire and release a lock. In that version of the adapter cards, ordering among writes *to the same physical memory* was guaranteed to be maintained across SCI due to the fact that each node only was able to have a single outstanding transaction at a time (limited by the amount of buffers available).

In the second generation SCI adapter cards (Sbus-2) even stores to the same memory can arrive out of order. The synchronization algorithms proposed by Dijkstra[4] and Lamport all implicitly assume that stores become visible to remote processors in program order (although stores from different nodes may be seen in different orders by the different nodes). Thus, as for message passing, the out-of-order SCI stores cause additional complexity. Since a load has the semantic of a store barrier (will not complete until all preceding stores from the same adapter is completed) most of the cases where reordering of stores could have been a problem are already taken care of by the algorithm. The potential problem lies in the cases of possibly consecutive stores from the same node.

Operation	C pseudo code
MASK_SWAP(cond, val)	new = (val & cond) | (old & ~cond)
FETCH_ADD(val)	new = old + val
BOUNDED_ADD(cond, val)	new = (old == cond) ? (val + old) : (old)
COMPARE_SWAP(cond, val)	new = (old == cond) ? val : old
WRAP_ADD(cond, val)	new = (old != arg) ? old + val : val

Table 3. Lock operations available on PCI/SCI

The sequence of stores needed for the Sbus-1 and Sbus-2 cases are shown in table 2. The first extra dummy read in the unlock operation is needed because otherwise someone else might read the new value of b[i], write to y as a result of attempting to acquire the lock which seems fully released to them according to y. When finally the unlock update of y arrives, it will overwrite the other processor's value and possibly allow for two nodes believing they have the lock simultaneously. The second dummy read is needed to protect b[i] from being corrupted by a late update from unlock that was bypassed by the write to b[i] as the result of the next attempt by this node to acquire the lock.

3.2 Hardware Supported Locks

Typically, synchronization operations on memory buses are issued using special CPU instructions. Unfortunately, in the case of I/O adapter based interconnects the host I/O buses seldom supports such instructions, that is, the CPU is free to issue these instructions in I/O space, but they are not visible to the I/O adapters. According to [8] Memory Channel avoids this problem by providing locks implicitly through utilizing the built in store order and other properties of the underlying reflective memory technology. With this implementation mutual exclusion can be achieved with only 1 remote store.

The SCI standard provides the locksb (lock selected byte) transaction type to enable implementations of hardware assisted locks. The PCI/SCI interface uses this transaction type to provide all the common atomic load/store operations. The available operations are listed in table 3. On PCI implementations that supports the PCI lock instructions, this functionality can be used directly to support mutual exclusion locks in the standard way giving similarly efficient locks as those provided by Memory Channel. The problem, however is that most PCI implementations do not support the use of PCI locks despite the presence of locks in the PCI standard.

Proposal for an Implementation of SCI Locks Without I/O bus Support. To enforce efficient locks despite lack of hardware support for locks on the I/O bus, the atomic properties of the lock operations must be ensured by the card instead of the I/O bus. Such an implementation is pictured in figure 5. An implementation that does not limit the number of available locks can be made by giving special semantics to certain regions of virtual addresses interpreted by the card. Writes to addresses in these mappings are interpreted as lock commands executed on designated memory allocated on one of the

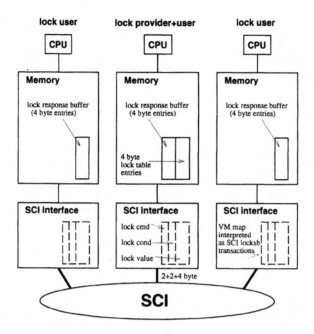

Fig. 5. A possible efficient implementation of SCI locks in absence of special support on the I/O bus

nodes. Each node keeps a separate set of memory locations, a *lock response buffer*, in local memory for the result of the lock operations.

A general SCI lock operation will contain an operation to perform (like those listed in table 3), the test condition and a value to store depending on the test. This information can easily be packed into an eight byte store where 2 bytes are used for the command option, 2 bytes are used for the condition and 4 bytes are used for the value. The PCI/SCI adapter will interpret this message, send the appropriate lock transaction, and when the transaction completes, save the result into the lock response buffer. The lock user can then poll the lock response buffer to see the result of the lock acquisition attempt. On the lock provider side, in the absence of atomic read/write cycles on the bus, the adapter itself will have to perform a read conditionally followed by a write itself and then depending on condition return the appropriate response back across SCI. This concept will work provided all accesses to the lock table are service by the lock provider adapter (see figure 5).

For the PCI/SCI adapter, to support this new functionality, minor hardware changes will be needed (the host bus interface is an ASIC), but the basic support (simple arithmetic) is already available. In the Sbus case, arithmetic support functions is not available, so the addition is more substantial, but the implementation is FPGA based, making changes less difficult. The lock implementations not requiring hardware support takes an average of around 50 μs on Sbus/SCI with no contention. The hardware changes suggested here have a potential to reduce this overhead to less than 8 μs. Efficient mutual exclusion is critical to the performance of for instance transaction handling in databases, an expected major application of distributed shared memory clusters.

4   Related work

Similar techniques to the valid flag in Algorithm 2 have been used in several hardware implementations. A good example is the Tera multiprocessor[1]. Tera and its predecessors Horizon and HEP have a full/empty bit associated with each memory location. This corresponds to the valid flag of Algorithm 2, but at a different granularity. Actually, Tera uses 4 extra bits for each memory word to distinguish between different memory states. One of these bits is the full/empty bit. In [3], extra cache line bits are used in a similar way. All these uses require special hardware, thus cannot be used in clusters based on off-the-shelf hardware. The valid flag algorithm however, is generally applicable to all shared memories where stores can be reordered on its way to memory, but at some extra processing cost and space usage.

The impact of memory ordering on the performance delivered to applications has also been pointed out in the Telegraphos work[10]. Telegraphos provides remote stores in a similar way as Dolphin SCI, but like Memory Channel guarantees that these stores are not reordered.

Technologies that are similar to Sbus/SCI and PCI/SCI in providing direct access to remote memory through off-the-shelf I/O adapters are Tandem's ServerNet[9] and the previously discussed Memory Channel[7, 8]. Memory Channel is based on reflective memory with separate write only and read only mappings. A store to a write only location is reflected in all participating nodes' local read only mapping of the same memory. ServerNet has an architecture even closer to Dolphin SCI. A detailed comparison could be an interesting option for future work, but requires more technical information about ServerNet than currently available. As the SCI adapters, I/O adapter based ServerNet provides shared memory by read- and writable I/O mappings to a specific remote memory region. Read and writes to these mappings will be directly reflected in the remote memory.

Several other works focus on providing lower latency of message passing to applications on clusters of workstations. A few examples of relatively comparable numbers from clustering with other off-the-shelf I/O adapters are presented in table 4. These adapters have no builtin hardware support for shared memory, but the low latency protocols U-Net[21] and Myrinet Fast Messages (FM)[18] use virtual memory mappings and alternate programming of the network device to reduce the operating system involvement. This requires attention to avoid compromising security by allowing one process to overwrite another process' data. In the SCI case, the shared memory mappings makes it easy, since each sender/receiver process pair can have completely independent data structures with access controlled by virtual memory protection. According to [24], Myrinet FM only support single process access to the network. U-Net uses the programmability of the devices and the device driver implementation to manage different device contexts transparently to different user processes. This requires extra operating

Platform	Interconnect	Protocol	Latency(μs)
133 MHz Pentium	DC21140 Fast Ethernet	U-Net[24]	30
Sparc-20	Fore ATM SBA-200	U-Net[21]	33
Sparc-20	Myrinet[2]	FM[18]	25

Table 4. One-way latency of low latency message passing protocols on some message passing technologies

system intervention to multiplex the use of the device, but much less than for implementations where every single message is sent and received through system calls.

Active Messages[22], a general mechanism for message passing on different hardware, emphasizes the technique of hiding latency by sending a part of the message and include a handle that provides enough information to extract the rest of the message from the interconnect. This technique is particularly useful when the interconnect efficiently supports pull based messaging. As discussed earlier, due to the implicit store barrier semantics, remote loads are much less efficient than stores on Sbus/SCI. In addition the largest possible remote load is 8 byte while remote stores can be as large as 64 bytes. Pull based messaging would then require the receiver to send a request back to the sender for the rest of the data with the increased latency this would give. The PCI/SCI board on the other hand provides options for prefetching of data, and large, pipelined remote loads. This should make the PCI/SCI board particularly interesting as a hardware platform for efficient implementation of Active Messages, an interesting topic for further work.

5 Conclusion

The way the hardware supports synchronization is of considerable importance when hardware performance is to be brought to user applications. This paper takes a closer look at the support for two types of synchronization on two different SCI adapters, and compares to similar support on Digital's Memory Channel. Both implementation of synchronization for message passing and for synchronization for mutual exclusion is affected by the weak memory model of SCI, where stores can be reordered across the interconnect. The bare hardware performance numbers (latencies of remote stores) are useful to show how well the hardware is able to shuffle data. Weaker orderings simplifies the hardware and gives easier scalability, but additional software is required to get failsafe application level performance with similar latencies and throughput. This paper shows that with some additional programming, message passing can be implemented efficiently even in presence of store reordering. This is achieved at a cost of some more software complexity as well as some CPU overhead. For the UltraSparc the extra CPU overhead gets minimized due to the hardware support for fast data moving and alignment.

Results show a significant reduction of latency, from 17.2 μs down to 8.9 μs for small messages, and an increase from 6 to 25 Mbytes/s in achievable throughput for many consecutive small messages. The analysis shows that error recovery and fault tolerant communication is possible, and that recovery (by switching to another interconnect) can be done very quickly, and with somewhat less delay than on Memory Channel.

Mutual exclusion without hardware support is a well known problem. A complex algorithm with a sequence of carefully applied loads and stores is required even for sequentially consistent memories. Such algorithms become even more complex and incurs higher latencies in presence of store reordering. This fact clearly justifies the extra effort to get suitable hardware support. The broadcast capability, the way reflective memory works, and the unfortunate lack of I/O bus lock implementations gives Memory Channel an advantage over PCI/SCI. However, this paper also demonstrates that SCI locks with minor hardware modifications could be made to work with similar efficiency as Memory Channel locks. Finally, it should be remarked that this paper only discusses problems related to synchronization, and that a complete and fair comparison will require closer examination of other properties of these interconnects.

6 Acknowledgments

I would like to thank Satyanarayana Nishtala for the inspiring discussions at Sun that gave me the initial idea to this work, and Greg Onufer for patiently answering all my questions related to the UltraSparc instruction set and debugging of assembly code. Thanks also to Haakon Bryhni, Øystein Gran Larsen, Stein Gjessing and the anonymous referees for valuable comments on different earlier versions of the paper. The implementational and experimental work was done during my stay at Sun Microsystems in 1996. Numerous people at Dolphin have answered questions and contributed in discussions related to the different versions of the SCI interfaces, most notably Bjørn Dag Johnsen, Marius Liaaen and Arne Sudgarden.

References

1. Gail Alverson, Brian Koblenz, Robert Alverson, Allan Porterfield, David Callahan, and Burton Smith. Exploiting Heterogeneous Parallelism on a Multithreaded Multiprocessor. Avaliable at http://www.tera.com/tera/ftp.html.

2. Nanette J. Boden, Danny Cohen, Robert E. Felderman, Alan E. Kulawik, Charles E. Seitz, Jakov N. Seizovic, and Wen-King Su. Myrinet: A Gigabit-per-Second Local Area Network. *IEEE Micro*, pages 29–36, February 1996.

3. David R. Cheriton and Robert A. Kutter. Optimized Memory-Based Messaging: Leveraging the Memory System for High-Performance Communication. Technical Report CS-TR-94-1506, Stanford University, 1994.

4. E.W. Dijkstra. Solution to a Problem in Concurrent Programming Control. *Communications of the ACM*, 8(9):569, September 1965.

5. Dolphin Interconnect Solutions. *SBus-to-SCI Adapter User's Guide, DIS303 SBus-2*, 1995.

6. Kourosh Gharachorloo, Daniel Lenoski, James Laudon, Philip Gibbons, Anoop Gupta, and John Hennessy. Memory Consistency and Event Ordering in Scalable Shared-Memory Multiprocessors. In *Proceedings of 17th International Symposium on Computer Architecture*, pages 15–26, May 1990.

7. Richard B. Gillett. Memory Channel for PCI. *IEEE Micro*, pages 12–18, February 1996.

172

8. Richard B. Gillett and Richard Kaufmann. Experience Using the First-Generation Memory Channel for PCI Network. In *Proceedings of Hot Interconnects IV*, pages 205–214, August 1996.

9. Robert W. Horst. TNet: A Reliable System Area Network. *IEEE Micro*, February 1995.

10. Manolis Katevenis. Telegraphos: High-Speed Communication Architecture for Parallel and Distributed Computer Systems. Technical Report TR-123, FORTH-ICS, Crete, Greece, May 1994.

11. Leslie Lamport. The Mutual Exclusion Problem: Part I – A theory of Interprocess Communication. *Journal of the ACM*, 33(2):313–326, April 1986.

12. Leslie Lamport. The Mutual Exclusion Problem: Part II – Statement and Solutions. *Journal of the ACM*, 33(2):327–348, April 1986.

13. Leslie Lamport. A Fast Mutual Exclusion Algoritm. *ACM Transactions on Computer Systems*, 5(1):1–11, February 1987.

14. Message Passing Interface Forum. MPI: A Message-Passing Interface Standard. (draft obtainable by ftp from info.mcs.anl.gov, directory pub/mpi), May 1994. Version 1.0.

15. Sun Microsystems. *UltraSparc Programmer Reference Manual*. SPARC Technology Business, 1995. Part No.:STP1030-UG.

16. Knut Omang. Preliminary Performance results from SALMON, a Multiprocessing Environment based on Workstations Connected by SCI. Research Report 208, Department of Informatics, University of Oslo, Norway, November 1995. Available at http://www.ifi.uio.no/~sci/papers.html.

17. Knut Omang and Bodo Parady. Performance of Low-Cost UltraSparc Multiprocessors Connected by SCI. In *Proceedings of Communication Networks and Distributed Systems Modeling and Simulation, Phoenix Arizona*, January 1997. Also available at http://www.ifi.uio.no/~sci/papers.html.

18. Scott Pakin, Mario Lauria, and Andrew Chien. High Performance Messaging on Workstations: Illinois Fast Messages (FM) for Myrinet. In *Proceedings of Supercomputing '95, San Diego*, 1995. Avaliable at http://www-csag.cs.uiuc.edu/papers/index.html#communication.

19. Stein Jørgen Ryan, Stein Gjessing, and Marius Liaaen. Cluster Communication using a PCI to SCI interface. In *Proceedings of IASTED Eighth International Conference on Parallel and Distributed Computing and Systems, Chicago*, October 1996. Available at http://www.ifi.uio.no/~sci/papers.html.

20. IEEE Standard for Scalable Coherent Interface (SCI), August 1993.

21. Thorsten von Eicken, Anindya Basu, Vneet Buch, and Werner Vogels. U-Net: A User-Level Network Interface for Parallel and Distributed Computing. In *Proceedings of 15th ACM Symposium on Operating Systems Principles*, December 1995.

22. Thorsten von Eicken, David E. Culler, Seth Copen Goldstein, and Klaus Erik Schauser. Active Messages: a Mechanism for Integrated Communication and Computation. In *Proceedings of 19th International Symposium on Computer Architecture*, pages 256–266, May 1992.

23. David L. Weaver and Tom Germond. *The SPARC Architecture Manual, Version 9*. Prentice-Hall, 1994.

24. Matt Welsh, Anindya Basu, and Thorsten von Eicken. ATM and Fast Ethernet Network Interfaces for User-level Communication. In *Proceedings of 3rd International Symposium on High-Performance Computer Architecture*, February 1997.

Load Balancing for Regular Data-Parallel Applications on Workstation Network

Maher Kaddoura

Architecture Technology Corporation
P.O Box 24344
Minneapolis, MN 55424

Abstract. A cluster of machines connected by a high-speed interconnection network is emerging as a new architecture for high-performance computing. Among the important issues that need to be addressed in this type of computing environment are adaptive load balancing and data partitioning. In this paper we discuss the parallelization of matrix multiplication and Gaussian elimination on adaptive and nonuniform environments. We present a simple strategy to reduce communication cost when remapping the arrays of these applications. We also develop CYCLIC distribution scheme for adaptive and nonuniform environments. Finally, we present performance results for the solution of the two applications on a cluster of heterogeneous workstations.

1 Introduction

Distributed computing environments made of clusters of machines connected by a high-speed interconnection network are becoming commonplace in scientific, academic, and business environments due to the fact that they provide high price/performance ratios. These Clusters are increasingly being used as an alternative to more expensive supercomputers for parallelization of data-parallel applications. In such a clusters of machines an individual machine can be dedicated to a single user's computation or shared by users. The former has the advantage of providing static computing capability for each machine, while the latter has a higher rate of utilization. The resources available to the user may be classified as:

1. Static: Computational resources are fixed throughout the completion of all tasks.
2. Dynamic: Computational resources vary dynamically throughout the computation because of sharing among users.
3. Adaptive: Computational resources remain fixed for a reasonable interval of time followed by a change.

There has been several research work targeted towards cluster of workstations. Nedeljkovic and Quinn [2] developed a data-parallel C compiler with dynamic load balancing for a network of workstations. Siegell and Steenkiste [6] implemented a runtime system that supports automatically generated programs with dynamic load balancing for workstations. Keyser, Lust, and Roose [5] implemented a parallel 2-D multiblock Euler/Navier-Stokes solver with adaptive block refinement and runtime load balancing for different parallel architecture, including clusters of workstations. Edjlali and et al. [1] developed a run time support for adaptive environment, where adaptive environment refer to an environment in which the number of processors available to a particular application changes due to the computational load of the workstations.

To effectively utilize Workstation Network for scientific data-parallel applications, several issues must be addressed. Among these issues are adaptive load balancing and efficient data partitioning. In this paper we discuss the parallelization of matrix multiplication and Gaussian elimination on cluster of workstations taking into consideration the above two issues. By nonuniform computational environment we mean an environment where the processors have different computational powers due to the load placed on them or due to their CPUs'. An adaptive environment is also nonuniform environment because each processor will have different computation load placed on it.

The rest of the paper is organized as follows. Section 2 discusses the computational environment. Section 3 discusses arrays remapping in adaptive environments. Section 4 presents the adaptive load balancing technique used in this paper. Section 5 describes matrix multiplication algorithm. Section 6 describes Gaussian elimination algorithm. Section 7 presents the performance of the two applications on a cluster of heterogeneous workstations connected by Ethernet. We conclude in Section 8.

2 Computational environment

Our model is restricted to the Single Processor Multiple Data (SPMD) model of execution. In this model the same program is executed on all processors. Parallelism is achieved by partitioning the data structures and associated computations among processors. We are targeting a nonuniform computational environment where the computational resources available may change adaptively.

- These changes should be gradual enough that remapping is not required as soon as the computational resources adapt. Data-parallel programs execute by iterating through a sequence of several phases. There is an implicit synchronization at the end of execution of every phase. We assume that remapping can be performed after a phase is completed. The effect of the change in computational resources during the execution of one phase is not expected to cause the overall performance to deteriorate significantly.
- Minimal amount of computational resources are available for the remapping and redistribution of data. Clearly, one can terminate the process as soon as it stops performing effective computation for the given data-parallel application. However, when the resource is available again this may require spawning a new process that may be considerably more expensive.

3 Remapping for Arrays

For an adaptive computational environment there is a need to remap the array according to the changed computational power of the machines as available computational resources change. The array could be remapped from scratch by using best algorithms available in the literature [3]. However, the computational cost may be prohibitively high if the array adapts frequently. By partitioning an array one-dimensionally into contiguous blocks, remapping becomes simple and fast, since partitioning is equivalent to assigning contiguous blocks of the array to each partition. The size of each block is proportional to the weight of the partition. When available computational resources change, the array can be remapped by repartitioning it along the dimension along which it was originally partitioned.

There are several ways to achieve the repartitioning of an array such that contiguous blocks are assigned to every processor. We will use the term *arrangements* to represent each of the possible ways of partitioning. There are $p!$ arrangements for p processors.

---

procedure $MCR(L,P,L2)$

```
/* P is the number of processors.
L is the array which has the arrangement of the processors.
The function COST given two different
arrangements of processors returns the cost of
data redistribution.
L2 is the array which contains the arrangement
of processors generated by the procedure
*/
```

$\quad$ **for**$(1 \leq i \leq P)L2[i] := L[i]$
$\quad min := +\infty.$
$\quad$ **for**$(1 \leq i \leq P)$
$\quad\quad$ **for**$(1 \leq j \leq P)$
$\quad\quad\quad MOVE(L2, L[i], j).$
$\quad\quad\quad temp := COST(L, L2).$
$\quad\quad\quad$ **if** $(temp < min)$
$\quad\quad\quad\quad min := temp. \; jmin := j.$
$\quad\quad MOVE(L2, L[i], jmin).$
end.

Fig. 1. MCR Algorithm

The amount of data movement can be reduced by finding a new arrangement that maximizes the overlap between the original intervals and the new intervals.

---

procedure $MOVE(L, C, D)$

/* Move the element C in L to location D and rearrange the remaining
elemnts. */
/* $MOVE(\{1, 3, 5, 4, 6\}, 5, 0) = \{5, 1, 3, 4, 6\}$ * /

    find the location of C in L. We shall refer
    to this location as X.
    if $(X < D)$
        shift the elements in location $X + 1$ to
        D to the left.
    if $(X > D)$
        shift the elements in location D to
        $X - 1$ to the right
    put C in location D.
end.

Fig. 2. Rearranging a list

For example, consider a list of 100 elements and 5 processors with the following ratios of computational capabilities: $P_0 = 0.27, P_1 = 0.18, P_2 = 0.34, P_3 = 0.07$, and $P_4 = 0.14$. Let us assume that the one-dimensional list is divided among the processors using the arrangement $(P_0, P_1, P_2, P_3, P_4)$. If the computational capabilities of the processors adapts to 0.10, 0.13, 0.32, 0.24, 0.21, respectively, then dividing the list according to the original arrangement $(P_0, P_1, P_2, P_3, P_4)$ will yield 34 overlapped elements (i.e., 66 elements have to be moved across the network). On the other hand, if the list is divided using the arrangement $(P_0, P_3, P_1, P_2, P_4)$, the number of overlapped elements will increase to 67. The cost of the number of messages generated can also be taken into account by incorporating it into the cost of redistribution. Using the first arrangement, the number of messages needed to redistribute the data is 5; the number of messages needed to redistribute the data for the latter arrangement is only 4.

Choosing the best arrangement by trying out all cases is feasible only for a small number of processors. In [4] we developed an algorithm (Minimize-CostRedistribution (MCR)) that generates only a subset of all the arrangements, considering data overlap and number of messages generated (see Figure 1). The algorithm MOVE, which is used by MCR, is described in Figure 2. The time requirement for this algorithm is $O(P^3)$, where P is the number of processors.

4 Adaptive load balancing

When the available computational resources adapt, a remapping of data items may be required to maintain good load balance. This can be divided into four phases:

- Monitoring local load on each processor.
- Exchanging load information between processors.
- Making a decision to remap; if remapping is required, choosing the appropriate partitioning of the array to minimize data movement.
- If remapping is required, performing the data movement.

In our current implementation each processor monitors its own load and sends it to a *controller* processor, which makes the decision about repartitioning the data. Centralized load-balancing algorithms are suitable for an environment with a small number of processors. This currently requires sending the load information as separate messages to the controller, which broadcasts the decision to all the processors. When better resource management tools are available, we hope to have distributed strategies.

The goal of a good parallelization for the targeted environment is to minimize the idle time on any given processor. Using information from the current phase, the data (and associated computations) should be redistributed such that the idle time for the next phase is minimized. This assumes that the computational resources allocated for the data parallel computation are the same as for the previous phase.[1] The controller determines from time to time whether the remapping of data is profitable. Remapping is considered profitable if its cost is offset by an improvement in time for the next phase. If it is not profitable, the controller broadcasts an appropriate message to all the processors, and computations are resumed for the next phase. Otherwise, the controller computes new data intervals for each processor based on its estimated computational capability in the previous phase. The new intervals are broadcast to all the processors and the data is redistributed among the processors.

The frequency of this load-balancing check has to be set based on the following:

- The overhead of load balancing. This should represent a small fraction of the time between successive load-balancing steps
- The rate at which the underlying computational resources adapt. If the computational environment adapts slowly, the frequency can be low. Clearly, if the computational resources adapt very frequently, effective parallelization will not be possible.

Techniques to choose the best frequency are outside the scope of this paper.

5   Matrix Multiplication

In this section we give a description of the matrix multiplication algorithm that we used to perform our experiments. Since the network is Ethernet (bus) decom-

---

[1] This could be extended to techniques that would predict the available computational resources based on more than one previous phase. If the operating system can guarantee that a process will be allocated a particular amount of resources for the next phase, this can also be used to predict the amount of computational resources available in the next phase.

posing the matrixes into two-dimensional blocks will only increase the number of messages without reducing the amount of data that needs to be transferred between the processors. Dividing the matrix along one dimension into continuous blocks will thus yield the best decomposition in this case. Also, by decomposing the matrix into one-dimensional blocks, one can take advantage of broadcast, and it becomes simple to remap the matrix in an adaptive environment by using MCR algorithm. The algorithm assume that the matrixes are divided along the rows. Let A, B, and C be the matrixes such that $C := A \times B$. The algorithm has P iterations, where P is the number of processors. In each iteration one of the processors (starting with the smallest ID) would broadcast its local A (A_l)to all the processors. Then the processors would multiply the rows in A_l with the corresponding columns in its local B and store the result in the appropriate location in its local C. In an adaptive environment when remapping is required we need only to remap matrixes B and C.

6 Gaussian Elimination

Parallelization of Gaussian elimination on a uniform computational environment is done by mapping the rows of a coefficient matrix in a CYCLIC fashion. In a uniform computational environment, data elements are mapped onto processors in a round-robin manner, assuming N elements in a dimension of the array and P processors. Every i^{th} element is mapped onto processor P_i, where $1 \le i \le P$.

In a nonuniform computational environment, processors have different computational power. To best utilize all the processors, the number of data elements assigned to a processor should be proportional to its computational power. For example, assuming the number of elements is 20, if there are four processors with computational power of 1, 2, 3 and 4 units, then the computational power fractions for processors P_1, P_2, P_3, P_4 are 0.1, 0.2, 0.3, 0.4, respectively, and the number of elements assigned to processors P_1, P_2, P_3, P_4 will be 2, 4, 6, 8, respectively. The problem then becomes how to choose these elements from among the data domain for each processor. We solve this problem using a two-step process:

1. Finding the minimal window retaining load balance
2. Repeating the minimal window across the whole data domain

In nonuniform computational environments, the size of the minimal window is larger than P since the number of elements assigned to each processor is not identical. Let a_i be the fractional power for processor P_i, $1 \le i \le P$, where $1 \le i \le P$ and $\sum_{i=1}^{P} a_i = 1$. The number of total elements assigned to processor P_i is approximately N_i, where

$$N_i = \lceil N * a_i \rceil, 1 \le i \le P. \tag{1}$$

In the minimal window the number of elements assigned to a processor is proportional to its computational power. Thus, the size of the minimal window is

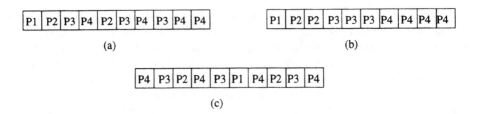

Fig. 3. Three 1-D CYCLIC Distributions in the minimal window

dependent on the fractional power of the processors. If n_i is the number of elements assigned to processor P_i in the minimal window and W is the size of minimal window, then

$$W = \sum_{i=1}^{P} n_i. \tag{2}$$

Our goal is to minimize the minimal window and to keep the load balance so that the number of elements assigned to each processor is proportional to its computational power in the minimal window. There might be many solutions for this problem. Our approach is to calculate g, the gcd of all N_i, $1 \le i \le P$,

$$g = \gcd(N_i, 1 \le i \le P). \tag{3}$$

Thus,

$$n_i = \frac{N_i}{g}, 1 \le i \le P, \tag{4}$$

and

$$W = \sum_{i=1}^{P} \frac{N_i}{g}. \tag{5}$$

In the above example, we have: $N_1 = \lceil 20 * 0.1 \rceil = 2$, $N_2 = \lceil 20 * 0.2 \rceil = 4$, $N_3 = \lceil 20 * 0.3 \rceil = 6$, and $N_4 = \lceil 20 * 0.4 \rceil = 8$. The gcd of all N_i, $1 \le i \le P$, is $g = \gcd(2, 4, 6, 8) = 2$. Therefore, $n_1 = 1$, $n_2 = 2$, $n_3 = 3$, and $n_4 = 4$. And the size of the minimal window, W, is $W = 1 + 2 + 3 + 4 = 10$. The above approach works fine only when $g > 1$. Otherwise, the minimal window is of the same size as the data array. To maximize the value of g, one may use approximations of different N_i's so that the size of the minimal window can be further reduced. Finding the optimal window size with the above issues is a difficult problem and is out of the scope of this paper.

Once we find the size of the minimal window, there are several ways to distribute elements in the minimal window. Three examples are shown in Figure 3 (a), (b), (c), where (a) distributes elements in a round-robin fashion, (b) distributes n_i consecutive elements to the processor P_i, and (c) distributes elements onto all processors as evenly as possible.

In this paragraph we give a a high level description of Gaussian elimination algorithm. The coefficient matrix is distributed into continuous blocks among

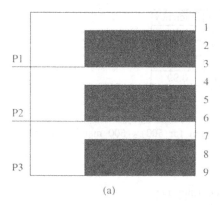
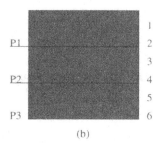

(a)   (b)

Fig. 4. Remapping of a matrix: (a) Original matrix, where $k = 3$ and $N = 9$. (b) The renumbering of the non-zero parts of the matrix before remapping it.

the processors (see Figure 4 (a)). The size of these blocks in proportional to the computational power of the processors. However, the order of the computation (the location of the row being eliminated) is done according to the minimal window generated by the method described in this section. This approach has the advantage of minimizing load variation between the processors by using CYCLIC distribution, while at the same time enabling the programmer or compiler to take full advantage of the adaptive load balancing scheme that we developed (MCR). In an adaptive environment only the non-zero parts of the matrix are remapped. The non-zero parts of the matrix are logically renumbered such that each processor has a continuous number of rows, and these numbers start at 1 and end at $k - N$, where k is the number of rows eliminated so far and N is the number of rows in the matrix (see Figure 4).

7   Experimental Results

The two applications were evaluated on a cluster of SUN4 workstations connected by Ethernet using the P4 message-passing environment. We first evaluated the Two algorithms in a static environment. Tables 1 and 2 gives the execution time of the two applications in a static environment. These results show that high efficiency was maintained in all cases.

We used the same environment to measure the performance in a controlled adaptive environment. A check was made after the processing of every 10 rows of the matrix. Using the information gathered for the first 10 rows, a remapping of the matrix was performed and was used for the remaining of the algorithm. The performance was measured using the following initial conditions:

1. A constant competing load was added to one of the processors (processor 1).
2. The matrixes were decomposed assuming all the processors had equal computational ratio.

Workstations	Time	Efficiency
1	437.20	1
1,2	228.34	0.96
1,2,3	149.32	0.98
1,2,3,4	110.02	0.99
1,2,3,4,5	98.05	0.89

Table 1. Execution time of matrix multiplication for 500×500 matrixes in static environment (in seconds)

Workstations	Time	Efficiency
1	197.04	1
1,2	88.86	1.11
1,2,3	63.91	1.03
1,2,3,4	66.96	0.74
1,2,3,4,5	59.63	0.66

Table 2. Execution time of Gaussian elimination for 500×500 matrixes in static environment (in seconds)

Workstations	Execution Time with Load Balancing	Execution Time without Load Balancing	Load Balance Check	Load Balancing Cost
1	434.72			
1,2	254.81	457.23	0.005	0.96
1,2,3	177.73	300.04	0.007	0.96
1,2,3,4	129.01	218.42	0.009	0.72
1,2,3,4,5	110.09	176.31	0.011	0.89

Table 3. Execution time of Matrix multiplication for 500×500 matrixes in a controlled adaptive environment (in seconds)

Workstations	Execution Time with Load Balancing	Execution Time without Load Balancing	Load Balance Check	Load Balancing Cost
1	393.51			
1,2	163.51	213.60	0.005	0.85
1,2,3	106.52	133.33	0.007	0.66
1,2,3,4	98.17	110.39	0.009	0.55
1,2,3,4,5	77.58	81.79	0.011	0.39

Table 4. Execution time of Gaussian elimination for 500×500 matrixes in a controlled adaptive environment (in seconds)

Workstations	Execution Time with Load Balancing	Execution Time without Load Balancing
1,2	386.39	513.19
1,2,3	271.18	345.94
1,2,3,4	212.21	227.33
1,2,3,4,5	188.43	221.24

Table 5. Execution time of Matrix multiplication for 500 × 500 matrixes in an uncontrolled adaptive environment (in seconds).

Workstations	Execution Time with Load Balancing	Execution Time without Load Balancing
1,2	141.18	157.41
1,2,3	110.16	115.45
1,2,3,4	95.31	111.80
1,2,3,4,5	81.21	78.34

Table 6. Execution time of Gaussian elimination for 500 × 500 matrixes in an uncontrolled adaptive environment (in seconds).

Tables 3 and 4 presents the results for matrix multiplication and Gaussian elimination in a controlled adaptive environment, and Tables 5 and 6 presents the results for the two applications in an uncontrolled adaptive environment. An uncontrolled adaptive environment is an environment where we did not have exclusive access to the workstations and network. These results show that remapping substantially improves the time required for execution. The cost of load balancing is close to the time required to process a few rows, while the cost of performing the load balance check is an order of magnitude lower. These results show that even if a check is done after every 10 rows, the overhead for performing this check will be small compared to the total execution cost; however, if the environment adapts during that time, the potential advantages of remapping can be substantial.

8   Conclusions

In this paper we have described efficient techniques for the parallelization of matrix multiplication and Gaussian elimination on a cluster of workstations. The techniques are a simple strategy to redistribute data when the computational load of the processors in the environment changes, and a CYCLIC distribution method for nonuniform environments. The techniques are general and can be applied to a wide class of data-parallel applications. The two applications were evaluated on a cluster of workstations using P4 in static and adaptive environments. In both cases good performance was obtained.

References

1. Edjlali, G., Agrawal, G., Sussman, A., Saltz, J.: Data-Parallel Programming in An Adaptive Environment. Proceedings of International Parallel Processing Symposium. April (1995) 827–832.
2. Nedeljkovic, N., Quinn, M.: Data-Parallel Programming on a Network of Heterogeneous Workstations. Proceedings of the First International Symposium on High-Performance Distributed Computing. September (1992) 28–36
3. kaddoura, M., Ranka, S., Wang, A.: Array Decompositions for Non-Uniform Computational Environments. Journal of Parallel and Distributed Computing. **36** (1996) 91–105
4. kaddoura, M., Ranka, S.: Run-time Support for Parallelization of Data-Parallel Applications on Adaptive and Non-Uniform Computational Environments. Proceedings of High Performance Distributed Computing. August (1996) 30–39.
5. Keyser, J., Lust, K., Roose, D.: Run-Time Load Balancing Support for Parallel Multiblock Euler/Navier-Stokes Code with Adaptive Refinement on Distributed Memory Computers. Parallel Computing. **20** (1994) 1069-1088
6. Siegell, B., Steenkiste, P.: Automatic Generation of Parallel Programs with Dynamic Load Balancing. Proceedings of the Third International Symposium on High-Performance Distributed Computing. August (1994) 166–175

A Comparison of Three High Speed Networks for Parallel Cluster Computing*

Henri Bal   Rutger Hofman   Kees Verstoep

Vrije Universiteit
Dept. of Mathematics and Computer Science
Amsterdam, The Netherlands

Abstract. Many high speed networks have been developed that may be suitable for parallel computing on clusters of workstations. This paper compares three different networks: FastEthernet, ATM, and Myrinet. We have implemented the Panda portability layer on all three networks, using the same host machines and as much the same software as possible. We compare the latency and throughput for Panda's point-to-point and multicast communication on the three networks and analyze the performance differences.

1 Introduction

The suitability of a cluster of workstations for parallel computing depends strongly on the local area network (LAN) that interconnects the machines. Whereas massively parallel processors (e.g., the SP-2) use efficient, specially-designed switching networks, workstation clusters typically use off-the-shelf LANs. With traditional LANs such as 10 Mpbs Ethernet, the relative communication overhead is high and will even get worse as processors become faster. Fortunately, many high speed LANs have become available [6, 9, 19, 21]. An interesting issue, studied in this paper, is which LAN technology will give the best performance for parallel cluster computing.

Several experiments in parallel and distributed computing on high speed LANs have been described in the literature [1, 10, 15, 18, 22, 23, 25, 26]. However, these studies use a variety of networks, processors, operating systems, and communication software, making it hard to compare the results. Only few studies have been done that compare different networks using the same processors and software. The goal of our research is to evaluate the suitability of modern LANs for parallel processing, using a controlled experiment where only the LANs and low-level communication software are different.

The networks we discuss in this paper are FastEthernet, ATM, and Myrinet. Together, these represent an interesting range of alternatives for parallel cluster computing. FastEthernet basically gives a higher-bandwidth (100 Mpbs) Ethernet at low cost. ATM is originally designed for applications in the telecommunications industry, but it has also been used extensively for real-time, multimedia, and parallel applications. Finally, Myrinet was designed especially for parallel computing on collections of workstations. Unlike FastEthernet and ATM, it provides reliable communication in hardware.

---

* This research is supported in part by a PIONIER grant from the Netherlands Organization for Scientific Research (N.W.O.).

An important issue is at *which software level* to do the comparison. LAN manufacturers usually publish performance numbers for either the raw hardware or low-level software. For parallel cluster computing, such numbers are next to meaningless. To the parallel programmer, what really matters is the performance of the parallel language (or programming system) that is being used. Unfortunately, using a specific language to study LAN performance is not without problems either, since the results will depend strongly on the specific language and its implementation. Likewise, using parallel applications to compare the performance makes the results depend on the specific applications (in particular their grain size). Our approach is to study the communication performance at the abstraction level required by a parallel runtime system. We have developed a portable communication layer, called *Panda* [14], which provides reliable point-to-point and multicast communication. Panda has been used for implementing several parallel programming environments, including Orca [5], SR [2], PVM [16], and Nexus [8]. We will use the Panda system to compare the performance of FastEthernet, ATM, and Myrinet.

The outline of the paper is as follows. In Section 2 we describe the hardware and software environment used in our study. In Sections 3 and 4 we analyze the performance of Panda's point-to-point and multicast communication on the three networks. In Section 5 we discuss to what extent these results are relevant to higher-level parallel programming systems. In Section 6 we look at related work. Finally, in Section 7 we present our conclusions.

2   Hardware and Software Environment

The results of a performance study depend on the exact hardware and software being used. Therefore, in this section we provide enough detail about our hardware and software to understand the performance analysis in subsequent sections.

2.1   Hardware

The parallel system used in our study is a homogeneous cluster of SPARC processors. The entire system consists of 80 single-board computers, each consisting of a 50 Mhz MicroSparc with 32 Mbyte local memory, 4 Kbyte instruction cache, and 2 Kbyte data cache (both direct mapped). All machines are connected by a 10 Mpbs Ethernet, which we only use for starting the performance measurements.

For our performance study, three sets of eight processors each have been extended with a modern LAN. In this way, we get three subsystems that are identical except for the LAN. The LANs we used are:

- A FastEthernet network with Sun 100BASE-T interfaces and a 3Com LinkBuilder FMS 100 hub.
- A Myrinet network with Myricom LANai-4.1 interfaces and an 8-port Myrinet switch (the M2F-SW8).
- A Fore ATM network with SBA-200E interfaces and the ASX200-WG switch.

The hardware bandwidths of these networks are 100 Mbit/sec for FastEthernet, 1.28 Gbit/sec (full duplex) for Myrinet, and 155 Mbit/sec (full duplex) for ATM. ATM and Myrinet use a switched topology, so their aggregate bandwidths increase with the number of hosts; FastEthernet has a fixed bandwidth. It would have been possible to also use a switch (instead of a hub) for FastEthernet. A switch would give parallel application programs a much higher aggregate bandwidth than a hub, but FastEthernet switches are far more expensive than hubs. Also, for the performance measurements in this paper, the topology does not have a major impact, because our throughput tests use only a single sender.

With all three LANs, the Network Interface is an adaptor card that is inserted in each host and that communicates with the host processor (the SPARC) over the SBus. For both Myrinet and Fore ATM, the Network Interface contains a processor that runs a control program (the 'firmware'). This control program communicates with the host and the network and processes all incoming and outgoing messages. With Myrinet, users can easily modify the firmware: all software interfaces are publicly available and all Myrinet software (including the firmware, device drivers, libraries, LANai compiler, and other tools) are distributed to customers in source form. With Fore ATM, on the other hand, the firmware should be regarded as a black box, since users are generally not given access to the sources. Consequently, in our study we will treat Myrinet as a system with a programmable Network Interface and Fore ATM as a system whose firmware cannot be changed. Many other ATM systems (and FastEthernet) do not use a programmable Network Interface at all.

The costs of the three networks also is an interesting issue. The ATM network is the most expensive, because of the high cost of ATM switches. We paid about a factor of two more for the ATM hardware than for the Myrinet hardware, mainly because the Myrinet switch is much cheaper. FastEthernet is somewhat less expensive than Myrinet. For the more popular PCI-bus systems (i.e., PCs), the difference between FastEthernet and Myrinet is much higher (FastEthernet PCI interfaces cost about US$ 150, while the Myrinet interfaces cost about US$ 1300).

2.2 Software

In addition to using identical hardware, we also use as much the same software as possible for all three networks. In our study, we use the Panda portability layer [14]. Panda provides high-level reliable communication primitives, including one-way message passing, two-way remote procedure calls, and totally-ordered multicast. Panda also supports threads, and all Panda communication primitives are thread-safe. Panda has been used to implement several parallel programming systems and parallel applications. Also, it is reasonably well tuned and it has been ported to a range of systems, including clusters of workstations and MPPs [3, 14].

Before we give more detailed information about the Panda software, we first discuss some general issues. To obtain high performance on fast networks, it is necessary to remove the standard kernel protocol stack from the critical path. One way of doing this is via device mapping: the network device is mapped into *user space* and is accessed without any intervention from the operating system. We use this approach for all three networks. Our software does not support protected access to a shared network device,

Host	Panda protocols
	Illinois Fast Messages
	Network device driver
Network interface	Firmware (on Myrinet and ATM)
	Hardware

Fig. 1. Structure of the Panda-based system.

so we do not share the device among multiple users. (Techniques for allowing shared and protected access to the network are described in [23].)

Another well-known critical issue is whether to receive incoming messages through polling or interrupts. Although our software supports both forms, all performance tests in this study use polling, because they only do communication and no useful computation.

The operating system used on our cluster is Amoeba [17]. Given the assumptions above, however, the impact of the OS on the results has become neglectable. The OS is only involved in initializing the system, but not in communication.

The structure of our system is shown in Figure 1. The firmware is the software that runs on the Network Interface processor (for Myrinet and ATM). The lowest software layer that runs on the host is the device driver, which is different for each network.

The Panda protocols do not directly invoke the device driver primitives. Instead, we use Illinois Fast Messages (FM) [13] as a device-independent interface for all three networks. We have used the original FM system for Myrinet from the University of Illinois [13] and extended it as discussed below. In addition, we have implemented the same interface on ATM and FastEthernet. On ATM and FastEthernet, the FM primitives are *unreliable*, because FM does not itself provide a reliability protocol; on Myrinet, FM provides reliable communication, since the network is reliable. On all three systems, FM takes care of fragmentation and reassembly of messages. Below, we describe our software in more detail.

Firmware For Myrinet, we use the LANai control program (Version 1.1) of FM [13] with the extensions described in [20]. The most important extension is a reliable and efficient spanning-tree multicast protocol. This protocol runs entirely on the Network Interfaces, so it forwards multicast messages without involving the host processors. To avoid buffer overflow, it implements a credit-based flow control scheme. Another extension is a primitive to get a sequence number for the totally-ordered multicast protocol, using the firmware. This primitive sends a message to a centralized sequencer machine; the Network Interface firmware on that machine replies with the next sequence number.

For ATM, we use the standard Fore firmware (Version 4.0.0), for the reasons described above. FastEthernet does not have a programmable CPU on the Network Interface, so it does not use firmware.

Device Drivers The device drivers provide primitives for sending and receiving message fragments. The drivers run in user space, and directly access the Network Interface (NI).

Our Myrinet device driver is based on that of FM. It uses the same approach as described in [13]. The host uses programmed I/O for sending messages to the NI. Incoming fragments are received using DMA, which is initiated by the NI processor. The message fragments are transferred through DMA into a fixed-size DMA-area on the host. As with the original FM driver, our driver uses small, fixed-size message fragments to optimize latency. On our system, we have set the fragment size to 256 bytes.

The ATM and FastEthernet interfaces cannot be accessed with programmed I/O. Therefore, the sender copies each fragment into a DMA area and also puts a small descriptor for the fragment in a command queue in the DMA area. The NI will then initiate a DMA to read the fragment. (With FastEthernet, the driver sets a control bit on the device; with ATM, the NI processor polls the command queue.) Incoming fragments are handled in the same way as on Myrinet, using DMA from the NI to the host DMA area. The ATM driver uses message fragments up to 4 Kbytes. These are fragmented on the NI into AAL5 ATM cells, but this is transparent to the driver. On FastEthernet, we use message fragments up to 1500 bytes.

A subtle issue is where to allocate the DMA area. With the MicroSparc architecture, the cache may become inconsistent after a DMA transfer. For ATM and FastEthernet, we solve this problem by allocating the DMA area in uncached memory. On Myrinet, however, our NI firmware guarantees that all incoming fragments are always stored in consecutive locations in the DMA area. The Myrinet driver treats the DMA area as a circular buffer that is always read sequentially. Since the cache is direct mapped and the size of the cache is much smaller than the DMA area, the cache lines for a message in the DMA area will have been overwritten before the driver reads the message. Also, we have chosen the fragment size to be a multiple of the cache line size, so reading a fragment from the DMA area does not fetch the first few bytes of a still unreceived fragment into the cache. As a result, on Myrinet the cache consistency problem can be avoided and the DMA area can be allocated in cached memory.

Multicast messages are handled by the device drivers in much the same way as point-to-point messages. For Myrinet, the firmware takes care of forwarding the message. For ATM, we have set up a number of special Permanent Virtual Circuits on the switch; fragments sent to these PVCs will be multicast by the switch. For FastEthernet, we use multicast addresses, as with 10 Mbps Ethernet.

Fast Messages The Fast Messages layer provides a standard interface for all three networks to the Panda layer. Messages are received by calling the FM polling primitive, which processes all queued messages (if any); for each message, a handler function that is passed as part of the message is executed. The FM layer does message fragmentation and reassembly, thus allowing Panda to send messages of arbitrary size. The fragmentation and reassembly code is the same for all three networks, except that they use different fragment sizes (as described above). On Myrinet, the FM layer also does flow control for point-to-point messages, to avoid losing messages due to buffer overflow [13]. On ATM and FastEthernet, we did not implement flow control; since the network is unreliable, a retransmission protocol must be provided by higher layers. Such a protocol is integrated with flow control in the Panda layer.

Panda The goal of the Panda system is to implement high-level communication primitives on top of whatever primitives are provided by the underlying system. Internally, Panda has a highly modular structure [14]. Panda can be configured statically to use the protocols that best match the underlying system. For example, it only uses a reliability protocol if the communication primitives of the underlying system are unreliable.

On systems that already provide reliable message passing, Panda's point-to-point messages are easy to implement. On systems with unreliable message passing (i.e., FastEthernet and ATM), Panda uses a credit-based reliability protocol. Credit updates also serve as acknowledgements, so flow control and reliability are integrated. Credit updates are piggybacked on data messages whenever possible. A time-out mechanism is used for retransmissions. Retransmissions can also be requested by a receiver that detects a missing message.

Besides point-to-point communication, Panda also supports totally-ordered multicast, which guarantees that all multicast messages are received by all destinations in the same order. These strong semantics are highly useful for implementing distributed shared memory systems; it is used extensively in the Orca system [4, 5].

The multicast protocol uses a centralized *sequencer* machine to order all messages. If the underlying system already provides reliable multicast, the protocol is simple: the sender first gets the next sequence number from the sequencer and then multicasts the message with the sequence number tagged on it. We use this protocol on Myrinet. Recall that we extended Myrinet's firmware with support for reliable multicast and for getting a sequence number.

On systems with unreliable multicast (i.e., ATM and FastEthernet), we use the negative acknowledgement protocol of Kaashoek [12]. This protocol uses only two messages for each reliable multicast (one point-to-point message and one unreliable multicast), which is far more efficient than having each receiver return an acknowledgement. If a machine misses a message, the protocol is able to retrieve it. All receivers keep track of which multicast messages they have received and piggyback this information when they send a multicast message. This information is used to determine if all machines have received a given message. More details about the protocol can be found in [12].

3 Performance of Point-to-point Communication

We will now discuss the performance of Panda on the three networks. We look at point-to-point communication in this section and multicast communication in the next section. We will present performance data for latency and throughput, since both are important for parallel programming.

The latency for point-to-point roundtrip messages was measured with a simple ping-pong test: a process on one host sends a message of varying data size and the receiving process on the other host replies with a message containing 32-bytes of data. (All data sizes are excluding data in the headers.) The unidirectional throughput was measured

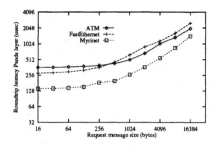

Fig. 2. Panda roundtrip latency.

Fig. 3. Panda throughput.

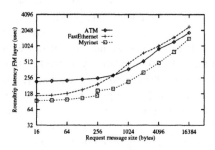

Fig. 4. FM roundtrip latency.

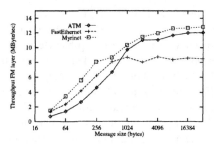

Fig. 5. FM throughput.

by letting a process on one host transmit a long stream of messages of a given size to a process on another host. The results are shown in Figures 2 and 3.

To analyze the performance results, we have run a similar ping-pong test using the lower-level FM primitives. This program aborts when it detects a lost message (which did not occur during our measurements). The results are shown in Figures 4 and 5.

Several observations can be made from these experiments. Myrinet has by far the lowest latency for Panda point-to-point messages. For 32-byte messages, for example, the roundtrip time is 143 μsec on Myrinet, 287 μsec on FastEthernet, and 365 μsec on ATM. A large fraction of this difference can be attributed to the fact that Myrinet is reliable, whereas on ATM and FastEthernet we need to use a reliability protocol at the Panda level. At the FM layer, the roundtrip latencies for 32-byte messages are 96 μsec on Myrinet, 120 μsec on FastEthernet, and 222 μsec on ATM.

The difference in latency between the Panda and FM layers for ATM and FastEthernet is about 155 μsec. This difference is the price paid for reliability, thread synchronization, fragmentation, and flow control. We have also determined that the high overhead (155 μsec) is partly due to the poor performance of the very small cache. (In some other cases, we have measured up to 40 μsec less overhead for the reliability protocol, while executing exactly the same code.) The most important reason for the high overhead, however, is the fact that the MicroSparc processors we use are slow. We have measured that the reliability protocol takes only 10 μsec on a 200 MHz Pentium Pro, which we currently have at our disposal.

Fragmentation is the cause for some discontinuity when measuring the latency for messages that are slightly larger than the network's fragment size. In Figure 4 this effect is responsible for the small jump in the Myrinet latency of 256 byte messages.

On Myrinet, the Panda latency is 47 μsec higher than the FM latency, which is due to the usage of synchronization primitives (condition variables), a higher procedure call and register window overflow overhead, and extra header data that the Panda protocol adds to the FM header (for multiplexing). ATM exhibits a high latency at the FM layer. Research performed by the U-Net project at Cornell University has shown that this is caused by the relatively high delay introduced by the current Fore firmware [23]. The ATM switch also adds a delay of about 10-15 μsec one way. (The delay of the Myrinet switch is less than 1 μsec.)

The latency we obtain with FM on Myrinet is higher than that reported in other papers (e.g., [13, 7]). There are two important reasons for this difference. First, we use much slower processors (50 Mhz MicroSparcs). To determine the impact of processor speed, we have done a loop-back test with a single 200 Mhz Pentium Pro machine with a Myrinet PCI interface. This test shows that the FM roundtrip latency on the Pentium Pro will be about 28 μsec, compared to 96 μsec on the MicroSparc. Secondly, our FM primitives provide somewhat more functionality than the original FM system. The impact of our FM extensions is described in [4]. Our FM primitives are thread-safe and they support more flexible fragmentation. Also, we use a larger message size than that of the original FM system, to increase the maximum throughput on our hardware.

Myrinet also obtains the highest throughput for Panda point-to-point messages, although the difference with ATM becomes small for large messages. For messages of 16 Kbytes, Myrinet obtains a sustained throughput of 12.6 Mbyte/sec and ATM obtains 11.3 Mbyte/sec. One of the reasons why the Myrinet throughput is higher is the fact that the DMA receive area is in cached memory for Myrinet and in uncached memory for ATM (see Section 2.2). Reading data from cached memory is substantially faster (even if the data are not in the cache), because the data will be read with entire cache lines (of 32 bytes) at a time; uncached memory is read one word at a time. With an uncached DMA area, Myrinet obtains a throughput of 9.9 Mbyte/sec. This is lower than the throughput for ATM, because of the smaller fragment size. FastEthernet exhibits a sustained throughput of just over 8.6 Mbyte/sec.

For ATM and Myrinet the throughput on our hardware is bounded by the receiving host, which has to reassemble incoming fragments out of the DMA area. The host fragment processing and copying overhead combined causes the maximum throughput to be limited to the values measured. For comparison, we have measured that the maximum achievable throughput for copying data over the memory bus is about 25 Mbyte/sec, and about 17 Mbyte/sec when the source data is in uncached memory (as is the case for ATM in our system). We have determined that the host is not the bottleneck for FastEthernet: artificially decreasing both send or receive overhead by copying less data than required does not yield a higher throughput. The throughput of FastEthernet is probably limited by the particular Network Interface we use.

Panda and FM obtain a similar throughput on Myrinet; on FastEthernet and ATM, however, Panda requires larger messages than FM to obtain a high throughput. The FM layer for FastEthernet already achieves its best throughput for messages of 1024 bytes (which is smaller than the Ethernet fragment size), because the FM layer is very lightweight and because of the streaming nature of the throughput test. Note that all the throughput graphs have a 'dip' when the message size first exceeds the network's fragment size; these dips are due to message fragmentation and reassembly.

4 Performance of Multicast Communication

Although point-to-point communication is the most important primitive for parallel programming, multicast communication also is becoming more and more important. Many parallel programming systems (e.g., MPI, SR) provide a multicast primitive and several other systems (e.g., Orca) use it extensively in the runtime system. In this section we will study the performance of Panda's multicast primitive on the three networks. Recall that Panda supports totally-ordered multicast. In our analysis, we will also look at unordered multicast (at the FM level).

We have measured the latency of Panda multicast using a multicast group with eight members. Two of the eight members perform a ping-pong test, so they multicast a message when they receive a multicast message from the other sender; The remaining six members only receive messages. We have computed the average one-way multicast latency over all combinations of two members. The multicast throughput is measured by having one member in a group of eight sending messages as fast as possible to the other members. The results are shown in Figures 6 and 7.

To analyze these results, we have also measured the multicast performance at the FM level. At this level, the multicast is unordered. On Myrinet, FM multicast is reliable; on FastEthernet and ATM it is unreliable (as for point-to-point communication). The latency and throughput were measured using similar test programs as for Panda. The results are shown in Figures 8 and 9.

We can draw several conclusions from these experiments. A surprising result is that Panda multicast has a lower latency on Myrinet than on FastEthernet and ATM, even though Myrinet is the only of the three LANs that lacks hardware support for multicast. The reason for this is twofold. First, we have implemented an efficient spanning tree multicast in firmware [20]. Second, the hardware multicast of FastEthernet and ATM is unreliable, so an additional software protocol (see Section 2.2) is needed to make multicast reliable. On Myrinet, such a protocol is not needed.

On Myrinet, the multicast latency for 32-byte messages is 158 μsec for the Panda level and 55 μsec for the FM level. The Panda level multicast, however, is totally ordered, so it has the overhead of getting a sequence number from the sequencer. For ATM, the Panda latency is 372 μsec and the FM latency is 114 μsec; for FastEthernet, the Panda latency is 314 μsec and the FM latency is 89 μsec. The difference between the Panda and FM level thus is larger on ATM and FastEthernet than on Myrinet, because of the reliability protocol. We should point out that the reliability protocol we use for multicast is quite efficient. For example, Huang and McKinley [11] have recently proposed an alternative multicast protocol for ATM based on positive acknowledgements that are merged by the Network Interfaces. They simulated this protocol on Fore ATM hardware (similar to ours) and 20 Sparc 20 workstations. The tree-based acknowledgement merge

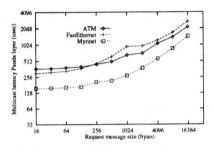

Fig. 6. Panda multicast latency.

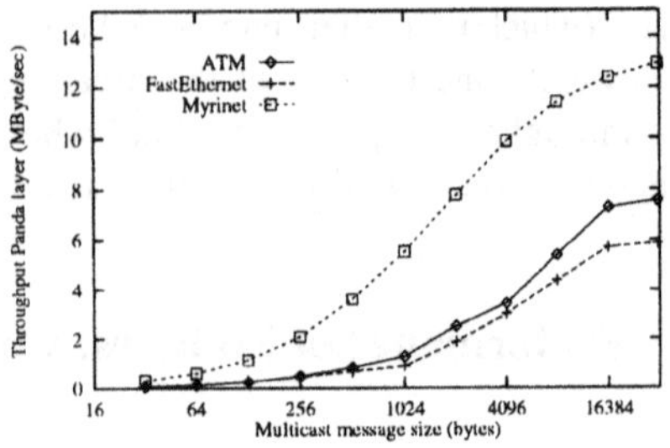

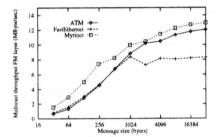

Fig. 7. Panda multicast throughput.

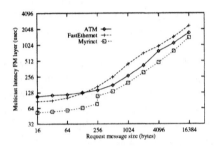

Fig. 8. FM multicast latency.

Fig. 9. FM multicast throughput.

alone already costs over 600 μsec, which is more than a reliable totally-ordered multicast with our software.

The implementation of Myrinet also shows an overall highest throughput. For ATM and FastEthernet, the software protocol for making multicast reliable decreases the throughput. For all networks the maximum throughput for multicast is comparable to that for unicast. For ATM and FastEthernet this is to be expected, given the way multicast is supported in hardware. For Myrinet, given the firmware implementation, the relatively high throughput figures are more surprising.

Multicast communication requires larger messages than point-to-point communication to obtain the maximum throughput. This is explained by the way the synchronization takes place, and the general protocol overhead. The Myrinet implementation achieves high throughputs using relatively small messages, because its reliable multicast support allows the use of a more efficient protocol (with less overhead at the sequencer node) than unreliable networks.

The multicast measurements use groups with only eight members, which is the maximum number of machines that we have at our disposal for each network technology. An important question is what the performance would be on larger systems. On FastEthernet, we expect the multicast latency to remain the same, because the negative acknowledgement protocol of [12] basically uses two messages, independent from the number of receivers. (On 10 Mpbs Ethernet the constant latency has been validated experimentally using up to 64 machines.) For ATM, we expect a small increase in latency as more ATM switches are needed. With 64 processors, for example, multicast messages may have to go through 2 or 3 switches (depending on the number of ports per switch). Since multicast messages are forwarded by the switch hardware, the increase will be small (about 10-15 μsec per switch). On Myrinet, multicast messages are forwarded in firmware, using a binary spanning tree, so the latency will increase somewhat faster than on ATM. Simulations show that on 64 machines a latency of about 200 μsec can be expected for Panda multicast, which is still faster than on ATM and FastEthernet.

5 Performance of Higher-Level Systems

The previous two sections described and analyzed the performance obtained by Panda on point-to-point and multicast communication. An interesting issue is to what extent the Panda performance numbers are relevant to parallel cluster computing, in particular whether they are representative for higher-level systems as well. For this purpose, we have measured the latencies for point-to-point communication on two programming systems that have been implemented on top of Panda: the Orca parallel language and the PVM library. The results are shown in Table 1. For PVM we have measured the roundtrip message latency using a ping-pong test. For Orca, we have measured the latency for invoking an operation on a remote object (which also is implemented using two messages). For comparison, we also show the Panda point-to-point roundtrip latency. In each case, we use request and reply messages with 32-byte user data.

	FastEthernet	ATM	Myrinet
Panda message passing	287	365	143
PVM message passing	527	601	316
Orca remote object invocation	464	545	292

Table 1. Roundtrip latencies for Panda, PVM, and Orca point-to-point communication.

The two programming systems each add a significant overhead. The performance of Orca on Myrinet is studied in detail in [4]. For PVM, the overhead is due to extra thread switches and to differences in the Panda and PVM message interface [14]. Nevertheless, it is clear from Table 1 that the performance differences measured at the Panda level are also reflected at the PVM and Orca level. The differences at the higher levels are even larger than at the Panda level, but this is most likely due to caching effects.

6 Related Work

Several other interesting performance studies of high speed networks have been described in the literature. The NOW project at UCB uses LogP as a model to compare performance characteristics of several network interfaces (of the Intel Paragon, Meiko CS-2, and Myrinet) [7].

The U-Net project at Cornell University has developed an efficient model of communication that removes (most of) the kernel from the critical path while still supporting protection. The implementation of U-Net on a Fore ATM network is described in [23]. The paper also discusses the performance of several communication mechanisms on top of U-Net, including Active Messages, UDP, TCP/IP, and the Split-C language. The latency was improved substantially by modifying the Fore firmware on the Network Interface. As stated before, we (and almost all other users) use the standard Fore firmware.

Recently, U-Net has been ported to FastEthernet [24, 25]. On a 133 Mhz Pentium system (i.e., significantly faster than our hosts) the FastEthernet implementation using a broadcast hub achieved a 40-byte message latency of $57\mu sec$, which is significantly lower than the 89 μsec latency reported for ATM on the same platform. When a FastEthernet switch instead of a hub was used, the latency increased to 91 μsec, however. The U-Net latency on FastEthernet ($57\mu sec$) is much lower than the latency we obtain (120 μsec for FM), but we use much slower processors (50 Mhz MicroSparcs against 133 Mhz Pentiums) and a different network interface.

An earlier study [18] discusses low-latency communication on Ethernet, ATM, and FDDI networks, using several different host machines and network controllers. The study uses a highly efficient RPC implementation and analyses the costs of this protocol on the different platforms. In comparison, our study uses more recent network technology and more uniform hardware and software. In addition, we discuss both latency and throughput and we also deal with multicast communication.

7 Conclusions

We have compared three high speed networking technologies on a cluster of MicroSparc hosts. During our experiments, the network devices were completely programmed by low-overhead drivers from user space to avoid system call and device interrupt overhead. We have measured the performance of reliable point-to-point and multicast communication, using the Panda portability layer. To analyze the performance, we have also done measurements for the low-level FM primitives, which are unreliable on ATM and FastEthernet.

As with any experimental performance study, our study is limited by the hardware and software we use. For each type of network, we have selected one specific switch and interface, making it difficult to draw general conclusions about the network technologies. The results will also differ if other (faster) host machines are used. Finally, the software also has some impact on the results. In general, our approach has been to use as much the same hardware and software as possible, to allow a fair comparison.

For FastEthernet, the Panda roundtrip latency for 32-byte point-to-point messages is 287 μsec; the FM latency is significantly lower, so the software overhead of handling reliability and flow control is substantial. The maximum throughput is inherently bounded by the 100 Mbit/sec offered by the physical layer of this platform, but the Network Interface we used during the tests was not able to achieve this limit.

The ATM platform achieved a roundtrip latency for 32-byte Panda messages of 365 μsec, which is quite high. It achieves a throughput of about 12 Mbyte/sec, using messages of 16 Kbytes. The problem with the high latency is partly due to the slow firmware that comes with the Fore ATM Network Interface. Since ATM itself does not offer guaranteed delivery, higher level protocols must take care of flow control and reliability, which adds substantially to the latency (as with FastEthernet).

Myrinet is a consistent winner in our performance tests. It achieves a low latency (143 μsec) for Panda point-to-point communication and a high throughput (12.8 Mbyte/sec). Also, multicast is efficient on Myrinet, since it is implemented in the firmware, without causing overhead at the host. Moreover, since all communication is reliable at the lowest layer, higher level message passing layers can be more efficient than on the two other platforms.

Acknowledgements

We thank Andrew Chien and Scott Pakin for making the FM software available to us. We are grateful to Koen Langendoen, Andy Tanenbaum, Tim Rühl and the anonymous reviewers for providing useful comments on the paper.

References

1. C. Amza, A.L. Cox, S. Dwarkadas, P. Keleher, H. Lu, R. Rajamony, W. Yu, , and W. Zwaenepoel. TreadMarks: Shared Memory Computing on Networks of Workstations. *IEEE Computer*, 29(2):18–28, February 1996.
2. G.R. Andrews and R.A. Olsson. *The SR Programming Language: Concurrency in Practice*. The Benjamin/Cummings Publishing Company, Redwood City, CA, 1993.
3. H.E. Bal, R. Bhoedjang, R. Hofman, C. Jacobs, K. Langendoen, T. Rühl, and M.F. Kaashoek. Orca: a Portable User-Level Shared Object System. Technical Report IR-408, Vrije Universiteit, Amsterdam, June 1996.
4. H.E. Bal, R. Bhoedjang, R. Hofman, C. Jacobs, K. Langendoen, T. Rühl, and K. Verstoep. Performance of a High-Level Parallel Language on a High-Speed Network. *Journal of Parallel and Distributed Computing*, 19, February 1997.
5. H.E. Bal, M.F. Kaashoek, and A.S. Tanenbaum. Orca: A Language for Parallel Programming of Distributed Systems. *IEEE Transactions on Software Engineering*, 18(3):190–205, March 1992.
6. N.J. Boden, D. Cohen, R.E. Felderman, A.E. Kulawik, C.L. Seitz, J.N. Seizovic, and W. Su. Myrinet: A Gigabit-per-second Local Area Network. *IEEE Micro*, 15(1):29–36, February 1995.
7. D.E. Culler, L.T. Liu, R.P Martin, and C.O. Yoshikawa. Assessing Fast Network Interfaces. *IEEE Micro*, 16(1):35–43, February 1996.
8. I. Foster, C. Kesselman, and S. Tuecke. The Nexus Approach to Integrating Multithreading and Communication. *Journal of Parallel and Distributed Computing (to appear)*, 1996.
9. D.G. Gustavson. The Scalable Coherent Interface and Related Standards Projects. *IEEE Micro*, 12(1):10–22, February 1992.
10. C. Huang and P.K. McKinley. Communication Issues in Parallel Computing Across ATM Networks. *IEEE Parallel and Distributed Technology*, 2(4):73–86, Winter 1994.
11. Y. Huang and P.K. McKinley. Effective Collective Communication with ATM Network Interface Support. In *1996 International Conference on Parallel Processing (Vol. I)*, pages 34–43, Bloomingdale, IL, Aug. 1996.

12. M.F. Kaashoek. *Group Communication in Distributed Computer Systems*. PhD thesis, Vrije Universiteit, Amsterdam, December 1992.

13. S. Pakin, M. Lauria, and A. Chien. High Performance Messaging on Workstations: Illinois Fast Messages (FM) for Myrinet. In *Supercomputing '95*, San Diego, CA, December 1995.

14. T. Rühl, H. Bal, G. Benson, R. Bhoedjang, and K. Langendoen. Experience with a Portability Layer for Implementing Parallel Programming Systems. In *International Conference on Parallel and Distributed Processing Techniques and Applications*, pages 1477–1488, Sunnyvale, CA, August 1996.

15. D.J. Scales, M. Burrows, and C.A. Thekkath. Experience with Parallel Computing on the AN2 Network. In *10th International Parallel Processing Symposium*, Honolulu, Hawaii, April 1996.

16. V.S. Sunderam. PVM: A Framework for Parallel Distributed Computing. *Concurrency: Practice and Experience*, 2(4):315–339, December 1990.

17. A.S. Tanenbaum, R. van Renesse, H. van Staveren, G.J. Sharp, S.J. Mullender, A.J. Jansen, and G. van Rossum. Experiences with the Amoeba Distributed Operating System. *Communications of the ACM*, 33(12):46–63, December 1990.

18. C.A. Thekkath and H.M. Levy. Limits to Low-Latency Communication on High-Speed Networks. *ACM Transactions on Computer Systems*, 11(2):179–203, May 1993.

19. D.E. Tolmie. Gigabit LAN Issues: HIPPI, Fibre Channel, or ATM. In *Proc. High-Performance Computing and Networking (Lecture Notes in Computer Science 919)*, pages 45–53. Springer-Verlag, New York, NY, 1995.

20. K. Verstoep, K. Langendoen, and H.E. Bal. Efficient Reliable Multicast on Myrinet. In *1996 Int. Conference on Parallel Processing (Vol. III)*, pages 156–165, Bloomingdale, IL, August 1996.

21. R.J. Vetter. ATM Concepts, Architectures, and Protocols. *Communications of the ACM*, 38(2):30–38, February 1995.

22. T. von Eicken, A. Basu, and V. Buch. Low-Latency Communication over ATM Networks Using Active Messages. *IEEE Micro*, February 1995.

23. T. von Eicken, A. Basu, V. Buch, and W. Vogels. U-Net: A User-Level Network Interface for Parallel and Distributed Computing. In *ACM Symposium on Operating System Principles*, pages 303–316, Copper Mountain, CO, December 1995.

24. M. Welsh, A. Basu, and T. von Eicken. Low-Latency Communication over Fast Ethernet. In *Proc. Euro-Par'96*, Lyon, France, August 1996.

25. M. Welsh, A. Basu, and T. von Eicken. ATM and Fast Ethernet Network Interfaces for User-level Communication. In *Proceedings of the Third International Symposium on High Performance Computer Architecture*, San Antonio, Texas, February 1997.

26. H. Xu and T.W. Fisher. Improving PVM Performance using ATOMIC User-Level Protocol. In *Proc. First Int. Workshop on High-Speed Network Computing*, pages 108–117, Santa Barbara, CA, April 1995.

Understanding the Performance of DSM Applications *

Wagner Meira Jr.[1]   Thomas J. LeBlanc[1]   Nikolaos Hardavellas[1]
Cláudio Amorim[2]

[1] Department of Computer Science, University of Rochester, Rochester – NY – 14627
{meira,leblanc,nikolaos}@cs.rochester.edu
[2] COPPE Systems Engineering, UFRJ, Rio de Janeiro, Brazil – 21945-970
amorim@cos.ufrj.br

Abstract. Carnival is a performance measurement and analysis tool that assists users in understanding the performance of DSM applications and protocols. Using traces of program executions, Carnival presents performance data as a hierarchy of execution profiles. During analysis, Carnival automates the inference process that relates performance phenomena to specific causes in the source code or DSM protocol using techniques that focus on the two most important sources of overhead in DSM systems: *waiting time analysis* identifies the causes of synchronization overhead, and produces an explanation for each source of waiting time in the program; *communication analysis* identifies the sequence of requests that result in invalidations, and produces an explanation for each source of communication. We describe these techniques and their implementation in TreadMarks, and show how to use waiting time analysis and communication analysis to improve the running time of two programs from the SPLASH application suite when executed on DEC Alphas connected by a DEC Memory Channel network.

1 Introduction

Shared memory is an attractive programming model because it is easier to use than a distributed-memory model. Software DSM (distributed shared memory) systems offer the simplicity of the shared-memory programming model on cost-effective distributed-memory architectures (including networks of workstations). Although early DSM systems could only provide good performance for a limited class of applications, recent advances at both the protocol level [8, 7, 9] and the architecture level [5, 2, 3] have made DSM a practical and cost effective approach to parallel computing. Nonetheless, synchronization and communication are still major sources of performance degradation in DSM systems.

---

* This research was supported by NSF grant CCR-9510173, an NSF CISE Institutional Infrastructure Grant No. CDA-9401142, and an equipment grant from Digital Equipment Corporation's External Research Program. Wagner Meira Jr. is supported by CNPq–Brazil, Grant 200.862/93-6. Cláudio Amorim is a visiting professor at the University of Rochester and is supported by CAPES, Brazil.

Reducing or eliminating synchronization and communication in DSM systems is complicated by several factors. First, communication in a DSM system is dictated by the details of the coherence protocol, and therefore is not under the direct control of the user. As a result, the relationship between shared-memory references in the source code and the resulting frequency of invalidations, page requests, and diffs may not be understood by the programmer. Second, DSM systems support the shared-memory model on a range of architectures, where the costs associated with synchronization and communication vary widely. Implicit tradeoffs between the costs of various operations are embedded in the source code (including the data layout scheme, the scheduling strategy, and the degree of parallelism to be exploited), and thus are difficult to discover and change when porting code from one architecture to another. Third, the dynamic nature of synchronization and communication makes it difficult to associate runtime overhead with specific code segments or data structures. Often the cost of an operation is distributed in time (a write operation by one processor causes a subsequent invalidation on another, but only at a later synchronization point) and space (a request by one processor must be satisfied by another), making it difficult to understand the cause of excessive overhead observed during runtime.

There are many tools that help the programmer in understanding and tuning the performance of parallel applications. Many tools identify the location of performance problems. For example, Paradyn [12] measures performance bottlenecks, and presents the resulting performance information in an abstraction hierarchy. MTool [6] measures the time spent by processors waiting for memory requests to be satisfied, and relates memory behavior to code segments. MemSpy [10] identifies the data structures that cause remote memory references, and classifies the misses into various categories, such as invalidation misses and replacement misses. All of these tools measure performance effects and assist the programmer in finding the causes of performance degradation; however, the programmer is responsible for most of the inference process that links an observed effect to a specific cause.

There are two tools that focus on cause-and-effect relationships. Rajamony and Cox [14] implemented a performance debugger that automatically detects unnecessary and excessive synchronization by verifying data accesses between synchronization intervals. StormWatch [4] is a visualization tool for memory system protocols that presents multiple views of memory access operations, including performance slices that capture relationships between individual memory events, exposing causality in memory operations.

In this paper we present two techniques that help to automate the inference process between observed performance phenomena and underlying causes in DSM systems. *Waiting time analysis* is used to understand the causes of synchronization overhead; *communication analysis* is used to understand page reference and invalidation behavior. These techniques, which have been implemented as part of the **Carnival** performance visualization tool, can be used to understand an application's performance and tune the implementation.

In the next section we present two automated techniques that relate observed performance phenomena (synchronization and communication overhead) to underlying causes. Section 3 describes how these techniques are implemented within Treadmarks (a DSM system) and **Carnival** (a performance visualization tool). Section 4 shows how to use these techniques to understand and tune the performance of two Splash applications running under Treadmarks on a cluster of DEC Alpha stations connected by a DEC memory channel. Section 5 presents our conclusions and the directions of our future work.

2 Overview of Analysis Techniques

Waiting time analysis and communication analysis are both automated techniques that examine execution traces of DSM programs and produce explanations for parallel overheads in terms of the source code. Waiting time analysis examines traces to discover the set of basic blocks whose execution delayed one processor, causing another to wait at a synchronization point. Communication analysis examines the same traces to discover the access pattern that caused a page to be invalidated, and subsequently requested by another processor. Both techniques present the sources of parallel overheads in order of their relative contribution to the running time of the application, and highlight the portions of source code that must be modified to reduce the overheads, and hence improve running time.

2.1 Waiting Time Analysis

Many of the overheads associated with parallelism ultimately manifest themselves as *waiting time*; a processor is idle while it waits for another. Waiting time can be introduced at any synchronization point, such as locks and barriers, or whenever a request is issued by one processor that is served by another (e.g., page faults served remotely).

Consider two processors A and B that synchronize at a barrier, execute for some period of time, and then synchronize again at the barrier. Assume A arrives at the barrier before B. We can define the *cause* of waiting time suffered by processor A to be the differences in the execution paths of processor A and B since the last time they synchronized at the barrier. In order to understand why A must wait for B, we compare the execution paths of the processors leading up to the synchronization point, and determine why one path is longer than the other. Anything the two paths have in common is removed as a potential cause of waiting time, leaving only the differences between the two paths as an *explanation* for waiting time. These differences may represent code segments that were executed by one processor but not the other, or communication operations that were required by one processor but not the other.

Waiting time analysis is an automated technique that generates explanations for waiting time in an execution. (See [11] for a detailed description of waiting time analysis and its use in message-passing systems.) The implementation analyzes execution trace files, recording each occurrence of waiting time, and the set of basic blocks traversed by each processor leading up to a synchronization point. The result of this process is (1) a global execution-time profile of the program, which describes how much time is devoted to various forms of overhead (e.g., load imbalance, contention, insufficient parallelism) that result in idle processors; (2) a *waiting time profile* for each basic block in the program, which helps to identify portions of the source code that deserve special attention; and (3) an explanation for each source of waiting time in terms of the basic blocks that must be modified to reduce it.

Waiting time analysis complements profiling, which focuses attention on the code that appears to dominate the execution, but which cannot capture or quantify indirect effects on waiting time. Since the source code line at which we observe idle time may be distant from the actual cause, we need both waiting time analysis and performance profiles to isolate and understand the behavior.

2.2 Communication Analysis

In DSM systems, communication occurs when a page (the granularity supported by the coherence protocol) is accessed by a processor and that page is not available locally. The page may not be available because (1) this is the first reference to the page (e.g., a cold start) or (2) the page was invalidated as a consequence of write operations by another processor and a subsequent synchronization point. In order to understand why a page reference results in a remote request, we must know the operations that preceded the request (e.g., reads, writes, invalidations); the ordering and type of operations on a page that precede a remote request are the *cause* for that remote request. Analyzing the causes of remote requests is particularly important in DSM systems employing release consistency, since the cause of a remote request can involve multiple processors executing different portions of source code asynchronously.

Communication analysis examines the causes for remote requests (either from the point of view of an individual page or set of pages, or from the point of view of an individual source code line) and from that information infers the access pattern exhibited by a page or source code line. The access patterns are: (1) single-producer-single-consumer, (2) single-producer-multiple-consumer, (3) multiple-producer-single-consumer, (4) multiple-producer-multiple-consumer, (5) migratory, and (6) cold start.

To infer these access patterns, communication analysis uses traces of program executions that contain a record of every page fault and synchronization operation, with a global timestamp for each. Each page fault records the source code line that generated the fault, the nature of the fault (read or write), and the page number. Each synchronization operation records the list of pages that were invalidated as part of the operation. From these traces, the *immediate* cause of each remote request is determined automatically, where an immediate cause is the invalidation that preceded the page fault, and the write faults that generated the write notices at the synchronization point.

Requests to a particular page are usually chained (i.e., one page fault is the cause of another that happens later in time), corresponding to the migration of the page across processors. We represent causality between requests to a page as a directed graph, called the *communication graph*. We build this graph for each page while traversing the trace file and determining immediate causes for page faults. The nodes in the graph represent page faults (and their immediate cause), and edges in the graph represent causality relationships. There is an edge between two nodes if the write fault explained by one node generates a write notice that is an immediate cause for the fault in the other node. We assign weights to the edges according to the cumulative cost of the communication operations that the edge represents.

Since we are interested in learning why a processor faulted on a page that it owned in the past, we trace back through the edges in the graph until we arrive at a node representing the previous fault on the same page on the same processor. The explanation for the page fault is the set of paths leading back to the immediately previous page fault on the same processor.

We can merge explanations to understand reference behavior across pages. Similar explanations for different pages are combined, allowing us to generalize the reference behavior at a single source code location. The criteria for similarity takes into account the relative importance of each edge's weight in the graph.

The output of this process is, for each data structure, a list of sets of graphs that provide explanations for the page faults on that data structure. As described above, each set of graphs represents one or more pages that behave similarly. These explanations are augmented with communication profiles, which describe how the communication costs during execution are distributed among data structures, source code lines, and causes. With this information, the programmer can identify the source code, data structures, and access patterns that result in page requests, and thereby discover optimizations in data layout or scheduling to improve performance.

It is important to note that communication is a common source of waiting time, and therefore contributes to overhead both on the processor that performs the communication, and on any other processor that must wait for the communication to complete. Therefore, reducing the amount of communication can have the added benefit of reducing waiting time, so that the total savings during execution are much larger than the measured communication time. Waiting time analysis identifies the communication operations that contribute to waiting time; communication analysis identifies the access patterns (and associated pages and source code lines) that cause communication, so that both communication and waiting time can be reduced.

3   Instrumentation and Visualization

An implementation of waiting time analysis and communication analysis requires that we instrument an execution environment to capture the relevant trace information, and present the results of the analysis using an appropriate visualization. We instrumented the Treadmarks DSM system, and use **Carnival** for presentation and visualization. Treadmarks [1] is a DSM system for Unix systems developed at Rice University that uses a lazy release consistency protocol [8] to reduce communication and false sharing. **Carnival** is a performance analysis and visualization tool developed at the University of Rochester. We first describe the **Carnival** framework, and then describe our implementations of waiting time analysis and communication analysis within Treadmarks.

3.1 Carnival

Carnival is a performance measurement and analysis tool that supports hierarchical abstraction in the presentation of performance data, maintains links between dynamic measurements and the source code, and automates cause-and-effect analysis of performance phenomena. Performance analysis with **Carnival** consists of four steps: (i) instrumentation, (ii) program execution, (iii) automated analysis, and (iv) visualization.

During the instrumentation phase a preprocessor uses static information [11] or user hints, which identify the portions of the code where computation is replicated, to insert instrumentation calls into the application code, Each call records the occurrence of an important event, a timestamp, and the basic block (or data structure) in the source code where the event occurred. We link the instrumented code to a library that generates events in a trace file when the application is executed. After execution, the **Carnival** preprocessor analyzes the trace files, producing a hierarchy of performance profiles, and explanations for various performance phenomena. The results of this analysis (both profiles and explanations) are examined via a Tcl/Tk [13] interface (see figures 1 and 2). More details about the visualization resources provided by **Carnival** can be found in [11].

The instrumentation library is the only architecture-dependent code in **Carnival**. To use **Carnival** with Treadmarks, we only had to implement a global clock within Treadmarks (for recording timestamps) and define the relevant protocol events for our analysis. We implemented a global clock by broadcasting one processor's clock value using the DEC Memory Channel [5]. The accuracy of this global clock is on the order of tens of microseconds.

The relevant events in Treadmarks include lock operations, barriers, page requests, and garbage collection. At the application level we record two types of computation: parallel computation represents parallelized code executed by each processor on different data; replicated computation represents redundant execution performed on each processor as a side-effect of parallelization. Time spent during execution is divided into four categories for analysis: (1) computation, (2) idle time (waiting time), (3) local protocol overhead, and (4) daemon overhead caused by remote requests satisfied locally.

3.2 Waiting Time Analysis

In Treadmarks, processors may become idle while performing any one of four operations: (1) lock acquire, (ii) barrier entry, (iii) diff/page requests, and (iv) garbage collection.

We implemented waiting time analysis in **Carnival** using a pipeline of three independent tools. The first tool in the pipeline takes in trace file information and produces as output a pair of execution paths for every instance of waiting time in the execution. Each pair of matching events (such as the beginning and end of a Treadmarks library call) becomes a execution step that is identified by the processor where the events happened, the profiling category and location in the source code, and has a duration associated with it. An execution path is a set of execution steps, so the size is bounded by the product *processors* × *states* × *basic blocks*.

Another tool takes as input the list of waiting time steps and the pair of paths representing each such step, and creates a set of equivalence classes of execution paths (i.e., merges equivalent paths). The output of this tool is a list of waiting time steps expressed in terms of the representative path for an equivalence class. The waiting time step defines the duration of waiting; the representative path defines the percentage of that duration associated with each execution step on the path.

Finally, for each instance of waiting time, another tool removes any redundant steps between the pair of paths that characterizes it. This tool also acts as a filter on the set of characterizations, allowing the user to select individual execution steps for analysis.

3.3   Communication Analysis

Diffs and page requests are the Treadmarks operations that are the focus of communication analysis, which is also implemented as a pipeline of tools. The first tool takes as input a trace containing all page-related events (i.e., page faults, diff requests, invalidations) and maintains a per-page record of the latest operations to affect a page on each processor. When the tool encounters a request event in the trace, it outputs a summary of the request (i.e., processor, source code location, time to satisfy) and its cause, which is defined as the invalidation location and the preceding write-fault information (i.e., processor and source code location).

Another tool takes as input the page request summaries and their causes, and creates, for each page, a causality graph, where the nodes are locations in the code and the edges are causal relations. There is an edge from one node to another if the source location (basic block) associated with the first node caused an access fault in the source location associated with the second node. Both nodes and edges have attributes; the nodes describe the set of processors that read or wrote the page, and the access patterns exhibited, while the edges contain the cumulative request costs and the location of the synchronization operation that produced the invalidation.

The last tool in the pipeline creates a database of causality graphs, which summarize the access patterns in the program and the causes of remote page references. The causality graph for the program merges page causality graphs that are similar in terms of access patterns and causes. This last tool also creates the visualization interface for examining the access patterns to data structures and sets of pages.

3.4   Visualizing Performance with Carnival

Carnival presents performance profiles and waiting time analysis in the context of the source code. It helps the user quickly identify where in the source code a program spends the majority of its execution time, and where in the code important sources of parallel overhead are introduced.

The primary **Carnival** display window (Figure 1a) is divided into two parts. The source code (with line numbers) is presented on the right; information about each scope in the source code appears on the left. The line numbers are presented in a grey scale, where the intensity of the scale represents the percentage of execution time (summed across all processors) spent on a given line of source code. Users can quickly identify places in the code where the most time is spent by scrolling down the line numbers looking for the darkest portion of the scale. **Carnival** also provides other profiling displays, as described in [11].

Two pop-up windows are used for waiting time analysis. The **WT Map** (Figures 1b and 2b) provides a global perspective of all sources of waiting time; the **Characterization Map** (Figures 1c and 2c) presents an explanation for a single source of waiting time in terms of the two execution paths involved.

The WT Map lists each source of waiting time, the line number at which waiting occurred, the name of the scope involved, and the percentage of the total waiting time associated with that scope. The color-coded bar indicates the nature of the overheads that are causing the waiting time at that scope, such as load imbalance (LI), insufficient parallelism (IP), and communication and contention (CC). This map is used to navigate within the source code window and to initiate waiting time analysis. Clicking on an entry in the WT Map causes the main display window to shift to the relevant portion of the source code, and the WT Map presents statistics about each cause of that waiting time. These statistics include the percentage contribution of each cause to the total waiting time experienced at that statement, as well as the total waiting time explained by each cause.

Clicking on a characterization in the WT Map produces an explanation for that waiting time in the **Characterization Map**. Color-coded operations for the longer of the two paths are presented on the right side of the window, operations for the shorter path are on the left. The number of occurrences of each operations is given, as is the percentage of the waiting time associated with each scope. Clicking on an scope shifts the source code window to the relevant portion of the code.

The programmer inspects the results of communication analysis via the CA windows (Figure 2a), where information about a variable (or set of pages) is organized in a table form.

Each causality graph is represented as an incidence matrix, where the column header identifies the access pattern (using a color code), the source code location of the faults (R for request, I for invalidation, and W for preceding writes), and the percentage of total page fault cost in the graph associated with that node. The entries quantify the relative frequency of transitions between nodes in the graph. It is also possible to obtain per-processor information by clicking on the top of each column.

4 Examples

In this section we present examples of how **Carnival** can be used to tune applications running on Treadmarks. All experiments were performed on a cluster of eight DEC Alpha Server 2100 nodes connected by a DEC Memory Channel [5]. Each Alpha Server node has four 233 MHz Alpha processors with 256 Mb of memory. Applications are linked to an instrumented implementation of Treadmarks (version 0.9.6), which employs DEC's implementation of TCP/IP on the Memory Channel.

4.1 Excessive synchronization in Water

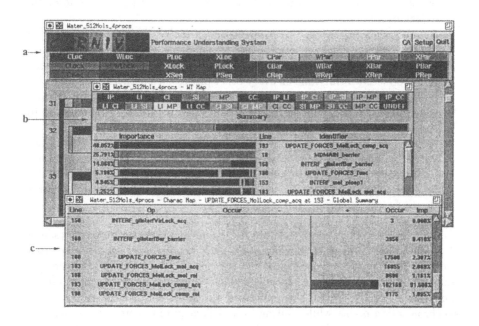

Fig. 1. Carnival visualization of Water

Our first example examines **Water**, a molecular dynamics simulation from the Splash suite [15] that is distributed as part of the Treadmarks release. **Wa-**

ter evaluates forces and potentials that occur over time in a system of water molecules. It uses one large, shared array to represent the molecules being simulated.

We executed three iterations of a 512 molecule simulation of **Water** on four processors and collected the execution traces. The execution took 272 seconds of real time, or 1088 processor seconds. The global execution-time profiles showed that almost 60% of the total processor time was spent waiting for locks and barriers. Waiting time analysis (as shown in the WT Map in Figure 1b) shows three major sources of waiting time, which together account for nearly 90% of all waiting time in the application (and thus over 50% of the execution time):

1. Nearly half of the total waiting time is associated with the lock acquire operations that control access to individual molecules in the simulation (UP-DATE_FORCES_MolLock_comp_acq). The explanations produced by waiting time analysis (shown in the Characterization Map of Figure 1c) show that waiting time at a lock acquire operation is not caused by the actions of another processor (since the left-hand, or negative, side of the explanation is empty); it can be attributed almost entirely to the cost of the lock acquire operation itself (which appears on the right-hand, or positive, side of the explanation).

2. Roughly one quarter of the total waiting time occurs at a barrier (MD-MAIN_barrier). The explanation for this waiting time (not shown in the figure) is the code associated with initialization, which is serialized and therefore produces waiting time on every other processor. Furthermore, the serialized code (which, for simplicity, exploits the same loops used by the parallel code, and therefore includes unnecessary lock operations) is dominated by the cost of lock operations.

3. About 14% of the waiting time occurs at a barrier at the end of the routine INTERF, where processors wait until all the forces are updated. Although the explanation suggests some load imbalance among the processors in the function UPDATE_FORCES, the majority of the waiting time is again explained by the cost of acquiring and releasing locks.

Our analysis shows that lock acquire operations are the dominant source of overhead for **Water** on Treadmarks. Each acquire operation is expensive and therefore results in overhead. What is surprising, and is only discovered by waiting time analysis, is the extent to which expensive lock operations on one processor indirectly affect other processors, which must wait at barriers or other synchronization points while waiting for a lock acquire to complete elsewhere.

To reduce both the direct and indirect effects of locks, we examined the execution profiles and the waiting time explanations to identify the source code that is causing the overhead. Most of the overhead is associated with two lock acquire calls, which are used to update molecule accelerations within an iteration. Since the modifications associated with the lock are only used in a subsequent iteration, we can modify the program to accumulate the changes locally within an iteration, and then update the global array of molecules. This modification, which reduces significantly the number of lock acquire operations and was already incorporated into Water in the Splash2 suite [16], improves the execution time by a factor of 17 on four processors.

The original version of **Water** was written for a shared-memory machine, where lock operations are relatively cheap and excessive synchronization is a small price to pay for simplicity. In DSM systems like Treadmarks the tradeoffs are very different, and locks should be avoided wherever possible. This example shows that **Carnival** is particularly helpful in analyzing parallel programs that are being ported to a DSM system from another architecture, since it identifies both direct and indirect consequences of tradeoffs made in one environment, and identifies the source code that must be modified to reflect different tradeoffs in the new environment.

4.2 Scheduling and Data Layout in Ocean

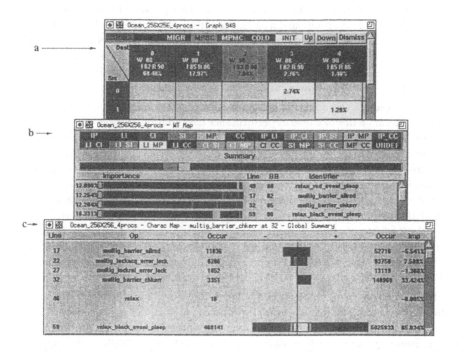

Fig. 2. Carnival visualization of Ocean

Our second example examines **Ocean**, an application in the Splash2 suite [16] that models large-scale ocean movements based on eddy and boundary currents.

The original Splash2 code was ported to Treadmarks by colleagues at the Federal University in Rio de Janeiro without any changes to the data layout scheme. We executed the program on four processors with a grid size of 258 x 258, a grid resolution of 20000, and a time between relaxations of 28800. This execution took 151 seconds.

The global execution-time profiles show that, for **Ocean**, processors are idle for 60% of the overall execution time, while another 31% of the execution time is spent in the Treadmarks protocol (including garbage collection). Of the overall waiting time, about half is spent by processors waiting for page requests to be satisfied, with the other half spent by processors waiting at a synchronization point. Waiting time analysis identifies two parallel loops (`relax_red_eveni_ploop` – basic block 88 and `relax_black_eveni_ploop` – basic block 90) as the source of most of the page requests, and two barriers as the source of most synchronization overhead (Figure 2**b**). Furthermore, the analysis shows (Figure 2**c**) that most waiting time spent at the barriers is caused by the communication in the loops. From this analysis we conclude that communication is responsible (directly or indirectly) for approximately 75% of the overall execution time.

The communication profiles show that the two parallel loops account for 62% of the overall communication in the program. The profiles also show that the variable `multi`, a shared data structure containing the various grids used in the red-black Gauss-Seidel multigrid equation solver, is the only shared variable accessed in those portions of the code. In fact, accesses to `multi` are responsible for 75% of the overall communication cost of the application.

At this point in the analysis, we know that the communication costs of two parallel loops are a major cause of performance degradation and the only variable involved in this communication is `multi`. We use communication analysis to examine the access patterns for `multi` and discover that each page in this data structure has multiple producers and multiple consumers (MPMC). In the graph presented in Figure 2**a**, we can see that 86% of the communication costs can be attributed to a MPMC access pattern (the sum of percentages in columns 0 and 1), and the two loops are always writing on each page (i.e., the data written in basic block 88 is requested by basic block 90 and vice-versa). Furthermore, each page is always accessed by the same set of processors. An examination of the two loops reveals that the boundary conditions do not overlap among processors, and therefore we attribute the MPMC behavior to false sharing.

The Splash2 implementation of **Ocean** adopts a tiling allocation policy to improve the communication-to-computation ratio [16]. Under this allocation, less than two percent of all accesses are to boundary entries shared with another processor. However, using a tiling allocation of sub-matrices of 500K each, coupled with the 8K page size in Treadmarks, means that **every** access to multi under Treadmarks is a shared access. Since the boundaries of `multi` sub-matrices are not aligned on page boundaries, every write access to a page in this data structure generates an invalidation. Adopting the blocked allocation policy of the original Splash version of **Ocean**, and padding sub-arrays to align on 8K page boundaries, alleviates this problem, and improves the running time on four processors by a factor of 8.

It is not surprising that a program written for a shared-memory machine with relatively small units of coherency exhibits false sharing on a DSM system with large units of coherency, nor is it surprising that padding of data structures in such a program improves performance on a DSM system. The point of this example is to illustrate how waiting time analysis and communication analysis can be used to find the sources of excess communication in the source code, and suggest changes. In this particular example, our analysis lead us to focus on communication in the two loops, even though a global profile would have suggested a focus on synchronization at two barriers elsewhere in the program.

5 Conclusions

In this paper we presented two automated techniques for analyzing the performance of DSM applications: waiting time analysis (which determines the causes of idle processor cycles) and communication analysis (which determines the causes of page requests). We described how these techniques are implemented within **Carnival**, a performance visualization tool, and Treadmarks, a DSM system. We used the **Carnival** interface and our techniques to analyze the performance of two Splash applications, Water and Ocean, on a DEC Alpha implementation of Treadmarks. Our experience demonstrates that these techniques can be used effectively to understand the causes of poor performance, and to identify specific improvements in the source code.

We are continuing to analyze applications using these techniques, to better understand the limits of our techniques, and to improve the way in which performance information is presented to the user by **Carnival**. Furthermore, we plan to compare the performance of applications under Treadmarks and Cashmere [9] (a DSM system under development at Rochester), and consider how best to apply our techniques to understanding tradeoffs in the protocols.

Acknowledgements

We would like to thank Sandhya Dwarkadas for her comments on this work. We also would like to thank Cristiana Seidel and Lauro Whately of the Federal University in Rio de Janeiro for the Treadmarks version of Ocean.

References

1. C. Amza, A. Cox, S. Dwarkadas, P. Keleher, H. Lu, R. Rajamony, W. Yu, and W. Zwaenepoel. Treadmarks: shared memory computing on networks of workstations. *IEEE Computer*, February 1996.
2. R. Bianchini, L. Kontothanassis, R. Pinto, M. De Maria, M. Abud, and C. Amorim. Hiding communication latency and coherence overhead in software DSMs. In *Proceedings of the 7th International Conference on Architectural Support for Programming Languages and Operating Systems*, Boston,MA, October 1996.

3. M. Blumrich, C. Dubnicki, E. Felten, K. Li, and M. Mesarina. Virtual-memory-mapped network interfaces. *IEEE Micro*, 15(2):21–28, February 1995.
4. T. Chilimbi, T. Ball, S. Eick, and J. Larus. Stormwatch: A tool for visualizing memory system protocols. In *Proceedings of Supercomputing'95*, San Diego, CA, December 1995. IEEE.
5. R. Gillett. Memory channel network for PCI. *IEEE Micro*, pages 12–18, February 1996.
6. A. Goldberg and J. Hennessy. MTool:an integrated system for performance debugging shared memory multiprocessor applications. *IEEE Transactions on Parallel and Distributed Systems*, 4(1):28–40, January 1993.
7. L. Iftode, C. Dubnicki, E. Felten, and K. Li. Improving release-consistent shared virtual memory using automatic update. In *Proceedings of the 2nd IEEE Symposium on High-Performance Computing Architecture*. IEEE, February 1996.
8. P. Keleher, A. Cox, and W. Zwaenepoel. Lazy release consistency for software distributed shared memory. In *Proceedings of the 19th International Symposium on Computer Architecture*, pages 13–21, Gold Coast, Australia, May 1992. ACM.
9. L. Kontothanassis and M. Scott. High performance software coherence for current and future architectures. *Journal of Parallel and Distributed Computing*, 29:179–195, November 1995.
10. M. Martonosi, A. Gupta, and T. Anderson. Memspy: Analyzing memory system bottlenecks in programs. *Performance Evaluation Review*, 20(1):1 – 12, June 1992. Reprint of a paper presented in Sigmetrics' 92.
11. W. Meira Jr., T. LeBlanc, and A. Poulos. Waiting time analysis and performance visualization in Carnival. In *Proceedings of SPDT96: SIGMETRICS Symposium on Parallel and Distributed Tools*, pages 1–10, Philadelphia, PA, May 1996. ACM.
12. B. P. Miller, M. D. Callaghan, J. M. Cargille, J. K. Hollingsworth, R. B. Irvin, K. L. Karavanic, K. Kunchithapadam, and T. Newhall. The Paradyn parallel performance measurement tool. *IEEE Computer*, 28(11):37–46, November 1995.
13. John K. Ousterhout. *Tcl and Tk Toolkit*. Addison Wesley, 1994.
14. R. Rajamony and A. Cox. A performance debugger for eliminating excess synchronization in shared-memory parallel programs. In *Proceedings of the 4th International Workshop on Modeling, Analysis, and Simulation of COmputer and Telecommunication Systems (MASCOTS)*, February 1996.
15. J. P. Singh, W. Weber, and A. Gupta. SPLASH: Stanford parallel applications for shared memory. *Computer Architecture News*, 20(1):5–44, March 1992.
16. S. Woo, M. Ohara, E. Torrie, J. Singh, and A. Gupta. The SPLASH-2 programs: Characterization and methodological considerations. In *Proceedings of the 22nd Annual International Symposium on Computer Architecture*, pages 24–36, Santa Margherita Ligure, Italy, June 1995. ACM.

Performance Metrics and Measurement Techniques of Collective Communication Services

Natawut Nupairoj and Lionel M. Ni

Department of Computer Science
Michigan State University
East Lansing, MI 48824-1027
{nupairoj,ni}@cps.msu.edu

Abstract. The performance of collective communication is critical to the overall system performance. In general, the performance of the collective communication is dependent not only on the underlying hardware, but also its implementation. To evaluate the performance of collective communication accurately, identifying the most representative metrics and using correct measurement techniques are two important issues that have to be considered. This paper focuses on the measurement techniques for collective communication services. The proposed techniques can provide an accurate evaluation of the completion time without requiring a global clock and without having to know the detailed implementations of collective communication services. Experimental results conducted on the IBM/SP at Argonne National Laboratory are presented.

1 Introduction

Collective communication is frequently invoked in parallel programs to communicate and coordinate a group of participating processors. The MPI standard [1] classifies this communication class into three subclasses: one-to-all (one source, all processors are destinations), all-to-one (all processors are sources, one destination), and all-to-all (all processors are both sources and destinations). Note that all processors in the group could be a subset of processors in the system. Thus, one-to-all and all-to-one from group point-of-view are actually one-to-many and many-to-one from system point-of-view, respectively.

The performance of collective communication is critical to the overall system performance. In general, the performance of the collective communication is dependent not only on the underlying hardware, but also its implementation. Thus, to measure the performance of the collective communication accurately, the following issues must be considered.

- For a given computing-platform, can we claim one implementation is better than the other implementation ? Consider the example in Figure 1. The binomial multicast tree finishes sooner than the chain multicast tree. On the other hand, processors in the chain multicast tree have more idle time waiting for messages than processors in the binomial multicast tree. Theoretically, if a program can distribute its workload such that no processor is waiting due to communication, all implementations will make no difference. By dynamically balancing the workload, programmers can perform machine-dependent tuning to allow their programs to achieve the best performance. However, dynamic workload balancing is a very complicated issue, and in some high-level data parallel programming language, such as HPF [2], it is assumed that a vector data is evenly-distributed across all processors (e.g. block and cyclic distributions). Moreover, machine-dependent dynamic load balancing prohibits program portability due to different implementations of collective communication services. Thus, under the assumption that the workload is evenly-distributed, a good implementation of collective communication should minimize the waiting time due to communication.

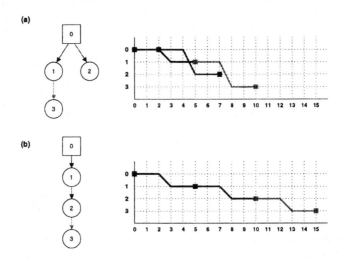

Fig. 1. One-to-many communication: (a) binomial multicast tree, (b) chain multicast tree.

- What is the most representative metric(s) for a collective communication service? In order to evaluate a collective communication service, the chosen metrics must be able to characterize the actual overhead of the service when it is invoked in applications. Moreover, the definitions of metrics must be clearly defined. In this paper, we consider the *completion time* as the most representative metric for collective communication services. Although other metrics can also be used to quantify the performance of collective communication services, the completion time is simpler and can be used to to estimate the communication overhead in a wider range of applications. The definition of the completion time is provided in Section 2.

– What is the correct technique to measure the metric? One of common mistakes in performance evaluation is using incorrect measurement techniques. The results from incorrect techniques can be very misleading. Thus, it is necessary to verify that the techniques are actually measuring the desirable metrics.

The objective of this paper is to propose metrics and measuring techniques to evaluate one-to-many and many-to-one collective communication services. Our proposed technique are quite simple, more accurate, and have less limitation than other techniques. We also provide definitions and theorems to verify the correctness of our measurement techniques. Our experiment is based on MPI library due to its popularity. However, the proposed technique can also be applied to other communication libraries. For the measurement purposes, all processes are executed in distinct processors. Thus, process, processor, and node will be used interchangeably in this paper.

This paper is organized as follows. Section 2 defines the point-to-point communication model and collective communication flow model which will be used as a basis in our measurement techniques. Section 4 discusses the measurement techniques for one-to-many collective communication. In Section 5, we present the measurement techniques for many-to-one collective communication. We then use the proposed techniques to measure the collective communication services on IBM/SP at Argonne National Laboratory whose results are presented in Section 6. Finally, the paper is concluded in Section 7.

2 Models

2.1 Point-to-Point Parameterized Communication Model

The point-to-point communication model used in this paper is the parameterized communication model which is the extension of the LogP model [3]. Basically, the model involves five parameters: sending latency (t_{send}), receiving latency (t_{recv}), network latency (t_{net}), holding latency (t_{hold}), and end-to-end latency (t_{end}), as shown in Figure 2. The parameter t_{send} is the software latency required in processing the sending message at the sender which includes the overhead of packetization, checksum computing, and, possibly, memory copying. Similarly the parameter t_{recv}, is the software overhead at the receiver. The parameter t_{net} is the time required to transmit the message across the network. In general, several significant factors contribute to the value of t_{net}, such as network bandwidth, underlying switching mechanism, and blocking time due to network contention. In order to measure the network latency accurately, benchmarking must be conducted in a controlled environment so that the effect of network contention due to other unrelated messages is avoided.

Measuring t_{send}, t_{net}, and t_{recv} individually is rather difficult. In order to obtain the accurate measurement, some special techniques, such as using hardware monitor and software probe, are required. Thus, two additional parameters are

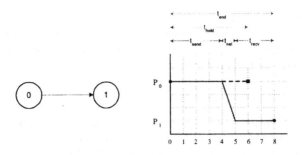

Fig. 2. The point-to-point communication model.

defined: end-to-end latency (t_{end}) and holding time (t_{hold}). The parameter t_{end} is the interval between the time when the sender starts sending a message and the time when the receiver finishes receiving. Hence, t_{end} is

$$t_{end} = t_{send} + t_{net} + t_{recv} \qquad (1)$$

The parameter t_{hold} is the minimum time interval between any two consecutive send or receive operations. In most cases, the communication performance can be predicted based on t_{hold} and t_{end} since most communication services are based on the send and receive operations. Observe that t_{hold} represents the latency of invoking the send operation, and t_{end} reflects the delay of delivering a message across the network. In [4], we explain how to evaluate both t_{hold} and t_{end} at the user-application level.

2.2 Collective Communication Flow Model

In this study, we consider an implementation of the collective communications based on the MPI standard which all participating processes form a group and forward messages among them. A process in the group is considered to *start participating* a collective communication service when it calls the collective communication routine. When the call is returned, the participation in the operation of the process is considered *finished*. Based on the MPI definition, the whole collective communication operation may not be completed. Hence, the time that each process spends in the operation does not reflect the actual performance of the collective communication and it is not a good performance metric. Therefore, in this study, we use the *completion time* as the performance metric of all collective communication services.

Definition 1. Let all processes simultaneously call the collective communication routine at time t_0. The **completion time** of the collective communication operation (t_c) is the elapsed time between t_0 and the time when all processes finish the call. And let the set of critical destinations (D_c) be a set of destinations that finish the call last.

The main problem of the completion time is that it is not possible to make all processes call the communication routine at the same time without using a special hardware. To make the completion time measurable, our measurement techniques are based on the *communication flow model*.

Definition 2. A **communication flow** $f(s, d)$ is a chain of unicast operations propagating messages from the source s to the destination d.

Definition 3. The **flow latency** $t_f(s, d)$ is the elapsed time between the source s calls the collective communication routine and the destination d returns from the call.

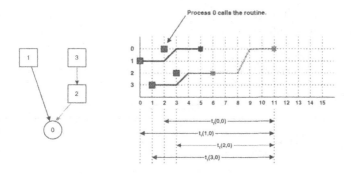

Fig. 3. An example of the reduction communication service for 4 processes. Processes 0, 1, 2, and 3 call the reduction routine at time instance 2, 0, 3, and 1, respectively.

Figure 3 demonstrates an example of the reduction communication service for 4 processes where process 0 is the root processes. In this example, there are 4 flows including $f(0,0)$, $f(1,0)$, $f(2,0)$, and $f(3,0)$. The flow latencies of each flow are 9, 11, 8, and 10, respectively. Note that we consider process 0 as both source and destination.

3   Pitfalls of Ping-Based Benchmarking

In order to construct the measurement techniques of collective communication services, we study the problems of ping-based benchmarking which has been used by some researchers. Algorithm 1 shows a ping-based multicast benchmarking code which measures the average multicast latency at the root process (t_{root}) and the maximum multicast latency among all participating processes (t_{max}). The results can be a big misleading when comparing different multicast implementations. As shown in Figure 4, the results mislead us to conclude that the performance of the chain multicast tree is better than the binomial multicast tree in term of both latency and scalability, which is obviously wrong.

Algorithm 1.   **The ping-based multicast benchmark.**

begin
    t_{start} := GetTime();
    for i := 1 **to** N **do**
        MPI_Bcast(message);
    endfor;
    t_{local} := (GetTime() - t_{start})/N;

    t_{root} := t_{local} from process 0;
    t_{max} := maximum reduce (t_{local});
end.

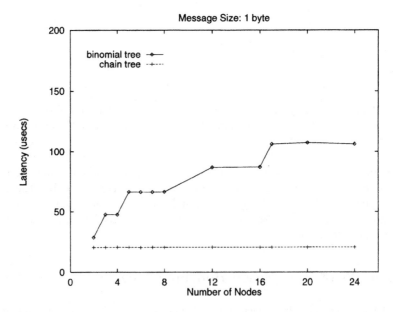

Fig. 4. Ping-based measurement results of multicast (t_{root}) on the IBM/SP.

There are two problems with the ping-based benchmark, pipelined effect and cross-iteration contention. If we roll out the loop in Algorithm 1, this algorithm measures the average latency of N consecutive multicast operations. Based on

MPI definition, the return from MPI_Bcast call does not guarantee that the whole operation is actually finished. Thus, some processes may start the next call to MPI_Bcast routine even before all processes finish the current MPI_Bcast operation. This creates a pipelined effect, and hence, the measured latency is less than the actual MPI_Bcast latency. The other problem is the contention between MPI_Bcast executed on different iterations. As mention earlier, some processes may start the next call to MPI_Bcast routine while the current MPI_Bcast operation is not finished. The overlap of MPI_Bcast from different iterations may create network contention which can further skew the measurement results.

4 One-to-Many Communication

To measure the completion time of one-to-many communication services, we have to utilize the fact that there is only one source (called the *root process*) and all other processes in the group are the destinations. Typically, all processes, except the root process, have to receive a message before forwarding the message to other processes. Therefore, we can derive the following theorem.

Definition 4. Let r be the root process of the one-to-many operation. Let $t'_f(r, d)$ be the flow latency of $f(r, d)$ where all processes simultaneously call the routine.

Theorem 5. *If r is the last process to call the one-to-many communication routine, for all destination j:*

$$t_f(r, j) = t'_f(r, j)$$

Theorem 5 implies that if the root is the last process to call the routine, the completion time can be measured from $t_f(r, d_c)$ where r is the root process and d_c is a critical destination. By calling a many-to-one communication such as reduce before the measurement, it is guaranteed that the root process is always the last one to call the routine. Thus, the key is to identify the critical destinations.

One property of a critical destination is that it is always finishes last. Hence, if we measure the flow latencies between the root process and all other processes, a process i who has the longest flow latency ($t_f(root, i)$) is a critical destination. Therefore, we measure all flow latencies and choose the longest one. The chosen latency is also the completion time of the operation. Algorithm 2 illustrates the code to measure the completion time. Without the loss of generality, we assume that the participating processes are $\{0, 1, \ldots, k - 1\}$. Hence there are k flows (1 source and k destinations). To measure a flow latency $t_f(root, responder)$, We measure the time before the root process call the one-to-many routine and the time after the root process finishes the call and receives a message from a responder which indicates that the responder has already finished the call. The elapsed time $t_m(root, responder)$ in Algorithm 2 is the flow latency $t_f(root, responder)$ (Theorem 5). After measuring all flow latencies, a responder who has the longest flow latency is a critical destination and its flow latency is the completion time.

Algorithm 2.   **Measuring one-to-many communication.**

input: process_id where $0 \leq$ process_id $\leq k - 1$.
begin
   for *responder* := 0 **to** $k - 1$ **do**
        {Synchronize.}
        MPI_Reduce(*root*); {The root process finishes the last.}

        {Measurement.}
        if process_id == *root* **then**
           t_{start} := GetTime();
        endif;
        for i := 1 **to** N **do**
           One_to_Many_Routine();
           if process_id == *root* **then**
              Wait for a respond from *responder*;
           else if process_id == *responder* **then**
              {Dummy loop goes here.}
              Send a one_byte ack to the *root*;
           endif;
        endfor;
        if process_id == *root* **then**
           t_{ack} := $t_{end}(one\_byte)$;
           $t_m(root, responder)$:= (GetTime() - t_{start})/N - t_{ack};
        endif;
   endfor;
   $t_c = \max_{i=0}^{k-1}\{t_m(root, i)\}$;
end.

Typically, the system clock resolution is not fine enough to measure the latency of a single call of a one-to-many operation accurately. Thus, we measure the elapsed time of N repeatations of the inside loop, compute the average, and subtract the overhead of an ack message (which can be predetermined by using the traditional one-to-one ping-pong technique). Suppose that the responder is not a critical destination. It is possible that the responder may send an ack message to the root before the operation being measured is actually ended. The transmission of the ack message and the not-yet-completed operation may cause channel contention in the network. The delay introduced to the ack message may mistakenly consider the responder as a critical destination and leads to a wrong measurement.

To avoid the unexpected network contention, each responder has to wait t_{dummy} time before sending the ack message back. Let the worst case measured latency in Algorithm 2 be t_{worst}. By choosing $t_{dummy} \geq t_{worst}$, it can guarantee that there is no contention between the ack message and the operation messages. t_{dummy} can be easily implemented by executing a dummy loop with some harmless computations. The relationship between the number of iterations in the dummy loop and t_{dummy} can be easily predetermined. After critical destinations are identified. The completion time can be measured by using one of the critical destinations as the responder and performing one more measurement without the dummy loop. The placement of the dummy loop in the code is shown in Algorithm 2.

5   Many-to-One Communication

As many-to-one communication service usually involves more than one source, measuring its completion time is quite difficult. In this study, we assume that the internal implementation of a many-to-one communication service being measured is based on a tree of messages where processes are considered to be nodes in the tree and messages are propagated from sources to a single destination called the *root* process. The tree-based structure has been used to implement many-to-one communication services in both hardware [5] and software [3, 6].

A tree-based many-to-one communication service can be represented by a directed graph, or *digraph*, G(V,E) with the node set V(G) and the arc set E(G). A node u in V(G) represents the process u and an arc (u,v) is E(G) represents a unicast to propagate a message from u to v.

Definition 6. Let G(V,E) be a digraph and let u, v, and w be nodes in V(G). A node u is reachable from node v if and only if one of the following conditions holds.

1. $v = u$.
2. (v, w) is in E(G) and u is reachable from w.

Definition 7. A tree-based many-to-one communication service represents by a digraph G(V,E) satisfying the follow conditions:

1. There is one node, called the root node, which has out-degree = 0.
2. Other nodes have out-degree = 1.
3. The root node is always reachable from all nodes.

Definition 7 implies that the root process always finishes the call last. In other words, the root process is always the critical destination. We can also conclude two additional properties of the flow latency of tree-based many-to-one communication services in the following theorems. Due to the limiting spaces, the proof of these theorems can be found in our technical report [7].

Theorem 8. *If a source i is the last process that calls the tree-based many-to-one communication routine, $t_f(i, r) \leq t_c$ where r is the root process of the operation.*

Theorem 9. *There exists at least one source s that if it is the last process that calls the tree-based many-to-one communication routine, $t_f(s,r) = t_c$ where r is the root process of the operation. We also called s a critical source.*

Algorithm 3. **Measuring many-to-one communication.**

input: process_id where $0 \le$ process_id $\le k - 1$.
begin
    for *timer* := 0 **to** $k - 1$ **do**
        {Synchronize.}
        MPI_Reduce(*timer*); {The timer finishes the last.}

        {Measurement.}
        if process_id == *timer* **then**
            t_{start} := GetTime();
        endif;
        for i := 1 **to** N **do**
            Many_to_One_Routine();
            if process_id == *root* **then**
                Send one_byte messages to all processes;
                {The last message is sent to the timer.}
            else
                Wait for a message from the *root*;
            endif;
        endfor;
        if process_id == *timer* **then**
            t_{sync} := $((k - 2) \times t_{hold}(one\_byte) + t_{end}(one\_byte))$;
            $t_m(timer, root)$:= (GetTime() - t_{start})/N - t_{sync};
        endif;
    endfor;
    $t_c = \max_{i=0}^{k-1}\{t_m(root, i)\}$;
end.

We use Algorithm 3 to measure the completion time of the many-to-one communication services. Similar to one-to-many measuring technique, the program measures flow latencies between all sources and the root process (single destination). We measure the time at a designated source called *timer* before it calls the many-to-one routine. After the timer finishes the call and receives a message from the root process to indicate that the call at the root process is finished (hence the operation is completed), we measure the time and compute the elapsed time $t_m(timer, root)$. When all flow latencies are measured, the timer with the largest $t_m(timer, root)$ is the critical source and its flow latency is the completion time (Theorems 8 and 9).

When the root process finishes each call, it informs all other processes. This synchronization prevents the sources from starting the next iteration before the collective communication routine of the current iteration is actually finished. It is important that *timer* process must always be the last one to be informed which guarantees that it is the last process that calls the routine. The cost of the synchronization can be estimated from t_{hold} and t_{end} (see t_{sync} in Algorithm 3).

6 Experiments

We conducted the experiments on the 128-node IBM/SP at Argonne National Laboratory. Each node has an IBM/RS6000 processor (62.5 MHz) with 128 MB memory and 1 GB local disk. The peak performance is 125 MFlops per node. Both Algorithm 2 and Algorithm 3 are implemented using MPI-F library version 1.41 [8]. In order to fully utilize the high-performance switch, the library euilib with option us is used. Each data point in our results is the minimal value of 128 measurements to reduce the overhead due to network contention from other programs [1] Thus, the results represent the best performance possible to achieve without the effects from the overhead produced by other programs. However, if the sustained performance is desirable, the average values can be used instead.

6.1 One-to-Many Communication

Figure 5 illustrates the completion time of the MPI-F multicast, the binomial multicast, the sequential multicast, and the optimal multicast [9] when the message is 1024 bytes. When the number of processes is small, all multicasts exhibit the same performance. As the number of processes increases, the completion time of all multicasts increases. The sequential multicast shows the worst performance and does not scale. MPI-F multicasts perform slightly better than the binomial multicast, but still worse than the optimal multicast. This indicates that the performance of the current MPI-F multicast implementation can be further improved.

We compare the performance of three different scatters with respect two different message sizes. Figure 6 illustrates the completion time of the MPI-F scatter, the binomial scatter, and the sequential scatter when the message size is 1 byte. Obviously, the current MPI-F scatter implementation is based on a sequential tree where the root process sends a separated message to each of destinations in turn. The results also indicate that when the message size is small, the scatter implementation based on a binomial tree is more efficient. However, as shown in Figure 7, if the message size becomes 1024 bytes, the scatter implementation based on a sequential tree performs better. To fully understand the results, let consider the scatter implementation based on a binomial tree. The root process sends a message to its first child. Then both processes send

---

[1] It is difficult to reserve the whole machine for our measurement.

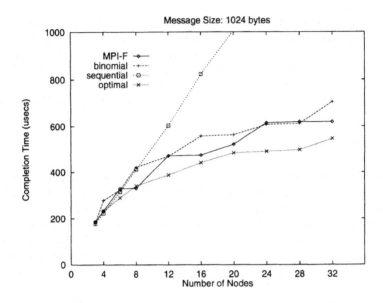

Fig. 5. The completion time (t_c) of four multicast algorithms with message size being 1024 bytes.

messages to the other two processes. Thus, the number of processes that have already received the message increases by a factor of two. Since each destination receives a distinct message from the root process, the root process has to send all messages that its first child need to send to its successors. For example, suppose the root process scatters eight 1-kbyte messages to eight processes. The root process sends a 4-kbyte message to its first child since, based on an 8-node binomial tree, the first child has four successors. The root process then sends a 2-kbyte message to its second child and a 1-kbyte message to its last child. As a result, the scatter implementation based on a binomial tree can perform worse than the implementation based on a sequential tree.

6.2 Many-to-One Communication

In Figure 8, we use Algorithm 3 to measure the completion time of the MPI-F reduce, the binomial reduce, and the sequential reduce with message size being 512 bytes. The results lead us to conclude that the MPI-F reduce implementation is similar to a binomial-based reduce algorithm. However, the MPI-F reduce implementation performs better than a pure binomial-based implementation. This is probably because the MPI-F reduce is customized to perform well on the IBM/SP. Due to the limiting spaces, the performance of the gather operation can be found in our technical report [7].

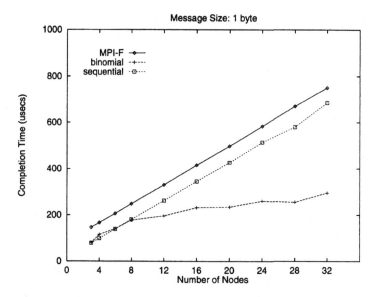

Fig. 6. The completion time (t_c) of three scatter algorithms with message size being 1 bytes.

7 Conclusion

Evaluating the performance of collective communication services is a challenging problem. Using improper performance metrics and incorrect measurement techniques can produce results which are very misleading. This paper proposes the metric and the measurement techniques for one-to-many and many-to-one collective communication. We also present the experimental results conducted on the IBM/SP at Argonne National Laboratory.

The other interesting problem is how to evaluate the performance of many-to-many collective communication services. It is more difficult to measure the completion time since all processes are both sources and destinations at the same time. One possible solution is to use the combination of both measurement techniques presented in this paper. We are investigating the verification of this technique.

Acknowledgments

The authors wish to thank the Mathematics and Computer Science Division at Argonne National Laboratory for granting us to use their 128-node IBM/SP system. This research was supported in part by NSF grants CDA-9121641 and MIP-9204066, and DOE grant DE-FG02-93ER25167.

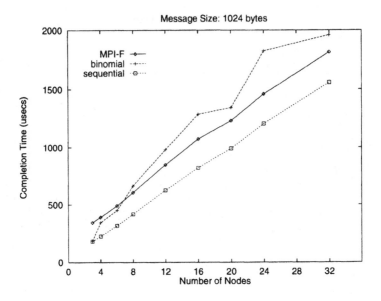

Fig. 7. The completion time (t_c) of three scatter algorithms with message size being 1024 bytes.

References

1. M. P. I. Forum, *MPI: A Message-Passing Interface Standard*, Mar. 1994.
2. High Performance Fortran Forum, "High Performance Fortran Language Specification (version 1.0, draft)," Jan. 1993.
3. D. Culler *et al.*, "LogP: Towards a realistic model of parallel computation," in *Proc. of the 4th ACM SIGPLAN Sym. on Principles and Practice of Parallel Programming*, May 1993.
4. N. Nupairoj and L. Ni, "Benchmarking of Multicast Communication Services," Tech. Rep. MSU-CPS-ACS-103, Department of Computer Science, Michigan State University, Apr. 1995.
5. C. E. Leiserson *et al.*, "The network architecture of the Connection Machine CM-5," in *Proceedings of the ACM Symposium on Parallel Algorithms and Architectures*, (San Diego, CA.), pp. 272–285, Association for Computing Machinery, 1992.
6. C. Huang and P. K. McKinley, "Communication Issues in Parallel Computing across ATM Networks," Tech. Rep. MSU-CPS-94-34, Michigan State University, June 1994.
7. N. Nupairoj and L. M. Ni, "Performance Metrics and Measurement Techniques of Collective Communication Services," Tech. Rep. MSU-CPS-ACS-96-12, Michigan State University, Department of Computer Science, East Lansing, Michigan, Dec. 1996.
8. H. Franke, P. Hochschild, P. Pattnaik, and M. Snir, "MPI-F: An Efficient Implementation of MPI on IBM-SP1," in *Proceedings of the 1994 International Conference on Parallel Processing*, vol. III, (St. Charles, IL), pp. 197–201, Aug. 1994.

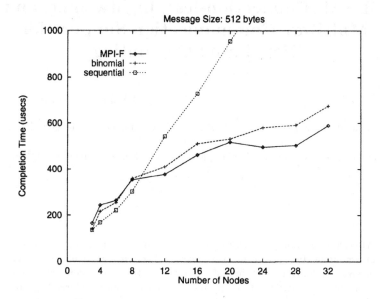

Fig. 8. The completion time (t_c) of three reduce algorithms with message size being 512 bytes.

9. J.-Y. L. Park, H.-A. Choi, N. Nupairoj, and L. M. Ni, "Construction of Optimal Multicast Trees Based on the Parameterized Communication Model," in *Proceedings of the 1996 International Conference on Parallel Processing*, pp. 180–187, Aug. 1996.

CLAM: Connection-less, Lightweight, and Multiway Communication Support for Distributed Computing*

Juan Carlos Gomez[1], Vernon Rego[1], and Vaidy Sunderam[2]

[1] Department of Computer Sciences, Purdue University, West Lafayette, IN 47907, USA
[2] Department of Mathematics & Computer Science, Emory University, Atlanta, GA 30322, USA

Abstract. A number of factors motivate and favor the implementation of communication protocols in user-space. There is a particularly strong motivation for the provision of scalable, multiway and connectionless transport for distributed computing, multimedia, and conferencing applications. This is also true of high speed networking, where it is beneficial to keep the OS kernel out of the critical path in communication. User-space protocol implementations may hold the key to optimal functionality and performance. We describe the Connectionless, Lightweight and Multiway (CLAM) communications system which provides efficient and scalable user-space support for distributed applications requiring multiple protocols. The system supports heterogeneous networked applications with irregular or asynchronous communication patterns and multimodal data. We focus on motivating and describing the CLAM architecture and present some experimental results that evaluate an specific protocol module inside this architecture.

1 Introduction

Distributed computing has undergone rapid and profound changes in recent years, both with respect to the paradigms used and also with respect to implementations and hardware. Active messages [31], Optimistic Active Messages [33], and Active Networks [30] have appeared as flexible and versatile alternatives to more traditional approaches like message passing, shared memory, and message driven computing. Communication hardware and software architectures have reduced workstation-cluster latencies from milliseconds to microseconds [32]. New applications requiring efficient many-to-many transfers, not supported by traditional protocols, have stimulated design and implementation of novel application-specific protocols [24]. With advances in software technology, distributed computing systems have begun to accommodate threads-based computing models [1, 9, 10, 21].

---

* Supported in part by ONR-9310233, ARO-93G0045 and BMDO-34798-MA.

Traditional distributed computing software architectures that are based on in-kernel protocols cannot fully deliver to an application the low latencies and high bandwidths offered by current network technology. To overcome this limitation, new software and hardware architectures have been proposed [2, 15, 22, 32] that depart from the traditional approach by moving the kernel out of the critical path in communication. The idea is to implement protocols in user space, with user-level processes having direct access to network devices. As a result, such architectures have reduced message latencies from milliseconds to tens of microseconds, and in some cases, round-trip times in the order of microseconds have been reported [22]. There are several reasons for implementing communication protocols in user space: to keep the kernel simple [29] (i.e. Mach, Amoeba), to obtain functionality not available with traditional in-kernel protocols (e.g., many-to-many communication [24]), to increase scalability, and to make protocols more sensitive to application needs [6].

Partly motivated by concerns of performance, and partly pressured by available software technology, designers of distributed systems have begun to exploit lightweight threads as application-level interfaces [9, 10, 14, 20, 21]. This is also the result of a general acceptance that threads can enhance application development, support unpredictable data access patterns, mask communication and I/O latencies, enable dynamic computation schedules, facilitate fine-grained concurrency in shared memory multiprocessors, and potentially provide for load balancing. It must be recognized, however, that these are all constructs that exploit concurrency at the application level, and coexisting threads must still rely on the old communication framework (e.g., TCP/IP or reliable UDP) for message delivery. Most importantly, threads enable a smooth and efficient integration of communication protocols and application code, in keeping with the needs of current day applications and technology.

There is an alternative to the simple top-down use of threads in application-level constructs. This is a bottom-up view in which the communication framework relies entirely on threads for transaction-level communication, eliminating much of the protocol layering separating computing threads from communicating threads. In such a view, the communication subsystem is free to interact with the computation subsystem in any way that is beneficial to a distributed application. Further, locating all threads in user-space has the added advantage of placing the controllable part of the communication framework in user-space and offering the often undervalued benefits of application portability and system flexibility [6, 8]. Finally, the use of threads at both the application and the protocol level enables the efficient integration and scheduling of communication and user computation inside a single OS process. With such support, an application need not use distinct OS processes for communication and computation. With user-space protocols, there is no need for communication daemons.

The Connectionless, Lightweight, and Multiway environment (CLAM) [11, 12, 13] combines the advantages of threads, user-level protocols, and multiprotocol support to provide an efficient and scalable framework for integrating collaboration and computing on heterogeneous networks. CLAM improves efficiency by reducing expensive OS-level context switches, and by optimizing the message polling used to retrieve data from in-kernel protocols or network interfaces. CLAM augments the message passing environment with its user-level protocol modularity, providing support for reliable point-to-point, real time, and other types of traffic. Because of its scalability, multi-protocol and threads support, CLAM covers a potentially wider spectrum of distributed applications than most other runtime platforms.

Though a few systems provide support for multithreaded distributed computing at the application level [9, 14, 21], CLAM is the only platform that supports threads-based computing and communication in a fully integrated manner, including threads in protocol and message passing software. CLAM's protocol modules support a wider functionality than that provided by the traditional protocols used to support distributed computing (i.e. TCP/IP and UDP), including out-of-order delivery, remote thread activation, active messages, etc. Finally, CLAM was designed to be portable and easy to deploy, requiring no kernel coding or modification.

In the following section (Section 2), we describe the CLAM environment and, in Section 3, we present some experimental results comparing the performance of the reliable protocol module of CLAM to well-known message passing libraries. We conclude in Section 4 with a mention of future work.

2 The CLAM Environment

We expect future applications to exhibit a host of communication requirements, including low-latency, high-bandwidth, scalability, flexibility, multiple-protocol support, multimodal data, multiway transfers, and realtime and isochronous transport, among other things. CLAM is a connectionless, lightweight and multiway communications architecture designed to address the requirements listed above and, in particular, to support scalable, high-performance and collaborative applications that manage multimodal data (see Figure 1). To avoid heavy and cumbersome functionality, CLAM offers a plug-and-play methodology with its protocol suite [11]. It is layered on top of the Ariadne threads library [21] and the UDP protocol. It consists of a software layer that offers runtime support for global process management, and three native protocol modules: an unreliable module that provides efficient unreliable unicast and multicast, a reliable multicast module, and a reliable point-to-point module. Each protocol module is implemented with a specific set of communicating threads, depending on the functionality required. For example, the reliable point-to-point module requires three threads (i.e., a *receive*, a *send*, and a *timer* thread). The *send*, and *timer* threads handle asynchronous events, such as transmissions delayed by flow and congestion control algorithms, retransmissions, etc. The *receive* thread handles polling of the underlying communication layer. The unreliable module requires only a *receive* thread.

The CLAM system can be structured in one of two ways: a uniprocess model and a multiprocess model (see Figure 2). In the uniprocess model, all of the

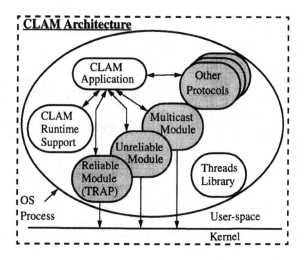

Fig. 1. Process View of CLAM

CLAM functionality is integrated with an application and runs within a single process at the OS level. The Ariadne scheduler is in charge of doling out CPU quanta between the different runnable threads. The multiprocess model may be used on shared memory multiprocessors, so that available parallelism can be exploited. Here, all threads reside in shared memory and may be scheduled to run in distinct OS-level processes (and thus, processors) to enable concurrency. A third model is currently under development, and it involves the use of kernel threads to exploit parallelism in shared memory multiprocessors. Benefits of this approach include reduced Operating System related costs, and the fact that no special software version has to be maintained for the multiprocessor architectures.

The reliable protocol module, that is, the Transaction-oriented Realiable and Point-to-point protocol (TRAP), is a key component of the CLAM protocol suite, designed to either augment or even replace TCP/IP in those situations where it cannot deliver the requisite performance or functionality. TRAP provides unreliable, reliable in-order, and reliable out-of-order at-most-once transmission. Further, each message may be delivered as a regular passive-message, an active-message, or a thread-activation. UDP datagrams may be lost, delivered out of order, or may get replicated. CLAM's reliable layer (TRAP) tackles these problems and provides a reliable, in-order, message oriented service on top of UDP or any other best-effort network protocol. TRAP is a sliding window protocol based on packets. This makes it highly suited to messaging applications. Positive acknowledgments, timed retransmission, and a modified version of the Fast Retransmit algorithm [17] are used to deal with packet loss. TRAP uses selective acknowledgments. Sequence numbers are used to detect packet replication and guarantee in-order delivery. TRAP computes retransmission timeouts using an adaptive algorithm proposed in [7]. Karn's algorithm, with binary-exponential

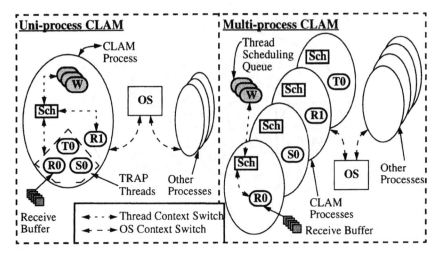

Fig. 2. Integrating CLAM to the OS

back-off, is used to modify the retransmission timeout on retransmissions [19]. TRAP also provides flow and congestion control. To improve the performance of our TRAP implementation, we used well-known optimization techniques such as the "Last-Received Cache" scheme proposed by Mogul [23], schemes suggested by Clark [4, 5], and the header prediction scheme [16].

The multicast module, currently under development, is intended to support reliable, totally-ordered multicast on a LAN or a set of locally interconnected LANs. By restricting the protocol to these environments, we expect to be able to achieve good performance through use of a simple multicast algorithm.

In a typical distributed computing application, a program explicitly specifies where sends and receives must occur in its execution sequence. This enables *send* and *receive* threads to run. Automatic polling strategies, based on compiler support, are likely to be inefficient. With threads support, however, a communications library may run *send* and *receive* threads with or without user-knowledge, enabling transparent message transmission and latency hiding. When they run, communication threads run at a higher priority than application threads. Each protocol module has a *receive* thread that polls the underlying protocol session for incoming messages. The scheduling of the *receive* thread is adaptively tuned to minimize polling overhead and datagram loss [11, 12, 13]. Adaptation is accomplished by adjusting the frequency of activation of the *receive* thread, based on a recent history of the datagram arrival rate.

As stated earlier, each protocol in CLAM supports active messages and remote thread activations. An active message carries an index that points to a function previously registered at the destination. Upon receipt of an active message, the protocol module invokes the function pointed-to, and passes it the message as a parameter. If the received message is a remote thread activation, the protocol module creates a new thread with the function pointed-to by the index, and passes the message to the new thread at creation time. The sender decides, through a flag set in the message header, whether the message is to be executed as a thread or as a function upon arrival at its destination.

Applications supported by CLAM consist of one or more threads that can access any of the protocol modules or any other in-kernel protocol provided by the host OS. Each of these protocol modules can have simultaneous sessions to many remote sites. Although the CLAM environment provides a broad range of communication support, applications on top of CLAM may still make use of in-kernel protocols like TCP/IP. This may be useful in applications where reliable stream oriented transfer is required.

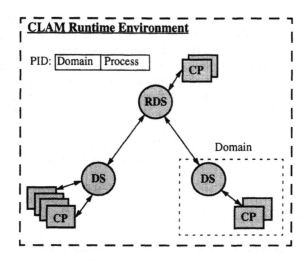

Fig. 3. Global View of CLAM

Figure 3 shows a global perspective of the CLAM environment. On top of the basic protocol modules, CLAM provides the additional runtime support necessary for the implementation of distributed applications. This support includes process management and message routing. CLAM's processes are structured in a three-level hierarchy, with three types of processes: Root Domain Server process (RDS), Regular Domain Servers processes (DS), and Computing Processes[3] (CP). This hierarchy divides CLAM's processes into domains. A CLAM domain is defined as a set of processes consisting of a Domain Server, with Computing Processes that depend on this Domain Server. Domain Servers are processes that enable user computation through a set of services (e.g., initial routing, global naming). The Root Domain Server is a special Domain Server process that is authorized to assign domain identifiers. Computing Processes enable user or application code to execute.

---

[3] What is referred to here as a process may, in fact, be a set of OS processes if the multi-process model is used.

All processes, including the Domain Servers, are addressed through a process identifier number (pid). The upper half of this pid defines the domain, and the lower half identifies a specific process in the given domain. Each Domain Server is named by a pid in which the process specific part is zero. It is responsible for a number of Computing Processes, all of which are located (preferably) on the same local area network. Pids are dynamically mapped to IP address and UDP port number tuples with the help of the Domain Servers.

3 Implementation Performance

We report the results of a set of experiments that we conducted to measure TRAP's performance. The intent is to determine how TRAP-based communication compares to popular TCP/IP- or UDP-based software systems for message-oriented computations on heterogeneous networks. Because these popular environments offer only single-threaded process executions, we made every effort to keep the comparison fair. In particular, we did not exploit the advantages of TRAP's support for multithreaded processing. We compare TRAP's communication performance to communication in version 1.4 of P4 [3], version 3.3.9 of PVM [28], and version 6.0 of LAM-MPI [25]. Our proposed message-passing interface (CMPI) is based on the TRAP multithreaded and user-level protocol library.

3.1 Experimental Methodology

All experiments presented here were conducted on homogeneous networked platforms; the message-passing libraries were *not* configured to do data conversions (PvmDataRaw option and LAM -O switch). Latency is measured from the viewpoint of the application. That is, we consider a message to be delivered *only when* it arrives at an application's buffer and is detected by the application. The $-nger$ switch was used during the LAM-MPI tests to turn off the Guaranteed Envelope Resources feature [26]. The experiments were performed on SPARCstation-5 machines, running SunOS Solaris 5.5, with cpu clock rates of 70 and 85 MHz.

We used two different types of environments in our experiments. The LAN experiments were conducted on a 10-Mbit/sec Ethernet and an ATM LAN composed of two workstations connected through a Fore Switch 200wg running version 4.0.0 of the switch software. The ATM interfaces used were the SAB-200E/UTP5 running at 155 Mbits/sec (OC3) over unshielded twisted pair. While conducting the experiments, it was ensured that "other" network and CPU load was low. The hosts used in these experiments ran NFS and shared the same file system.

In all cases, the experiments involving different libraries were run consecutively and not simultaneously. The interval of time between consecutive runs was kept low so as to complete all tests under similar conditions. Each message passing library was compiled using the *Makefile* contained in its distribution package.

All test programs, except for the ones using the LAM library, were compiled using *gcc* version 2.7.2 with the $-O$ optimization switch. Applications using the LAM-MPI library were compiled with the library-provided *hcc* command and the $-O$ optimization switch. The Ariadne threads library was compiled with the same *gcc* compiler, but with no optimizations. The TRAP library was compiled with the same version of *gcc* using the $-O$ switch.

To ensure that factors like initial ARP [27] cache miss and connection establishment did not bias measurements, at least one message was initially transmitted before timing-statistics were initiated. The function *gettimeofday* was used for all timing measurements. Since the overhead of invoking this function is about two orders of magnitude smaller than the minimum measurement obtained (i.e., μ-secs versus msecs), we ignored this effect in our measurements. The size of the maximum window used by TRAP in all the experiments was set to 32 packets, except where stated otherwise. For the other libraries, default send and receive protocol buffer sizes were used.

3.2 Round-trip Time

Low communication latency is a feature that can be crucial to the performance of distributed and collaborative software. To measure such latency we measure the amount of time it takes for one host to send a message of a fixed size to, and receive a reply from, another host. This test is commonly referred to as the ping-pong test.

The results of experiments conducted on Ethernet and ATM LANs are shown in Figure 4. We experimented with two variants of TRAP. With the first, labeled simply as TRAP, the user invokes message-passing primitives using application-buffers that are completely independent of the communication system. With the second variant, labeled TRAP-NC, the user puts application-level data directly into buffers initially allocated through communication-library primitives. As can be seen in Figure 4, the extra copy between application-space and communication-library space consumes a small amount of time that increases with message size. Observe that on an Ethernet, TRAP's message-latency is virtually the same as that offered by PVM-TCP (see Figure 4(a)). On an ATM LAN however, TRAP's latency is smaller than most of the other systems even in the presence of the additional copy operation (see Figure 4(b)). Further, both TRAP and TRAP-NC yield a performance that is significantly superior to that exhibited by the other UDP-based systems. The low latency achieved by TRAP is related to the use of a larger segment size at the transport protocol level. The average round-trip time estimate is based on 10,000 samples. The error, based on a 90% confidence interval, was found to be negligible relative to graph dimensions. The step seen in the PVM-UDP graphs (see Figures 4(a) and (b)) is a consequence of buffer handling overheads due to fragmentation. The spike seen in the LAM-TCP graph (see Figure 4(b)) recurred over several independent runs of the test program. We are unable to explain its cause.

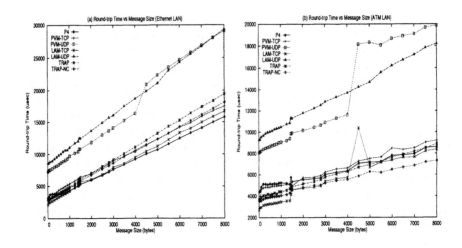

Fig. 4. Round-trip time (LAN)

3.3 Transaction-oriented Traffic

Distributed applications with irregular communication patterns require an asynchronous send and receive functionality. To measure TRAP's performance at handling asynchronous messages from different sources we designed the following test. A server process handles transactions that are sent by up to n clients. Each client process repeatedly sends the server a 100-byte message and awaits a reply to this message before sending the server a next message. The server's reply consists of a 1-byte message. The clients synchronize with one another during startup, with the help of the server. Client messages are sent to the server only after the synchronization, when all clients are known to be ready. Each client obtains an estimate of the average round-trip time (for its send-reply activity with the server) based on 10,000 messages. All nodes involved in this experiment were located on the same 10 Mbits/sec Ethernet LAN.

The server collects a round-trip time estimate from each client and computes a grand average, at the end of the test. We used up to 53 clients in this experiment: up to 43 clients on hosts with clock rates of 85 MHz and the rest on hosts with cpu clock rates of 70 MHz. The average number of transactions executed by the server per second, and the overall average round-trip time obtained by the server are shown graphed against the number of clients in Figures 5(a) and (b), respectively. In Figure 5(a), error-bars are shown in those situations (i.e., for TRAP, P4, PVM-TCP and LAM-TCP) where the size of the 90% confidence interval around the estimate is significant relative to graph dimensions.

In terms of the server's transaction processing rate, it is clear (see Figure 5(a)) that TRAP outperforms the other communication libraries we studied. P4 was not able to operate with more than 27 clients. This was the case even when the maximum number of file descriptors per process was 64. PVM-TCP

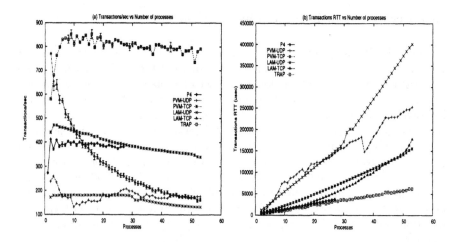

Fig. 5. Transaction Throughput and Delay (LAN)

and LAM-TCP were fully operational for all the values of n tested. This may be because PVM and LAM use a smaller number of file descriptors per session with a remote host. As shown in Figure 5(b), the experiment indicates that a TRAP-based server exhibits better scalability characteristics, with respect to the number of clients it can handle, than a server implemented with the other systems. Further, TRAP yields the smallest round-trip time, which implies the best support for rapid process interactions.

At first glance it may appear that TRAP's significant performance difference, as seen in Figure 5, is due to communication and computation overlap. A closer look at the situation, however, will show that TRAP's scalability is due to reasons other than user-threads based communication and computation overlap. In all the test programs, TRAP's transactions were found to be atomic; that is, the server sends a reply to each message received before the next arriving message is processed. This was due to the 10 ms time-slice length in the TRAP test program, and the small 100-byte messages. In further investigating causes for the performance difference we found that the TCP/IP-based libraries look for incoming messages using the *select* call. This call requires about 40 μ-secs to poll a single socket on a host with cpu clock rate of 70 MHz. Further, this time increases at the rate of about 10 μ-secs for *each* additional socket polled . In TRAP, sockets are polled with the help of non-blocking receives; the cost of each unsuccessful receive is roughly 60 μ-secs. Thus, with more than three clients, the TCP/IP libraries incur a polling cost that is larger than TRAP's polling cost. Further, the TCP/IP-based libraries incur an additional cost in that the *select* call they use must be followed by a *receive* or *read* at every socket that has input data available to read. In contrast, TRAP's non-blocking receives may directly retrieve such data.

3.4 Iterative Solution of a Linear System

To test TRAP's performance on a typical application, we implemented a distributed version of the Jacobi [18] iterative method for solving linear systems. The algorithm is explained as follows. A set of n slave processes are made to synchronize with one another through a master process. After this, each slave iteratively computes a piece of the solution vector. After the i-th iteration, each slave computes its contribution to the difference $|X_i - X_{i-1}|$ and sends the result of this computation to the master process. Each slave also multicasts (using point-to-point communication) its portion of the solution vector to the other slave processes, so that distributed iteration can continue, if necessary. The master process computes the total value of $|X_i - X_{i-1}|$ and uses this value to decide whether iteration must continue. If so, the slaves proceed with the next iteration and the process is repeated. Otherwise, the distributed computation is terminated.

The application was implemented in a uniform manner using four different systems: CLAM-based message passing, P4, PVM, and LAM. We used the versions of P4 and LAM indicated earlier, but used version 3.3.11 in the case of PVM. In each case, compilation was done with version 2.7.2 of *gcc* and optimization option $-O$, except for the case of LAM, where the library-provided *hcc* command was used. Each process ran on a distinct host. All hosts were interconnected through a 10 Mbit/sec Ethernet. We sampled execution times for 30 runs, and estimated an average with a 90% confidence interval. This was repeated for different numbers of slave processes and different vector sizes. The results are presented in Figure 6. Observe that, along with LAM, TRAP exhibits the best performance for this application.

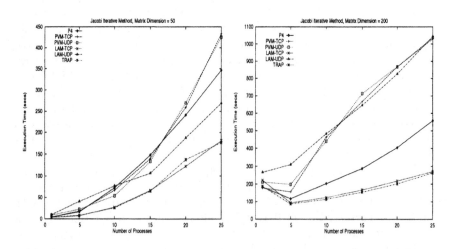

Fig. 6. Execution time vs Number of processes (Distributed Jacobi)

4 Conclusions and Future Directions

Based on our experiences with the design, implementation and testing of the TRAP protocol, we conclude that UDP-based user-level protocols are highly competitive in their ability to provide communication support for distributed computing. Indeed, in our experience, this support is almost as efficient as in-kernel protocol support, and even more valuable in terms of portability, scalability and flexibility. Further, integrating user-space protocol actions with user-space threads enables us to avoid problems inherent to TCP/IP-based and single-threaded message passing systems, including problems of deadlock with unrestricted two-way traffic and low throughput on ATM LANs. Threads also enable the hiding of programming complexities which may result from the use of single-threaded asynchronous calls in distributed computing.

Our experiments show that TRAP's polling mechanism exhibits scalability characteristics that are significantly better than the *select*-based polling mechanism used in most TCP/IP-based distributed computing systems. There are other important features of the TRAP implementation that were discussed, but were not experimented with in this paper. Such features may lead to improved performance, and include its fast connection-establishment scheme, its support for active-messages, and its support for threads-based concurrency on shared memory multiprocessors. Experiments involving these features are a subject of our ongoing work. The overhead of using threads also proved to be insignificant during our experiments. Using a profile tool we found this overhead to be of the order of 1% of the total execution time for a CLAM process that is actively sending or receiving messages.

Our plan is to implement a scalable and reliable multicast protocol, with low-level support for active-messages and remote thread activations. This protocol will enhance CLAM's TRAP module and its unreliable module, and will provide a versatile and efficient protocol-level communication platform for distributed computing and collaboration on heterogeneous networks. In addition, we intend to layer TRAP directly upon AAL5 to reduce latency and increase throughput in ATM LANs. Based on this support, our goal is to provide an interface for efficient collaborative and distributed computing with multimodal data.

References

1. R. Bhoedjang, T. Ruhl, and R. Hofman. Panda: A Portable Platform to Support Parallel Programming Languages. In *Symposium on Experiences with Distributed and Multiprocessor Systems IV*, pages 213–226, September 1993.
2. M. Blumrich, C. Dubnicki, E. Felten, K. Li, and M. Mesarina. Virtual-Memory-Mapped Network Interfaces. *IEEE Micro*, pages 21–28, February 1995.
3. R. Butler and E. Lusk. Monitors, Messages, and Clusters: The p4 Parallel Programming System. *Parallel Computing*, 20(4):547–564, April 1994.
4. D. Clark. Modularity and Efficiency in Protocol Implementation. RFC-817, July 1982.

5. D. Clark, V. Jacobson, J. Romkey, and H. Salwen. An Analysis of TCP Processing Overhead. *IEEE Communications Magazine*, 27(6), June 1989.

6. D. Clark and D. Tennenhouse. Architectural Considerations for a New Generation of Protocols. In *ACM SIGCOMM*, 1990.

7. S. Edge. An Adaptive Timeout Algorithm for Retransmission across a Packet Switching Network. In *ACM SIGCOMM*, March 1983.

8. A. Edwards and S. Muir. Experiences Implementing a High Performance TCP in User Space. In *ACM SIGCOMM*, 1995.

9. A. Ferrari and V. Sunderam. Multiparadigm Distributed Computing with TPVM. Technical Report CSTR-951201, Department of Math and Computer Science, Emory University, 1995.

10. I. Foster, C. Kesselman, and S. Tuecke. The Nexus Approach to Integrating Multithreading and Communication. Journal of Parallel and Distributed Computing. (To appear).

11. J. Gomez, V. Rego, and E. Mascarenas. The CLAM Approach To Multithreaded Communication on Shared-memory Multiprocessors: Design and Experiments. Technical Report TR-96-036, Purdue University, West Lafayette, IN 47907, 1996.

12. J. Gomez, V. Rego, and V. Sunderam. Efficient and Reliable Multithreaded Transport in User-space: The Design and Implementation of the TRAP Protocol. Technical Report TR-96-X, Purdue University, West Lafayette, IN 47907, 1996.

13. J. Gomez, V. Rego, and V. Sunderam. On Tailoring Thread Schedules in Protocol Design: Experimental Results. Technical Report TR-96-018, Purdue University, West Lafayette, IN 47907, 1996.

14. M. Haines, P. Mehrotra, and D. Cronk. Chant: Lightweight Threads in a Distributed Memory Environment. Technical report, ICASE, June 1995.

15. R. Horst. TNet: A Reliable System Area Network. *IEEE Micro*, pages 37–45, February 1995.

16. V. Jacobson. 4BSD Header Prediction. *ACM Computer Communications Review*, 20(2):13–15, 1990.

17. V. Jacobson. Modified TCP Congestion Avoidance Algorithm, April 1990.

18. J.Rice. *Matrix Computations And Mathematical Software*. McGraw-Hill, 1981.

19. P. Karn and C. Partridge. Improving Round-Trip Time Estimates in Reliable Transport Protocols. In *ACM SIGCOMM*, August 1987.

20. E. Mascarenhas, F. Knop, and V. Rego. ParaSol: A Multi-threaded System for Parallel Simulation Based on Mobile Threads. In *Proceedings of the Winter Simulation Conference*, pages 690–697, 1995.

21. E. Mascarenhas and V. Rego. Ariadne: Architecture of a Portable Threads System Supporting Thread Migration. *Software-Practice and Experience*, 26(3):327–357, March 1996.

22. R. Minnich, D. Burns, and F. Hady. The Memory Integrated Network Interface. *IEEE Micro*, pages 11–20, February 1995.

23. J. Mogul. Network Locality at the Scale of Processes. In *ACM SIGCOMM*, September 1991.

24. T. Montgomery. *Design, Implementation, and Verification of the Reliable Multicast Protocol*. West Virginia University, Morgantown, West Virginia, 1994.

25. N. Nevin. The Performance of LAM 6.0 and MPICH 1.0.12 on a Workstation Cluster. Technical Report OSC-TR-1996-4, Ohio Supercomputer Center, March 1996.

26. Ohio Supercomputer Center. *MPI Primer/Developing with LAM*, December 1995.

27. D. Plummer. An Ethernet Address Resolution Protocol. RFC-826, November 1982.

28. V. Sunderam, G. Geist, J. Dongarra, and R. Manchek. The PVM Concurrent Computing System: Evolution, Experiences, and Trends. *Parallel Computing*, 20(4):531–545, April 1994.

29. A. Tanenbaum. A Comparison of Three Microkernels. *Journal of Supercomputing*, 9:7–22, 1995.

30. D. Tennenhouse and D. Wetherall. Active Networks. In *15th Symposium on Operating Systems Principles*, December 1995.

31. T. von Eicken. *Active Messages: an Efficient Communication Architecture for Multiprocessors*. PhD thesis, University of California Berkeley, 1993.

32. T. von Eicken, A. Basu, V. Buch, and W. Vogels. U-Net: A User-Level Network Interface for Parallel and Distributed Computing. In *15th Symposium on Operating Systems Principles*. ACM, 1995.

33. D. Wallach, W. Hsieh, K. Johnson, M. Kaashoek, and W. Weihl. Optimistic Active Messages: A Mechanism for Scheduling Communication with Computation. In *5th ACM SIGPLAN Symposium on Principles and Practice of Parallel Programming*, 1995.

Network-wide Cooperative Computing Architecture (NCCA)

Hiroyuki Yamashita[1], Toshihiko Suguri[1], Shingo Kinoshita[1] and
Yasushi Okada[2]

[1] NTT Information and Communication Systems Laboratories, 1-1 Hikari-no-oka.
Yokosuka. 239 Japan
[2] NTT Network Strategy Planning Department, 19-2 Nishi-shinjuku 3-Chome.
Shinjuku-ku, Tokyo. 163-19 Japan

Abstract. A network-wide cooperative computing architecture (NCCA)
is described that reduces communication-processing overhead in parallel
and distributed processing systems. Network-wide load balancing and
fault tolerance are achieved by interconnecting workstations, disks, and
other nodes in a logical ring topology over a high-speed network; by circulating service and information request messages over this network; then
having the messages accepted by the most suitable nodes that satisfy the
requests. In NCCA, the cooperative processing that used to be executed
by communications between applications is horizontally and vertically
migrated to a lower-layer communication protocol. By the control of this
communication protocol, system-wide cooperation is achieved through
autonomous operation of each node. Load balancing is achieved as each
node estimates its own load by monitoring received messages. compares
that value with an updated load threshold for the overall system, and
decides whether to accept processing request messages.

1 Introduction

Considerable progress is being made in parallel and distributed cooperative processing systems in which work is performed on multiple computers that communicate and cooperate with each other over a network, such as in the case
of multiple workstations connected in a cluster configuration. To increase the
efficiency of parallel and distributed cooperative processing, it is important not
only to increase the operating speed of computer hardware and the network,
but also to reduce the communication processing overhead needed to achieve
cooperation between applications running on computers. The authors have been
investigating one promising approach in which the cooperation-oriented application processing and upper-layer communication protocol processing are migrated
to lower-layer communication protocol processing in each node.

Horizontal migration involves distributing scheduling, process result merges.
and other centralized control functions to multiple nodes. This decreases the
number of communications between nodes. Vertical migration, on the other
hand, enables the functions of applications, the operating system (OS), and

upper-layer communication protocol to be performed by lower-layer communication protocols. This decreases the amount of upper-layer communication protocol processing at each node. The new lower-layer protocol resulting from these forms of migration is an intelligent protocol having the capability to support cooperation among computers, between computers and disks, and among disks.

The authors are now developing a network-wide cooperative computing architecture (NCCA) that achieves efficient parallel and distributed processing by locating the above intelligent communication protocol (ICP) at each node or at select locations within the network. The NCCA can evenly distribute the load among computers and can achieve fault tolerance in a relatively easy manner in a system of interconnected computers and disks provided by multiple vendors. This paper is organized as follows: Section 2 discusses the basic concept of the NCCA, and Section 3 describes the ICP. Sections 4 and 5 describe how NCCA achieve load balancing and fault tolerance. Section 6 discusses implementations of NCCA, and Section 7 summarizes the paper.

2 Basic Concept

2.1 Cooperative Processing in Parallel and Distributed Systems

In parallel and distributed computing systems, workstations, disks, and other kinds of nodes perform requested service processing while interworking cooperatively. Load balancing, fault tolerance, and other advantages can be achieved through this kind of cooperation between nodes. Cooperative work is achieved by applications in nodes communicating with other coordination-oriented applications in other nodes. Applications originating service requests, for example, collect performance and load information about other nodes through inquiries. By then using that information to select and send service request messages to the most appropriate node, system load balancing can be achieved.

2.2 Migration of Cooperative Processing

In the NCCA, communication overhead of parallel and distributed cooperative processing systems is reduced by horizontally and vertically migrating the cooperation-oriented application processing and upper-layer communication protocol processing to each configured node.

Horizontal Migration As shown in Fig. 1(a), horizontal migration is achieved when nodes are connected to a network configuring a logical ring or loop topology, and communication messages are circulated from node to node around the ring. Because ring topology networks result in little decease in throughput during times of high load, they are particularly well suited to high-speed areas. In this topology, cooperative processing that tends to be concentrated in the host originating service requests is distributed among other connected nodes. Cooperation-oriented applications at each node examine the contents of received messages, and autonomously determine if they will accept the messages for processing. This cuts down on the number of communications between applications, and thereby reduces the amount of communications for the overall system.

In this type of system, service and information request messages circulate around the ring topology network, and are accepted by the most appropriate nodes that satisfy the requests. The load balancing discussed above, for example, is achieved as follows. When a cooperation-oriented application in a node receives a service request message, it decides whether to perform the requested service based on the capability of the node and on the load status of the node and the whole system. If the node processes the message, it is accepted; if not, the message is sent on to the next downstream node on the ring. Among other ways, nodes are able to estimate the load status of the overall system by monitoring the flow of received messages. Since such a system-wide cooperation is achieved by node applications acting autonomously, it is called *autonomous cooperation.*

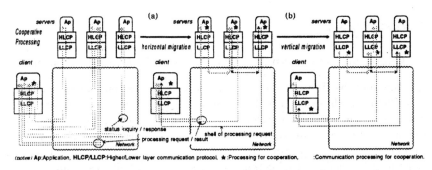

Fig. 1. Horizontal and vertical migration of cooperative processing

Vertical Migration Vertical migration, as shown in Fig. 1(b), involves shifting cooperative processing, such as acceptance judgment by each node, from the application to a lower-layer communication protocol. When processing is migrated in this way, the associated reference data is also moved. Consequently, messages received by nodes are not sent to the application, but rather are executed as cooperative processing at the lower-layer. This means that upper-layer communication protocol processing can be eliminated from the node.

The new lower-layer communication protocol resulting from this migration is an intelligent protocol endowed with cooperative functions. Here this protocol shall be referred to as an intelligent communication protocol (ICP).

2.3 Configuration

Fig. 2 shows an example of a system configuration based on the NCCA. Computers, disks, and other nodes are connected in a logical ring topology by a high-speed network. Then, by circulating service and information request messages around the ring and having them accepted by the most appropriate nodes through ICP control, load balancing and fault tolerance are achieved. In the example shown in Fig. 2, the client is external to the ring, but one of the computers directly connected to the logical ring topology network could also act as the client. In addition, although this capability is not indicated in Fig. 2, the ICP also has the ability to send messages on to another network if they are not accepted by a network within a specified time.

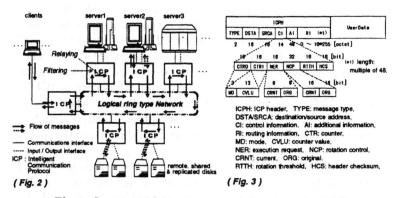

(Fig. 2)　(Fig. 3)

Fig. 2. System configuration example based on the NCCA

Fig. 3. ICP message format

3 Intelligent Communication Protocol

The ICP at each node examines the header area of the received message as to whether requested services can be executed or requested information is stored at the node, and accepts the message if it is judged that the node can service the message (*i.e.*, if the node is not down or overloaded). If the message is not accepted, it is sent on to the next node. When a message is passed on, the message status information in the header (*e.g.*, number of times the message has been accepted) of the message may be updated as necessary. The node status information (*e.g.*, load status) is also updated when a request message is accepted or a response message is sent. The information required for this processing is downloaded to the ICP layer in advance or as needed.

3.1 Message Format

The ICP message format is illustrated in Fig. 3. Based on the contents of the header area of received messages and the node status information held at the node, the ICP determines whether to accept a received message, whether to update the header area of the message, whether to update the node status information, and whether to relay the message on to another node in real time. All of the fields needed to make these determinations are located within the first 64 bytes of messages. The meanings of the main fields are summarized as follows:

1. Destination/Source address (DSTA/SRCA) : Identify the addresses of the destination and the origin of a message.
2. Message type (TYPE) : Indicates the type of message.
3. Control information (CI) : Contains information for determining together with the address fields (DSTA/SRCA) whether the message is accepted or passed on to another node. In addition, the field also includes information for determining if the message or node status is to be updated. When the message is sent on to another node, this field can be updated.
   (a) Counter 0-1 (CTR0-1) : Each of these is general-purpose field that is partitioned into two parts: update mode (MD) and counter value (CVLU). The result of comparing the counter value and node status value can be used as a credit value in determining whether to accept the message.
   (b) Execution request (NER) : Is split into two fields, current (CRNT) and origin (ORG), and indicates the number of nodes where the message has previously been accepted (*i.e.*, acceptance counter, number of acceptance request). When (ORG) is set to 0, this means the message can be accepted by any node.
   (c) Rotation control (NCP) : Is split into two fields, current (CRNT) and origin (ORG), and indicates the number of times the message has traveled around the ring (*i.e.*, loop counter, maximal number of permitted rotations).
   (d) Rotation threshold (RTTH) : Is used to determine how many times the message will go around the ring before it is sent on to another network.
   (e) Header checksum field (HCS) : Is used as an error detection code in the header area.
4. Additional information (AI) : Contains control information for registering / removing group addresses from a group address list stored on a node, etc.
5. Routing information (RI) : Contains address information for sending the message to a gateway so it can be relayed to another network.

3.2 Node Holding Information

The ICP processing entity in each node holds various kinds of information for cooperation-oriented processing including node status and load balancing control information. When received messages are accepted, this information is updated as necessary. The main types of information are summarized as follows:

1. Node address (ADIA) : A unique node address.
2. Computer functional address (NDFA) : Indicates the services provided by the node (computer). The service numbers corresponding to '1' bits in this address indicate the services provided by the node.
3. IO functional address (IOFA) : Indicates stored information for the node (I/O). The information numbers corresponding to '1' bits in this address indicate the information stored in the node.
4. Group address list (GAL) : Specifies the IDs (*i.e.*, group addresses) of a group to which the node belongs. If the instruction to "add group address"

is entered in the TYPE field of a received message, the group address in the AI field will be added to this address list before the next message is received. If the instruction to "delete group address" is entered, the group address will be deleted from this list regardless of whether the message is accepted or not before the next message is received. Group addresses are also either added or deleted from this list in response to commands from upper-layer entities.

5. Node failure flag (NDFL) : Indicates that services cannot be provided by the node because the node has failed.

6. Copy suppress flag (CS) : Indicates that received messages are not accepted for some reason.

7. Node load (NDLD) : Indicates the load status of a node. When a received message is accepted under specific conditions, only the addition to the node's load is added to this value. And only the reduction from the node's load is subtracted from this value in response to message send requests.

8. Node load add value (LDDF) : Indicates an addition to the node load when a received message is accepted.

9. Load threshold (LDTH): Indicates the load limit of a node. The load threshold is compared with the node load when messages are received. This value is updated in response to system-wide load fluctuations for load balancing control purposes.

10. Threshold update value (THDF) : Indicates an addition or a subtraction to the load threshold when the system-wide load fluctuations are detected.

11. Holding counter (HCTR0-1) : Is compared with the same number counter field in received messages, and is updated based on the results. For example, the credit value provided by the node is stored.

12. Gateway threshold value (RLTH) : Indicates the limit value of the message's NCP.CRNT field to determine whether the ICP gateway function accepts a received message. If the value of NCP.CRNT field exceeds the sum of this value plus the value of the RTTH field in the message, the message is accepted to be sent on to another network.

3.3 Functions

The ICP has the following functions :

1. Functional Addressing [1]

The ICP sets an address (called a *functional address*) indicating the service or function requested by a message in the destination address area of the message. Each node holds addresses of all services and/or functions that it is capable of handling. Then, if the functional address held by a node matches that of a received message, the node can accept the message and perform the service or function that is requested. The functional address can adopt a number of different formats : each bit in the address can represent a function, codes can be employed to represent functions, or a combination of these two approaches can be used. These formats can be used to represent the number of functions for the entire system, the existence of services made up of multiple functions, and other system-wide requirements.

2. Message Status Updating

When a message passes through a node, the message status is updated by the ICP as follows :

(a) Counter (CTR) : When a message is received at a node, this is incremented by 1 before the message is sent on to the next node.

(b) Acceptance counter (NER.CRNT) : When a message is accepted by a node, this is incremented by 1 before the message is sent on to the next node.

(c) Loop counter (NCP.CRNT) : When a message circles the ring without being accepted by the specified number of nodes, this is incremented by 1 at the node that originally sent the message.

3. Node Status Updating

When a message passes through a node, the node status is updated by the ICP as follows :

(a) Node load (NDLD) : When a node accepts a message, this is incremented by the node load add value (LDDF) before the message is sent on to the next node. When a message is sent from a node, this is decremented by a specified value.

(b) Load threshold (LDTH) : When a node accepts a message whose loop counter is larger than zero, this is incremented by the threshold update value (THDF) before the message is sent on to the next node.

(c) Holding counter (HCTR) : When a node receives a message, this is incremented by 1 before the message is sent on to the next node.

4. Message Filtering

Basically, only messages satisfying the following conditions are accepted and transferred to an application by the ICP in a node :

(a) The function requested by the message is included among the functions provided by the node (*i.e.*, the destination address matches).

(b) The message status is such that it is seeking acceptance by the node (*i.e.*, acceptance counter < number of acceptance requests).

(c) The credit provided by the node satisfies the credit requested by the message (*i.e.*, holding counter value ≥ requested counter value).

(d) The node load permits acceptance of the message (*i.e.*, node load < load threshold).

(e) The node is not down (*i.e.*, node failure flag = 0).

The node status information that is needed to make these determinations is downloaded each time it changes from the system management entity to the held information area maintained by the ICP. The exception is the node load status, which is updated in the ICP processing of the node when a message is received and sent.

5. Conditional Stripping

When a message circles the ring back to the node originating the message, its status (NER.CRNT) is examined by the ICP at the node, and if it hasn't yet been accepted by the requested number of nodes (NER.ORG), the message is not discarded but is sent around the ring again, unless the loop counter (NCP.CRNT) exceeds the permitted value (NCP.ORG). Nodes endowed with the message gateway function examine the status of received messages (NCP.CRNT), and if a message has exceeded its maximal number of round times (RLTH+RTTH), it is removed from the ring.

3.4 Types of Communication

Employing the various ICP functions listed in the previous section, the NCCA can support the following types of communication. These various kinds of communication are illustrated in Fig. 4.

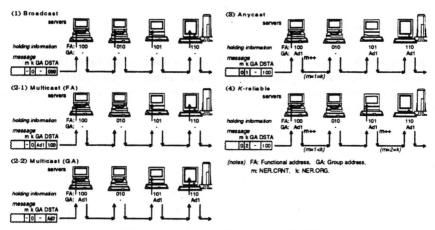

Fig. 4. Communication types in NCCA

1. Broadcast Communication

   A message is delivered to all nodes on the network. This is achieved by setting a broadcast address in the DSTA field of the message while setting NER.ORG to "0."

2. Multicast Communication

   A message is delivered to all members of a group of nodes satisfying some specified condition defined by *functional addressing* or *dynamic address registration*. With the former, a message is accepted at particular nodes if the functional address (FA) previously specified for the nodes matches the destination address (FA) in the message header. With the latter, group addresses (GAs) set in messages that were accepted by previous multicast communications are temporarily registered at those nodes, and a subsequently received message is accepted if the GA in its header matches one of the previously registered GAs. The latter approach in particular can be used to set up multicast connections. For sending a message to all members of a group of nodes, NER.ORG in the message must be set to "0."

3. Anycast Communication [2]

A message is delivered to only one node from among the members of a specified group. This is achieved by setting NER.ORG in the message to "1." Because (NER.CRNT) and (NER.ORG) coincide when the first node to accept the message increments (NER.CRNT) in the message by 1, the message is not relayed further downstream on the ring.

4. K-reliable Communication [3]

A message is delivered to only K nodes from among the members of a specified group. This is realized by setting NER.ORG in the message to "K." Nodes continue to accept the message, incrementing (NER.CRNT) by 1 and relaying the message downstream on the ring, until (NER.CRNT) and (NER.ORG) coincide.

4   Load Balancing

System-wide load balancing is achieved in NCCA not by exchanging information among nodes, but rather by autonomously controlling the acceptance of service request messages by individual nodes. The concept behind load balancing in NCCA is illustrated in Fig. 5.

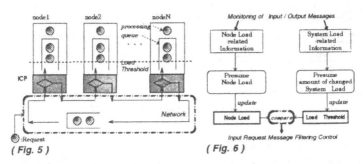

(Fig. 5)   (Fig. 6)

Fig. 5. Load balancing concept in NCCA

Fig. 6. Load balancing control scheme in each node

4.1   Algorithm

When a service request message is received at a node, the ICP compares the node load and the load threshold held in the node to determine whether to accept the message for service or to relay the message to another node. [4]

The load status of the node in question can be estimated from the difference between the number of input messages requesting service and the number of output messages conveying service results or from the number of active communication connections. It can also be obtained from the operating system. The load threshold can be calculated from the relative load status of the entire system and updated to accommodate the system-wide load fluctuations.

When the system-wide load is evenly balanced among nodes, the ideal threshold value at node k coincides with the load. This can be expressed by

$$\frac{\sum_i (processing\ amount\ of\ service\ request\ i)}{\sum_j (performance\ of\ node\ j)} \times (performance\ of\ node\ k) \quad (1)$$

As this formula makes clear, the load status of the entire system is relative, for it fluctuates according to the fault and recovery status of nodes in the system; the addition, deletion, and modification of nodes; and the input of service requests and output of their results. Load balancing in NCCA is based on more than just the load status of the entire system; it also involves estimating the relative amount of load fluctuation from the balanced state by monitoring received messages and then updating the threshold value accordingly. The variation in the threshold is proportional to the node performance. Fig. 6 is a schematic showing of the load balancing control scheme in each node.

The loop counter in the header of a service request message which has circulated the ring without being accepted by any node is updated by the ICP which originated the message, and the message is then relayed on. The ICP in each node is thus able to estimate the relative increase or decease of the system-wide load from the frequency with which messages are received with a non-zero loop counter. To prevent a specific node that is upstream on the ring from continually accepting service request messages, the copy suppress flag (CS) can be set in the node that suppresses the acceptance of messages for a fixed time interval, thus preventing succeeding messages from being accepted.

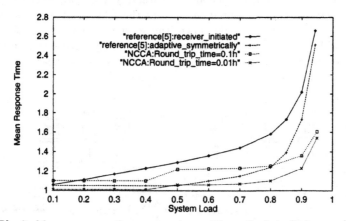

Fig. 7. Mean response time comparison with methods in Reference [5]

4.2 Performance Evaluation

The effectiveness of the load balancing method in NCCA was verified by computer simulation. Fig. 7 shows the simulation results comparing the average response time of the load balancing scheme evaluated in Reference [5] where service requests are transferred to other nodes and the NCCA approach. The comparison conditions are the same as those in [5] : each of the arrival time for a service request call and the service time has an exponential distribution in a system with 40 nodes of uniform performance connected to a 10 Mbit/s network . The total link length in the NCCA is 200 meters.

It will be apparent from Fig. 7 that, compared to the receiver-initiated scheme evaluated in [5], almost all of the system load for the NCCA method is evenly distributed, and therefore provides excellent performance in this regard. The NCCA method also outperforms the adaptive symmetrically-initiated method under high system-wide load conditions.

5   Fault Tolerance

5.1   Redundancy Configuration

Using the various types of communication described in Section 3, the following arbitrary (virtual) redundant configurations can be implemented for various processes. These configurations can even be mixed within the same system.

1. Shared Standby Redundancy

   Fig. 8 shows a schematic of the shared standby redundancy in NCCA. If the node receiving a service request message is down, the message will not be accepted but will be relayed to the downstream node. In the case where special service is performed by each node, a functional address (FA) can be set for each executable service and one standby node (which can even be an active node) can be prepared for setting the FAs of all services. Then, in the event that a node breaks down, the service-requesting message can be accepted by this common standby node and the requested service performed. Because the disks that store data for executing these services are shared by all nodes, they can be accessed by any node.

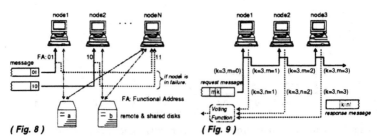

Fig. 8. Shared standby redundancy scheme

Fig. 9. Majority decision redundancy scheme

2. Majority Decision Redundancy

   To improve the reliability of processing results and other data, replies to sources of requests can be based on a majority decision taken from service execution results at multiple nodes or from results read from multiple disks. A schematic of the majority decision redundancy scheme in NCCA is shown in Fig. 9. To accomplish this, a voting function is created to select one result from a number of results by majority decision, and the functional address of this voting function is set to a specific node (which can even be the source of the request). A request message is then delivered to multiple nodes using K-reliable communication. The results of service execution and disk reading are then transferred by messages, whose FA is set to reflect the voting function in the destination address, so the node having the voting function accepts the message. Results that do not arrive within a set time are treated as abnormal, thus preventing the response time from increasing.

In place of majority decision, the order of arrival can also be adopted as a voting algorithm to realize a parallel redundancy configuration. Although this type of configuration does not increase the reliability of results, it does nevertheless shorten the response time.

3. Replicated disks

In disk accessing as performed in NCCA, FAs corresponding to file names or disk addresses are assigned to disk nodes. At that time, if the same FA is assigned to multiple nodes, replicated disks are achieved. In other words, identical data is written to multiple disks using multicast communication, and read data is obtained from one disk using anycast communication. Or, as described in 2. above, the reliability of read data can be increased by majority decision.

In addition, by relaying a message whose request for disk read has been denied by nodes already in disk-access processing and having the data read from another inactive disk, access time can be reduced.

5.2 Functional Evaluation

A pre-prototype system was used to verify the validity of the fault tolerance capabilities of the various configurations discussed in the previous section. The system was configured by connecting multiple PCs to an Ethernet. The ICP was implemented as a program running on the PCs, and the logical ring was configured using program control on a single Ethernet. For the disk access, SCSI commands were encapsulated and transmitted. In the majority decision redundancy, various voting algorithms such as majority, order of arrival, first two coincidence were verified.

6 Implementation

6.1 Variations

The ICP can be implemented in various ways : by incorporating it within a network interface controller (NIC) at each node, by incorporating it into add-on equipment interconnected by a communication or I/O interface, or by providing it as network-side functions in the switch or the hub. These various implementation approaches are illustrated in Fig. 10.

For the implementation of a logical ring topology on shared physical media or switching network, direct transmission was used to send service result messages to individual destinations without sending the message around the ring through other nodes. This made it possible to reduce the response time and also to reduce the network traffic.

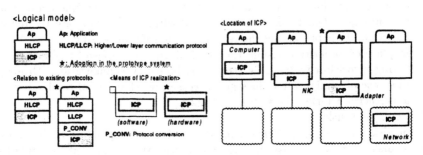

Fig. 10. Various implementations of NCCA

6.2 Prototype

Among the variations mentioned in the preceding section, the authors are now constructing a prototype system in which the ICP is implemented as hardware in a device (an adapter) connected to each node.

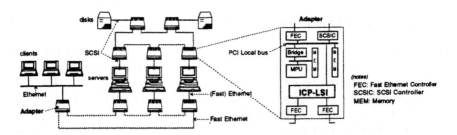

Fig. 11. Prototype system configuration

System Configuration Fig. 11 shows a schematic of the prototype system configuration. A physical ring topology is implemented by directly interconnecting each pair of adjacent two ICP adapters using a 100 Mbit/s Fast Ethernet link. Each adapter can also be connected to a Fast Ethernet shared hub or to a switching hub, which configures a logical ring. Incorporated in the adapter are two Fast Ethernet controllers for receiving/sending (DECchip 21140), an ASIC for ICP processing, an MPU (SPARClite) that runs protocol conversion processing firmware, 4 MB of buffer memory, a (Fast) Ethernet controller for connecting to computers, and a SCSI controller (MB86605) for connecting to computers and disks. These components are interconnected via a PCI local bus.

In this implementation of the prototype, computers and disks are interconnected by standard interfaces, and because the protocol conversion is performed by the adapters, modification of the computer applications and the operating system are not necessary. Multivendor-furnished equipment can be used for the nodes. Messages from clients are encapsulated by firmware in the entrance adapter and sent to the ring. Accepted messages are decapsulated and sent to the connected nodes after conversion of IP addresses. Node load data used for the load balancing control are inferentially derived as discussed earlier in the paper. Node failure is able to be detected by periodic *health checks* that are initiated by the adapters. The various types of address information is either downloaded from a special management node or is preset or updated as needed.

ICP-LSI The delay time for a message to circle the ring increases the more nodes are connected to NCCA-based systems, and this causes the communications overhead to also increase. This consideration thus led us to develop an ICP processing LSI to reduce the message relay delay in nodes.[6] The main parameters of the ICP-LSI are listed in Table 1.

Table 1. Characteristics of NCCA-LSI

item	Data
Process	0.35 μm triple-metal CMOS Gate Array
Clock Frequency	33 MHz
Number of Gates	400 $KGate$ (200$KGate$ Logic + 29$Kbit$ Memories)
Interface	5V-PCI × 3 $sets$, Others(TTL) : 19
Supply Voltage	3.3 V
Power Dissipation	2.2 W (design value)
Package	304 Pin QFP (PCI:146,TTL:19,Test:10(+13[$shared$]), VDD(3.3V):34,GND:69,VDD(5V):26)

The LSI examines the necessary fields by seizing them even while received messages are being transferred to a FIFO. Decisions to accept the message, update its contents, and relay it on to the next node are achieved through *on-the-fly* processing. A *cut-through* scheme is also implemented so that the updated message begins to be output immediately as soon as a relay decision is reached even though the entire message hasn't been received. The maximal relay delay time is about 2.5 μ s for the ICP-LSI and about 12 μ s including both Fast Ethernet controllers. Header checksums capability is not supported by the LSI.

7 Conclusions

In this paper we have presented an overview of a network-wide cooperative computing architecture (NCCA) that aims to horizontally and vertically migrate cooperative functions provided by applications and the operating system to a lower-layer communication protocol in each node, and to raise the efficiency of parallel and distributed processing through autonomous operation at each node. The NCCA realizes excellent load balancing and robust fault tolerance through the use of multicast and other types of communication provided by an intelligent communication protocol (ICP).

One point that must be addressed in future work on the NCCA is the relationship between system conditions such as the number of connected nodes, the volume of communications throughput and so on, and the bandwidth of ring topology networks. In addition, there are other issues calling for further work in the area of load balancing control. By measuring the effects under varying conditions, this will enable us to fine-tune key system parameters such as optimum load thresholds and message acceptance suppression periods. Following up on these results, we intend to apply the prototype system to video-on-demand and World-Wide-Web servers and to evaluate their performance.

Acknowledgment

The authors gratefully acknowledge the support and encouragement provided by their superiors, and also wish to thank their colleagues for their many useful contributions to this work.

References

1. IEEE Standards for Local Area Networks: Token Ring Access Method and Physical Layer Specification. IEEE Std 802.5-1989.
2. J. Bound, and P. Roque,: IPv6 Anycasting Service: Minimum requirements for end nodes. Internet-Draft, June 1996.
3. D. D. Kandlur, and K. G. Shin, : Reliable Broadcast Algorithms for HARTS. ACM Trans. on Computer Systems, Vol. 9, No. 4, Nov. 1991, pp. 374-398.
4. T. Suguri, H. Yamashita, S. Kinoshita, and Y. Okada.: Load Balancing Method for Autonomously Cooperative Distributed Systems. submitted to The Trans. of IEICE, D-I (*in Japanese*).
5. P. Krueger and N. G. Shivaratri,: Adaptive Location Policies for Global Scheduling. IEEE Trans. on SE., Vol. 20, No. 6, pp. 432-444, June 1994.
6. H. Yamashita, T. Suguri, S. Kinoshita, Y. Okada, K. Oguri, and S. Shiokawa, : Message Routing Latency Minimizing Method in An ASIC Design for Distributed Cooperative Communication Protocol Processing. submitted to The Trans. of IEICE, D-I (*in Japanese*).

Data Movement and Control Substrate for Parallel Scientific Computing[*]

Nikos Chrisochoides[1][**], Induprakas Kodukula[1] and Keshav Pingali[1]

Computer Science Department
Cornell University, Ithaca, NY 14853-3801

Abstract. In this paper, we describe the design and implementation of a data-movement and control substrate (DMCS) for network-based, homogeneous communication within a single multiprocessor. DMCS is an implementation of an API for communication and computation that has been proposed by the PORTS consortium. One of the goals of this consortium is to define an API that can support heterogeneous computing without undue performance penalties for homogeneous computing. Preliminary results in our implementation suggest that this is quite feasible. The DMCS implementation seeks to minimize the assumptions made about the homogeneous nature of its target architecture. Finally, we present some extensions to the API for PORTS that will improve the performance of sparse, adaptive and irregular type of numeric computations.

Keywords: parallel processing, runtime systems, communication, threads, networks

1 Introduction

The portability of programs across supercomputers has been addressed very successfully by MPI [8] which is intended to be an easy-to-use and attractive interface for the application programmer and tool developer. However, it is not intended to be a target for the runtime support systems software needed by compilers and problem solving environments, since this software requires an efficient (and perhaps inevitably, less friendly) substrate for point-to-point communication, collective communication and control operations. Issues not addressed by MPI, such as dynamic resource management, concurrency at the uniprocessor level and interoperability at the language level, need to be addressed by such substrates.

These issues are being addressed by a consortium called *POrtable Run-time Systems* (PORTS) [15] which consists of research universities, national laboratories, and computer vendors interested in advancing research for software

---

[*] This work supported by the Cornell Theory Center which receives major funding from the National Science Foundation, IBM corporation, New York State and members of the its Corporate Research Institute.

[**] Chrisochoides' current address is Department of Computer Science and Engineering, University of Notre Dame, Notre Dame, IN 46556.

substrates that provide support to compilers and tools for current and next generation supercomputers. Specific goals of the group are:

1. to promote the development of standard applications programming interfaces (APIs) in multithreading, communication, dynamic resource management, and performance measurement that will be used as a compiler target for various task-parallel and data-parallel languages,
2. to provide support for interoperability across parallel languages and problem solving environments, and
3. to encourage the development of a community code repository that will result from this consortium's activities.

To achieve these ends, the *PORTS* consortium has come up with several APIs. The first API, *ports_threads*, has already been agreed upon by the PORTS consortium. It comprises of a set of functions for lightweight thread management, modeled after a subset of the POSIX thread interface. An implementation of the *ports_threads* interface is available from Argonne National Laboratory [16]. In addition, a set of functions have been specified for timing and event logging, using the high resolution, synchronized clocks available on many shared and distributed memory supercomputers. The timer package is thread safe, but not thread aware. In other words, a correct implementation of this specification can be used in a preemptive thread environment, however the specification does not require threads. An extremely fast implementation of *ports_timing* is available from University of Oregon [24].

There is a proposed API for communication, and for the integration of communication with threads[17]. The *PORTS* consortium has been experimenting with four different approaches.

1. *Thread-to-thread* communication, supported by CHANT [2].
2. *Remote service request* communication, supported by NEXUS [11].
3. *Hybrid* communication, supported by TULIP [25].
4. The DMCS approach outlined in this paper.

In this context, our DMCS implementation accomplishes the following.

- We provide a simple mechanism for reducing the scheduling latency of urgent remote service requests, as well as the communication overhead associated with remote service requests for sparse, adaptive and irregular numeric computations.
- We isolate the interaction between threads and communication into a simple module which is easy to understand and modify, called *control.*
- We provide a global address space and a threaded model of execution that provides a common programming model for SMPs, clusters of SMPs and MPPs.
- We want a very lean and modular layer that allows us to "plug-and-play" with different module implementations from PORTS community.

The rest of the paper is organized as follows. In Section 2, we outline the architecture of the data-movement and communication substrate, including the interaction of the threads and communication modules. In Section 3, we discuss the implementation details of DMCS. Preliminary performance data for simple kernels from sparse and adaptive computations are given in Section 4. Finally, the related work and a summary with discussion are presented in Sections 5 and 6 respectively.

2 Architecture

DMCS consists of three modules: (i) a *threads* module (ii) a *communication* module and (iii) a *control* module. The threads and communication modules are independent, with some clearly defined interface requirements, while the control module is built on top of the point-to-point communication and thread primitives. The *threads* module supports the primitives defined by the PORTS consortium, *ports_threads*. We are using the implementation provided by the Argonne group, PORTS0 [16], augmented by an extra routine: *ports_thread_create_atonce*. The efficient implementation of this routine is necessary to minimize the scheduling latency of certain urgent, *remote service requests* [7]. Clearly, this extension can be implemented on top of the existing *ports_threads* primitives provided by PORTS0(for example, using the thread priority attributes), but for efficiency reasons, we choose to implement it, whenever possible, directly on the underlying thread package. A prototype is implemented on top of the QuickThreads [19], which has been ported to a wide variety of workstation and PC architectures.

The communication module provides the necessary support for the implementation of a global address space over both shared and distributed memory machines. Collective communication primitives are not considered in this paper. In the future, we plan to evaluate and use the "rope" primitives introduced in [10] and [20]. As in Split-C, NEXUS, TULIP and Cid, our communication abstraction is the *global pointer*. A global pointer essentially consists of a context number and a pointer to the local address space. The functionality of the communication module for point-to-point data-movement includes routines like *get/put* to initiate the transfer of data from/to a remote context to/from a local context. The interaction of the communication module and threads takes place in the *control* module which integrates the thread scheduler with the point-to-point communication mechanism. Figure 1 depicts the three modules of the DMCS and their interaction.

The *control* module provides support for remote procedure invocation, also known as *remote service requests* (RSRs). Remote procedures are either system/compiler procedures or user defined handlers. These handlers can be threaded or non-threaded. The threaded handlers can be either *urgent* (scheduled after a fixed quanta of time[3]) or can be *lazy* (scheduled only after all other computation and manager threads have been suspended or completed). The non-threaded

---

[3] The time interval of a timeslice or the time it takes for the next context-swithch of the current thread in the case of a non-preemptive scheduling environment.

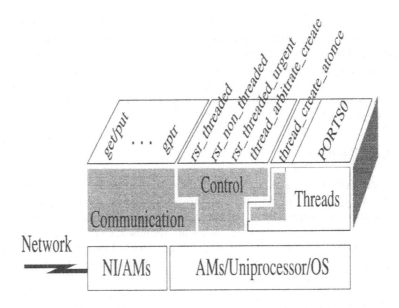

Fig. 1. Architecture

handlers are executed either as the message is being retrieved from the network interface[4], or after the message retrieval has been completed [1]. Finally, the control module provides some limited support for simple load balancing by allowing associating a window within which load on any processor can be balanced. This load-balancing support was chosen after experiments with the SplitThreads [23] system.

3 Implementation

In this section, we discuss the thread, communication and control modules of DMCS.

3.1 Thread subpackage

The underlying threads package consists of a user-level threads core called Quick-Threads, which is a non-preemptive user-level threads package for thread creation and initialization. It provides no scheduling policies or mechanisms. It also lacks semaphores, monitors, non-blocking I/O etc. It provides machine dependent code for creating, running and stopping threads. It also provides an

---

[4] This works by overlapping computation and communication in the instruction level by interleaving the computation and flow of control that corresponds to the incoming message and the load/store operations needed to retrieve the message from the network interface.

easy interface for writing and porting thread packages. The higher level thread package has the responsibility of providing any additional functionality. Since the QuickThreads package is very flexible, clients can be designed with specific applications in mind and can be selectively tuned very easily.

DMCS implements a non-preemptive threads package. The thread routines in DMCS can be classified into *scheduling routines* and *management routines*, depending on their functionality. In DMCS, thread creation is separated from thread execution. DMCS maintains a queue of runnable threads, and thread creation routines simply insert a new thread into this runnable queue. Two different creation mechanism are provided (*dmcs_thread_create_atonce, dmcs_thread_create*) corresponding respectively to a low priority and a high priority for the newly created thread. It is important to note that these routines simply create and initialize a new thread, but do not actually run the thread. Thread management routines are responsible for actually running any threads in the run queue maintained by DMCS. The *dmcs_run* routine examines the run queue to check if it contains any threads, runs all of them to completion and then returns. Since DMCS provides non-preemptive threads, a *dmcs_yield* routine is provided to enable a thread to voluntarily de-schedule itself. For the sake of efficiency, DMCS also preallocates stack segments, which can be used by a thread creation routines instead of allocating memory on the fly. This leads to a more efficient thread creation routine. Finally, threads in DMCS can have several attributes that can be configured on a per-thread basis. Attributes currently implemented are the stack size of a thread, and whether the thread should use a pre-allocated stack, or do a fresh allocation for its stack.

3.2 Communication subpackage

The communication subpackage is implemented on top of a generic active message implementation on the SP-2[1, 21]. Active messages are a mechanism for asynchronous, low-overhead communication. The fundamental idea in Active Messages is that every message is sent along with a reference to a handler which is invoked on receipt of the message. The generic active message specification provides for small messages as well as bulk transfer routines. The implementation of this specification on the SP-2[21] is optimized so that small messages are delivered as efficiently as possible; for sufficiently large messages, the bandwidth attained is very close to the peak hardware bandwidth.

DMCS provides a homogeneous, data driven, asynchronous and efficient runtime environment. The communication subpackage of DMCS consists of three modules:

- *global pointers module*: DMCS provides the notion of a global pointer through which remote data can be accessed. When a program using DMCS runs on a N processors, each processor is assigned a unique integer id (known as a *dmcs_context*, and returned by the routine *dmcs_mycontext()*) in the range $0 \ldots N - 1$. Any processor can access local data through a regular pointer. However, any remote data must be accessed through a *global pointer*. A global pointer is made up of a *dmcs_context* and a local pointer. Routines are provided to make a global pointer out of a local pointer and a *dmcs_context*, and also to extract these fields from a global pointer. This module is the only module that depends on the homogeneity of the underlying hardware (in the determination of unique context numbers).

Acknowledgement Variables: Since DMCS is asynchronous by nature, a mechanism is provided to enable programs to find out about data transfer completion. This mechanism is an acknowledgement variable. An acknowledgement variable is represented as a 16-bit integer for efficiency reasons. An acknowledgement variable can have three states: *cleared*, *set*, and *unitialized*. To use an acknowledgement variable, a program must first request one using the routine *dmcs_newack()*, which returns an unused acknowledgement variable. This return value can be used as a handle to perform various operations on the acknowledgement variable. For example, *dmcs_testack()* checks if the acknowledgement variable has been set or not, and return immediately. On the other hand, *dmcs_waitack()* waits until the variable in question has been set. It is also possible to clear an acknowledgement variable using *dmcs_clearack()*. Finally, it is possible to "anticipate" the use of an acknowledgement variable in future data transfer using the function *dmcs_anticipateack()*. The last routine has an important role in one-sided data transfer operations, which will be described later. Finally, it is possible to use the same acknowledgement variable in conjunction with multiple data transfer operations. Use of an acknowledgement variable is always optional and a value of NULL for an argument of this type indicates that the particular acknowledgement variable in question is not being used.

Get and Put operations: DMCS provides routines for one-sided communication. In other words, communication does not happen through a pair of matched sends and receives. Instead, get and put routines are provided for fetching remote data and storing remote data respectively. Both these operations are inherently asynchronous. Acknowledgement variables can be used to determine the state of one of these transfers. A Get operation transfers data from a source specified by a global pointer to a destination specified by a local pointer. A single acknowledgement variable passed as an argument to this routine is *set* when the data transfer operation is complete. A Put operation transfers data from a local buffer specified by a local pointer to a remote data buffer specified by a global pointer. A put operation has associated with it three acknowledgement variables: a *local_ack*, which is set when the local data buffer can be reused by the application program, a *remote_ack*, which is set on the processor that initiated the put operation to indicate that the put operation on the remote processor is complete, and finally a *remote_remote_ack* which is set on the remote processor to indicate that the put operation there has been completed. For the remote-processor intimation to work correctly, it must first anticipate this put operation by calling *dmcs_anticipateack()* on the acknowledgement variable specified as the *remote_remote_ack* in the put operation. As mentioned previously, all these acknowledgement variables are optional and a value of NULL can be passed as the corresponding argument to indicate dis-interest in that particular acknowledgement variable.

3.3 Control subpackage

The control subpackage is layered on top of the threads subpackage and the communication subpackage. The control subpackage consists of two sets of modules: remote-service requests and load-balancing routines.

– *Remote Service Requests*: DMCS provides several kinds of remote service requests. A remote service request consists of a remote context, a function to be executed at the remote context and the arguments to the function. In addition, a type argument is also passed, indicating the type of the remote service request. This type argument can take three possible values, and determines how the function at the remote end is executed. The function can be executed immediately on arrival, or it can be threaded. If the handler is threaded, then it can executed as either a low-priority thread or a high-priority thread. The type argument for the remote service request determines which of these modes of execution is performed.

DMCS recognizes that passing a function as part of the remote service request may not be always desirable. This is the case in adaptive mesh refinement, where the components of a mesh are distributed on various processors. Different processors use different "interpolation functions" to transfer data between different grids at different stages of the mesh refinement process. When data related to a mesh is sent to another processor that needs it, it is not always known at the sender what kind of interpolation function the receiver needs to apply. Also, in a non-SPMD environment, a function address valid at the center may not be valid at the receiver. To provide a solution to this problem, DMCS provides the notion of an indexed remote service request. At any processor, a function can be "registered" with an integer tag. When a message with that particular tag is received, the function registered with that tag is invoked as the handler for the message. This mechanism enables different processes to register different handlers with the same tag and allows great flexibility.

Some message passing system provide more efficient routines to transfer small amounts of data which are more efficient than using the generic bulk transfers. Keeping this in mind, DMCS optimizes the bulk transfer routines as well as the remote service request routines for small message sizes. For our implementation, this provides an improvement of almost 20% for small message sizes over the unoptimized case of using the same underlying generic bulk transfer routine. The generic form of the remote service request takes as arguments a remote context, a remote handler (either a function, or an index to one), a buffer of arguments and a length parameter counting the size of the arguments.

Finally, it is common in programs to transfer some data to a remote processor, followed by the invocation of a remote service request acting on the data just transferred. For such operations, it is more efficient to do the data transfer and the remote service invocation in one step, rather than transferring the data first, and then invoking the remote service request. This is because, the second approach usually involves some additional synchronization delays that can avoided by the first approach. For this purpose, DMCS provides *putw_rsr* routines, which combine the data transfer and the remote service action at the end of the data transfer. This is similar to the functionality specified in the generic active message specification.

- *Load balancing*: DMCS implements a simple parametrized load balancing primitive. The load on a processor is defined to be simply the number of threads on that processor. DMCS provides a primitive than enables a processor to start a new thread on the least loaded processor within a certain window size. The window size is a parameter that can be customized. Processors are divided into groups of size equal to the parameter. Load balancing is provided by DMCS within each of the groups. By tuning the window size parameter, load balancing can be confined to a small neighborhood or be over the entire machine. It may be noted that this load-balancing happens at thread creation, and a running thread is never migrated.

4 Performance Data

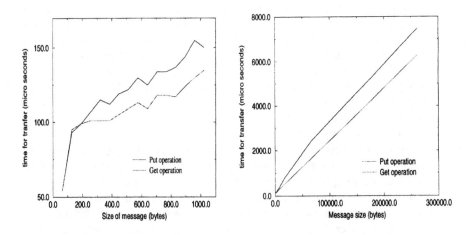

Fig. 2. Communication time as a function of message size: small message size(left), large message size(right)

In this section, we discuss the performance of our run time system on the IBM SP-2, comparing it with the performance of other systems.

The following are the basic parameters of our runtime system:

- Thread creation time = $12\mu s$
- Context switch time = $5.5\mu s$
- Peak Data transfer bandwidth = $33.6 MBytes/sec$
- One-way latency for a 0-byte message $29\mu s$.
- Time elapsed for a non-threaded null remote service request = $31\mu s$

The communication paramters of our runtime system parameters are very close (within 10%) of the underlying active message layer. For example, one-way latency for a 0-byte message in DMCS is $29\mu s$, which represents an overhead of 10% over the underlying active message latency of $26\mu s$. This compares with a handler to handler latency of $79\mu s$ in Nexus, which represents an overhead of 80% over the native MPL one-way latency of $44\mu s$. Similarly, the bandwidth achieved in DMCS for bulk transfers is $33.6 MBytes/sec$ for get operations, and $29 MBytes/sec$ for put operations. These numbers are also within 10% of the corresponding parameters of the active message layer. This verifies that the overhead introduced by the DMCS layer is quite small.

An advantage of the homogeneity of the target architecture is that it enables certain kind of optimizations in the runtime system implementation which are very hard otherwise. For example, in our implementation, we have recognized that certain kinds of remote service requests are very common. One such instance occurs in matrix vector multiplication, where the non-local portion of the vector needs to be fetched and then used in SAXPY operations. The usual manner to accomplish this is simply using a putw_rsr routine, with the remote service request handler taking care of the saxpy operations. However, by noting that the remote portion of the vector need not be stored, but can be simply used to compute the relevant portion of the matrix vector operations, after which only the results of the operations need to be stored, we can implement a more efficient matrix vector multiply operation in the runtime system itself. This routine avoids all buffering of the data and does the relevant computation in the hardware buffer itself. As can be seen from Figure 3, the performance saving can be quite substantial when the number of floating point operations is small for every data element, which is the case for sparse computations.

DMCS is being currently used to implement a task-parallel version of the Bowyer-Watson algorithm for mesh generation [14]. This algorithm provides an ideal mesh refinement strategy for a large class of unstructured mesh generation techniques on both sequential and parallel computers, by preventing the need for global mesh refinements. This application has been ported from an active message implementation to a PORTS implementation on top of DMCS. For the most part, this port was straightforward. The specialized matrix vector product routine of DMCS, described above, has been used to implement a sparse matrix-vector multiply routine for use in iterative solvers for large systems of linear equations.

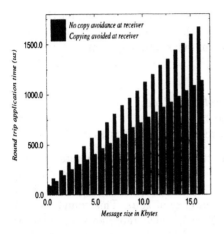
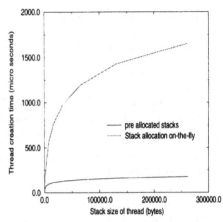

Fig. 3. Savings by copy avoidance at receiver(left), Comparison between preallocated and non preallocated threads(right)

5 Related Work

Three other software systems that integrate communication with threads are particularly interesting because they implement the same interface but have different design philosophies and objectives. CHANT implements thread-to-thread communication on top of portable message passing software layers such as p4 [13], PVM [18], and MPI [8]. The efficiency of this mechanism depends critically on the implementation of message polling or message delivery interrupt. There are three common approaches to polling for messages: (i) individual threads poll until all outstanding receives have been completed, (ii) the thread scheduler polls before every context switch on behalf of all threads, and (iii) a dedicated thread, called the *message thread*, polls for all registered receives. For portability, CHANT supports the first approach, since many thread packages do not allow their scheduler to be modified. Performance data in [2] indicate that there is little difference in performance between the first two polling approaches.

NEXUS decouples the specification of the destination of communication from the specification of the thread of control that responds to it. NEXUS supports the *remote service request* (RSR) driven communication paradigm which is based on the remote procedure call mechanism. The multithreaded system (or user) registers a message handler which is a new thread and is to be invoked upon receipt of an incoming message. The handler possesses a pointer to a user-level buffer into which the user wishes the message contents to be placed. The handler threads are scheduled in the same manner as computation threads. In a preemptive scheduling environment, each handler gets highest priority and will always get scheduled after a fixed quanta of time. In a non-preemptive environment, the handler thread gets assigned a low priority and gets scheduled only after other threads have suspended; thus, there is no bound on the waiting time for the handler in this case. The RSR driven communication paradigm is implemented in NEXUS which a portable multithreaded communication library for parallel language compilers and higher-level communication libraries [11].

TULIP's *hybrid* approach is essentially a combination of thread-to-thread and RSR driven communication paradigm [25]. The *hybrid* approach is essentially a combination of thread-to-thread and RSR driven communication paradigm and is supported by TULIP [25]. In the runtime substrate, TULIP provides basic communication via global pointers and remote service requests. Then, at the pC++ language level, there is the concept of threads and the notion of group thread actions [10, 20]. Communication is one module, the basic threads functions (i.e., creation, thread synchronization, etc) are in another module, and the two are combined into the *rope* module.

Finally, functionality similar to DMCS *threads* and *communication* and *control* modules are provided by a number of other runtime systems like Cid, Split-C, Cilk, and Multipol. Cid [3] and Split-C [22] are parallel extensions to C. Both systems support a global address space through the abstraction of the global pointer. They also implement asynchronous, one-sided communication, and multithreading (either in the language as in Cid, or through extensions as in SplitThreads [23]), and have mechanisms for overlapping computation with communication and synchronization latencies. Cilk [4] is similar but it targets a more restricted class of computations (*strict* computations). The scheduling policy is fixed, and for a certain class of applications is provably efficient with respect to time, space and communication. In contrast to the Cilk runtime system, Multipol [9] allows more flexibility to the programmer. For example, the programmer is free to use customized schedulers to accommodate application-specific scheduling policies for better performance, and can also specify how much of a thread state needs to be saved.

6 Conclusions

We have described the design and implementation of a data-movement and control substrate (DMCS) for network-based, homogeneous communication within a single multiprocessor, which implements an API for communication and computation defined by the PORTS committee. Unlike systems like Nexus, which are designed for a heterogenous environment, DMCS is targeted for a homogenous environment. Although the scope of DMCS is therefore restricted, it permits us to do optimizations which are difficult in heterogenous environments.

7 Acknowledgements

We thank Pete Beckman, Chi-chao Chang, Grzegorz Czajkowski, Thorsten von Eicken, Ian Foster, Dennis Gannon, Matthew Haines, L. V. Kale, Carl Kesselman, Piyush Mehrotra, and Steve Tuecke for valuable discussions.

References

1. Thorsten von Eicken, Davin E. Culler, Seth Cooper Goldstein, and Klaus Erik Schauser, Active Messages: a mechanism for integrated communication and computation *Proceedings of the 19th International Symposium on Computer Architecture,* ACM Press, May 1992.
2. Matthew Haines, David Cronk, and Piyush Mehrotra, On the design of Chant : A talking threads package, NASA CR-194903 ICASE Report No. 94-25, Institute for Computer Applications in Science and Engineering Mail Stop 132C, NASA Langley Research Center Hampton, VA 23681-0001, April 1994.
3. R.S. Nikhil, Cid: A Parallel, "Shared-Memory" C for Distributed Memory Machines. In Lecture Notes in Computer Science, vol 892.
4. Christopher F. Joerg. The Cilk system for Parallel Multithreaded Computing. Ph.D. Thesis, Department of Electrical Engineering and Computer Science, Massachusetts Institute of Technology, January, 1996.
5. L.V. Kale and M. Bhandarkar and N. Jagathesan and S. Krishnan and J. Yelon, CONVERSE: An Interoperability Framework for Parallel Programming, Parallel Programming Laboratory Report #95-2, Dept. of Computer Science, University of Illinois, March 1995
6. Nikos Chrisochoides and Nikos Pitsianis, FFT Sensitive Messages, to appear as Cornell Theory Center Technical Report, 1996.
7. Nikos Chrisochoides and Juan Miguel del Rosario, A Remote Service Protocol for Dynamic Load Balancing of Multithreaded Parallel Computations. Poster presentation in Frontiers'95.
8. MPI Forum, Message-Passing Interface Standard, April 15, 1994.
9. Runtime Support for Portable Distributed Data Structures C.-P. Wen, S. Chakrabarti, E. Deprit, Chih-Po Wen, A. Krishnamurthy, and K. Yelick. Workshop on Languages, Compilers, and Runtime Systems for Scalable Computers, May 1995.
10. N. Sundaresan and L. Lee, An object-oriented thread model for parallel numerical applications. *Proceedings of the 2n Annual Object-Oriented Numerics Conference - OONSKI 94, Sunriver, Oregon, pp 291-308,* April 24-27 1994.
11. I. Foster, Carl Kesselman, Steve Tuecke, Portable Mechanisms for Multithreaded Distributed Computations Argonne National Laboratory, MCS-P494-0195.
12. Ian Foster, Carl Kesselman and Steven Tuecke, The NEXUS approach to integrating multithreading and communication, Argonne National Laboratory.
13. Ralph M. Butler, and Ewing L. Lusk, *User's Guide to p4 Parallel Programming System* Oct 1992, Mathematics and Computer Science division, Argonne National Laboratory.
14. Nikos Chrisochoides, Florian Sukup, Task parallel implementation of the Bowyer-Watson algorithm, CTC96TR235, Technical Report, Cornell Theory Center, 1996.
15. Portable Runtime System (PORTS) consortium, http://www.cs.uoregon.edu/research/paracomp/ports/
16. PORTS Level 0 Thread Modules from Argonne/CalTech, ftp://ftp.mcs.anl.gov/pub/ports/
17. A Proposal for PORTS Level 1 Communication Routines, http://www.cs.uoregon.edu/research/paracomp/ports
18. A. Belguelin, J. Dongarra, A. Geist, R. Manchek, S. Otto, and J. Walpore, PVM: Experiences, current status and future direction. Supercomputing'93 Proceedings, pp 765-6.

19. David Keppel, Tools and Techniques for Building Fast Portable Threads Package, UW-CSE-93-05-06, Technical Report, University of Washington at Seattle, 1993.
20. Data Parallel Programming in a Multithreaded Environment, (**Need authors...**)*to appear i a Special Issue of Scientific Programming*, 1996.
21. Chichao Chang, Grzegorz Czajkowski, Chris Hawblitzell and Thorsten von Eicken, Low-latency communication on the IBM risc system/6000 SP. To appear in Supercomputing '96.
22. David E. Culler, Andrea Dusseau, Seth Copen Goldstein, Arvind Krishnamurthy, Steven Lumetta, Thorsten von Eicken and Katherine Yelick. Parallel Programming in Split-C. Supercomputing'93.
23. Veena Avula. SplitThreads - Split-C threads. Masters thesis, Cornell University. 1994.
24. Portable Clock and Timer Module from Oregon, http://www.cs.uoregon.edu/research/paracomp/ports
25. Pete Beckman and Dennis Gannon, Tulip: Parallel Run-time Support System for pC++, http://www.extreme.indiana.edu.

Author Index

Springer
and the
environment

At Springer we firmly believe that an international science publisher has a special obligation to the environment, and our corporate policies consistently reflect this conviction.

We also expect our business partners – paper mills, printers, packaging manufacturers, etc. – to commit themselves to using materials and production processes that do not harm the environment. The paper in this book is made from low- or no-chlorine pulp and is acid free, in conformance with international standards for paper permanency.

 Springer

Lecture Notes in Computer Science

For information about Vols. 1–1118

please contact your bookseller or Springer-Verlag